AT TRANSLATION'S EDGE

MEDIA MATTERS

Patrice Petro and Cristina Venegas, Series Editors

Media Matters focuses on film, television, and media within a transnational and interdisciplinary frame: environmental media, media industries, media and democracy, information media and global media. It features the work of scholars who explore ever expanding forms of media in art, every day, and entertainment practices. Under the co-direction of Patrice Petro and Cristina Venegas, the series is sponsored by the Carsey-Wolf Center at the University of California, Santa Barbara. The Center seeks to foster innovative and collaborative research that probes the aesthetic, political, economic, artistic, and social processes of media in the past and in our own time.

Nataša Ďurovičová, Patrice Petro, and Lorena Terando, eds., *At Translation's Edge*
Elena Gorfinkel and Tami Williams, eds., *Global Cinema Networks*

AT TRANSLATION'S EDGE

EDITED BY

NATAŠA ĎUROVIČOVÁ, PATRICE PETRO, AND LORENA TERANDO

RUTGERS UNIVERSITY PRESS
New Brunswick, Camden, and Newark, New Jersey, and London

Library of Congress Cataloging-in-Publication Data

Names: Durovicova, Natasa, editor. | Petro, Patrice, 1957–editor. | Terando, Lorena, editor.
Title: At translation's edge / edited by Natasa Durovicova, Patrice Petro, and Lorena Terando.
Description: New Brunswick, New Jersey : Rutgers University Press, [2019] | Series: Media matters | Includes bibliographical references and index.
Identifiers: LCCN 2018049876 | ISBN 9781978803381 (cloth) | ISBN 9781978803336 (pbk.)
Subjects: LCSH: Translating and interpreting. | Intercultural communication. | Mass media and language.
Classification: LCC P306 .A8 2019 | DDC 418/.02—dc23
LC record available at https://lccn.loc.gov/2018049876

A British Cataloging-in-Publication record for this book is available from the British Library.

♾ The paper used in this publication meets the requirements of the American National Standard for Information Sciences—Permanence of Paper for Printed Library Materials, ANSI Z39.48-1992.

www.rutgersuniversitypress.org

Manufactured in the United States of America

CONTENTS

AT TRANSLATION'S EDGE

INTRODUCTION

At Translation's Edge

NATAŠA ĎUROVIČOVÁ

In the last few decades, displacing "inter-," the Latinate prefix "trans-" has become among the more culturally responsive modifiers, yielding such common Latinate vocabulary as transnationalism and transculturalism as well as transgender, transdisciplinarity, transcreation, transhumance, transhumanism, and many other terms. Etymologically, "trans-, meaning "across," entails *movement*—in the examples above, across nations, languages, genders, disciplines, species. In today's seemingly ubiquitous and extremely rapid change of social, cultural, and scientific knowledge, "trans-" has come to be used as a semantic marker of flux, ungelled and multidirectional, signaling binaries dissolving into mutations.

The rise in status and ubiquity of translation studies may well be an index of this epistemic shift. Named and disciplined as a field, it emerged some four decades ago as an institutional space aiming to integrate both the large body of knowledge in practice-oriented training institutions and the millennial history of translation commentaries with more descriptive as well as more theoretical approaches. Whether linguistic in orientation—descriptive, comparative, or philological—or building on general ideas about literariness indebted to formalism and structuralism, "studies" established the institutional foundation for a requirement of systematicity (hence the weight of a Holmes map) on one hand and craft on the other.

The discipline's humanist housing was not a given in the United States: from the late 1940s on, translation had been extensively studied with the goal of achieving reliable machine translation (of large quantities of military materials from the Russian) and connected, in turn, to research in artificial intelligence. That intersemiotic base of translation—the numerification of language—continues today in departments of computer science and computational linguistics and is relied upon in the subfields of technical and commercial translation.[1] Here, the holy grail of measurable equivalency has remained central, and the process of translation is reconfigured as a calculation of probability.[2]

Both the structuralist and the mathematical efforts to precision-tool equivalency were upended by the insistence, in the approaching wave of poststructuralism, on the trope of *différance*—that is, nonidentity and noncorrespondence.[3] Acknowledging the distorting consequences of asymmetry between, for instance, a major and a minor language or a colonizing and a colonized language, the "cultural turn" put paid to the preferential treatment of communicability—opening translation studies, instead, to domains in which translation is embedded, or rather, more forcefully, in which it is constitutive without necessarily being raised to consciousness.

Some historians of the field's development in the United States, then, explain this disciplinary surge not only through institutional convergences, issuing from translation's natural "counterhegemonic," boundary-crossing impulse, but by pointing to the wider, more unruly, creative undersoil of the late 1960s and early 1970s.[4] On this account, translation studies arose within that moment's churning force field of intersemiotic hybridizations, migrations, and pervasive cultural transformation, in a general social upheaval and atmosphere of creativity rather than in search of any particular disciplinary rigor.[5] Hence, for instance, the rise of translation workshops modeled on "un-pedagogies" of creative writing, aiming to infuse the American literary scene with urgent-feeling poetry and prose from contested, even revolutionary, battlefields of what then went under the term "third world."[6] In this spirit, Anglophone translation studies soon took up double occupancy with deconstruction and postcolonial studies, determined to direct attention toward the difference end of the identity/difference spectrum along which Western translation discourse has moved ever since its earliest documents.

A next surge of disciplinary expansiveness, after this ferment of the 1970s, again breaching established institutional and national boundaries, came two decades later, at the very beginning of the new millennium, with the generalized use of the internet. The World Wide Web can after all be considered a technological embodiment of—among other things—the vast metaphorical apparatus applied to translation, the ultimate tool of continuous and ubiquitous communication, semiotic fluidity, debordering. In fundamentally undoing spatial (but not political) mapping, the virtual contact zone of the WWW offered a platform not only for translation itself but rather for the constant translat*ing*—that is, recoding and decoding—that makes up communication.

The present volume takes up translation in this expansive, transdisciplinary sense: "edge" signals here, for instance, that half of its contributors do not work as translation studies scholars proper but are, rather, disciplinary neighbors, commuters, for whom questions raised in and by translation serve to queer, as it were, their professional working terrain. Instances of such toggle effect, where translation is not the principal object of study but rather a uniquely sharp diagnostic tool for broader concerns, are Naoki Sakai's essay theorizing the political philosophy of "the nation" or the work of John Cayley, where translation, far from being considered as if a transparent bridge between natural languages, is included as a compositional procedure among many possible others that serve to lay bare the poetics of "programmed writing." The net effect of such approaches is to set the very idea of translation *on edge*, unsettled, exploratory.

At Translation's Edge is divided into three parts: "New Perspectives on Translation," "Translation at the Limits of the Nation-State," and "Translation's Practices and Politics." In many cases, the individual essays complement or implicitly comment on each other's positions in quite felicitous ways and so could have been grouped in different conversations. It is, after all, exactly such a "centrifugal" state of affairs in translation studies today that gave rise to this volume in the first place.

Part I, "New Perspectives on Translation," explores translation's methodological concerns in order to move disciplinary goalposts—of political and literary history for Lydia Liu, of literary aesthetics for John Cayley, and of rhetorical practice for Russell Valentino. For Liu, here as in her several books, the primary interest of translation is not that it allows transfers of meaning to occur but rather that, in certain historical situations, such "transfers" leave behind "translingual effects," enduring verbal seams of cultural confrontation, which make up modernity itself. These markers of the incomplete commensurability of languages—on her account language is always "heterolingual"—also signal occasions, or "events," as she has it, of unequal temporalities, of discourses reflecting historically distinct stages in each of the involved cultures. Thus, rather than present a historical narrative of the debates among the highly diverse group of men and women who, in 1947, worked to formulate a sufficiently universal Universal Declaration of Human Rights, Liu approaches the multilingual cowriting of the declaration as "a differentially distributed discursive event." In her analysis, this negotiated event is unpacked to show the valance of the Latin "human" as it competes in the English draft of the declaration with the Chinese character for "human" (*ren* 仁) derived from the character for "two-mindedness," a character regrounding the "idea [of the human] in the originary plurality of humanity, rather than in the concept of the individual." When the completed declaration (whose final draft was executed in English) was eventually translated into Chinese, *ren* returned as a more modern term, "denoting the empathetic endowment of the human psyche toward another human being prior to the formation of individual conscience." For Liu, this is one among the nearly endless examples of the dynamic, centripetal even force of "translingual plurality": a cultural shimmering between languages that standard procedures of translation are designed to dedifferentiate, make invisible—and which remain undescribed in what she sees as the normative, equivalency-driven, logocentric regime of mainstream translation studies.[7]

In contradistinction to approaches that assess translation diachronically/historically, as procedurally "the same" kind of activity over millennia (which is why Cicero and Saint Jerome are still the patron saints of its art), Cayley draws a decisive line at the mid-1990s. This he identifies as the point when linguistic practices of writing and reading enter a distinct phase of technics, moving over almost completely to what he calls "user-programmable devices." In the conceptual framework his essay outlines (i.e., in this new technical environment), translation taken as alternation between or among natural languages is downgraded to a problem that is, from an engineering standpoint, essentially "trivial": after all, technology processes natural language as generic information, as code. What isn't trivial, however, and what emerges here as new, is that natural language translations make up ideal comparative test material for demonstrating a "translation *of process*" (my italics) so that a comparison of translated literary artifacts provides raw material, as it were, for annotating and aesthetically grasping the program-like features of composed language, period. While comparative studies of retranslation, or of translation as rewriting, are a familiar procedure in hermeneutical terms, Cayley's theoretical argument here (as well as creative work elsewhere) rests on a program executing such comparisons by tracking minutely the fault lines of grammatological difference through individual literary translations. While, in the current environment, such generative processes are visible when executed by machines, Cayley demonstrates it on translations of experimental texts—of Oulipian work, for instance, or of John Cage's mesostic compositions—that can be accommodated in any material formations, if here exemplified by "extreme" formats of traditional (paper) publishing. The specific twinning of language, grammar, and style in each pairing yields insight in reverse, as it were: the translator works to bring into relief any and all appreciable 'strangeness' of form to recover the processes of composition in the guest (i.e., source) language. This commutational analytic of languages generated in the reading-and-writing-that-is-translation is indifferent to translation as a tool of communication: "We translate in order to try and reestablish . . . 'sameness' across linguistically distinct human communities, to reintegrate our . . . practices of language with an understanding that this should be shared by all who share *our species-being*" (my italics). On this account, the sifting and predicting mechanism involved in translation is not a building block for machine translation or a test of artificial intelligence (as Silicon Valley would have it) but rather a signal system among human *poiesis* makers.

Valentino, too, aims to reframe the two central problems in translation studies, those of communication and of equivalence, and does so in the enduring framework of rhetoric, taking these two terms to be *topoi*, commonplaces, which undergo changes depending on their context. The contexts in which he reevaluates them are translation's institutional neighborhoods—the teaching of foreign languages, the teaching of (literary) close reading, and the teaching of creative writing. The goal is to carve out a disciplinary space for *practitioners* along the full spectrum of interlingual transfer, from experimental literary to narrowly technical. Here, the translators' enterprise should be at once informed by, but distinct from, protocols of linguistic expertise (the domain of foreign language acquisition), the valuation of authorial originality (the domain of literary close reading and criticism), and ambitions of authorial autonomy (the domain of creative writing)—all so as to avoid conflating the ontological foundations of these three distinct disciplinary ideas of what, and whom, a text is *for*. As Valentino notes, the rhetoricity of the translatorial act is precisely what programmed machine translation (whether of the rules-based or the deep-learning type) simply isn't equipped for.

Cultural politics is at the center of the essays gathered together in part II, "Translation at the Limits of the Nation-State." Here, the authors move through debates about "thinking beyond the nation-state" and consider translation in polylingual spaces—diasporic, ethnolinguistic, or medial. A translatorial commonplace: that borders between cultures are defined by the line where the need to translate arises. Each of the four essays in this part tackles this commonplace from a different angle.

In Naoki Sakai's frontal attack, the study of translation begins by rejecting its communicative aspect, instead scrutinizing the ground on which the paradigm of communication rests—and which it thereby conceals. For Sakai, translation in the conventional sense of "bridging," "carrying over," is precisely a spatial "co-figuration" to be investigated. For taken in that sense, the concept of translation simply reinforces another, deeply naturalized but really only historically contingent concept, that of the sovereign nation-state (as in "one language = one country"). This is the view that Sakai sees as a key manifestation of a "homolingual" fallacy, one that ideologically displaces, represses, a historically and ontologically precedent "heterolingual" condition, embodied in a plural, the "we," of the intralingual translating subject in a dialogic situation and a *trans*national space. The difference inherent here in the prefix "hetero-" signals a supralinguistic category, one composed of a wide range of social discourses of power, not simply a series of plainly demarcated languages. For Sakai, translation figured, represented, as a binary "bridging" leads indirectly to the reification of "nation," which in turn leads to the disenfranchisement of its "others," externally (by confirming a space of "the inter-national") and internally (by internalizing assorted schemata of homogeneity). Instead, translation should be figured as *a bordering*.

In this sense, Deborah Folaron and Margaret Noodin's essays then provide perfect grist for the mill of Sakai's thesis, offering as they each do an instance of a nonstate social formation. The cases of the Romani *ethnos* and the deterritorialized Anishinaabeg group demonstrate vividly what an obstruction the very idea of homolinguality presents in real geopolitical conditions. In turn, Yiman Wang's reading of a pair of Hollywood silent films as the medium edges up toward sound exemplifies the turbulence that non-monolingualism, paired with what she terms "fake translation," causes in a transnational mediascape. Ultimately, all three scholars—in this sense converging with Liu—approach translating not as a normalized, specific, disciplinary procedure but more as an "event," which inevitably prompts scrutiny of the geopolitical power grid of each situation.

Folaron's detailed overview reflects on how Roma communities in today's Europe—unified by their ethnicity, but multilingual and transnational in their distribution—organize translation and interpreting practices to address their multiple language needs. "Carved out from a distinctive translational space," she argues, these practices "not only maintain a certain continuity with the Romani historical past, but also confront, as do other potentially endangered ethnolinguistic groups, new challenges in a fast-paced globalizing world configured by the dual hegemony of English and the internet, in its capacity as an information and communication technology." Showing how the ethnic communitarian Roma, unified by cultural ties, which are further strengthened by the groups' shared, ongoing cultural exclusion or direct racism, are also disaggregated by linguistic nonidentity, Folaron outlines the double bind of this and other "less-translated," minoritarian languages. For translation's various language-norm-stabilizing tools and institutions (dictionaries, laws, publishing) at once grant access to the dominant culture *and* potentially threaten to undo a group's identity—especially when its internal identity is plural and its territorial formation fluid, debordered. In this regard, the "distributed" Roma cultures with their "dialogical . . . relational" stance toward language have been uniquely well accommodated in the evolving translational space of the internet, which has provided them a virtual convergence space of their *bute droma*—"many roads."

Noodin takes up issues similar to Folaron's, similarly mapped across, or to some degree equally indifferent to, political borders of modern nation-states. Her interest in capturing twenty-first-century indigenous voices as they move between languages is part of the ongoing effort of Native American cultures to "intentionally modernize" oral and textual traditions, to retie threads of language frayed by the linguicide of the most recent colonization. This is in order to move indigenous language culture forward "through" English, making good, in the process, on the Anishinaabemowin/Ojibwe word for translation, *aanikanootan*, whose etymology stresses tying, making temporal connections backward and forward. Her main example, contemporary poetry by indigenous poets translated into Anishinaabe, moves between English and modern Anishinaabemowin as well as other native languages, and poetry is in fact a particularly suitable material foundation, for it is in formal attention that a language's vitality, its capacity to absorb, transform, and innovate, is tested and best demonstrated. As in Folaron's discussion, here too the historically oral aspect of indigenous language(s) is particularly well served by the complement of digital sound and image. Creating such double temporality—precisely Sakai's heterolinguality—may in turn yield a "collated" cultural space, where these two vastly different languages and their lifeworlds can coexist "pieced together" and a next generation of indigenous speakers and writers be accommodated.

The final essay in part II identifies transnational space as that of mixed media. Focusing her analysis on three "silent" Hollywood films, Wang attends to early cinema's linguistic dimension, starting with the conventional translation trope of intertitles on title cards lap-dissolving between two languages, here Chinese and English. What she finds in their counterfeit script/speech is "make-believe translation"—orchestrated code-switching without any actual translation, a rhetorical device with antecedents in the literary genre of pseudotranslation; at issue here is not, however, whether any given instance of such visual translation is accurate or "fake," but rather what performative processes are involved in generating meaning. As delivered by the complex persona of the bicultural Sinophone star Anna May Wong, however, the function of this language's graphemic "physiognomy"—its performative masque—is not, Wang argues, to convey particular semantic meaning but rather to "sift out" so as to then hail the "nonnormative" bilingual/bicultural viewer, able to make sense, partially or wholly, of the "foreign" discourse, from those who can't. In Wang's account, for all its location on the terrain of Anglophony, the discursive space of the movie theater can become, thanks to the active "overhearing" by the bilingual viewer, also a place of heterolinguality.

The volume's third and final part, "Translation's Practices and Politics," gathers themes from the first two parts but refracts them though the authors' practice—a reminder that when it comes to discussing translation, critique—make that theory—has a uniquely persistent relationship to craft/practice: there are few translation theorists who have not also done translation themselves (many more certainly than there are poets or novelists among literary scholars). In this sense, translators are similar to anthropologists, with their required experience of, and ongoing reflection on, their place in fieldwork—and similarly both center their discipline on issues of ethics, positionality, and agency. It is not by accident, then, that the two contributions written in a language other than English best fit in this particular part.

Martha Pulido's piece reflects on the necessary work and obligations of a translation history devoted to the emergence of various social and political strata in the (nation-)states of Latin America via the trope of *translatio studiorum* (i.e., the channel of translation determining the transfer of knowledge). Her examples move in two directions: those instances in Latin American history where a selection and influence of a specific foreign text affects cultural and political change—the colonial and also postcolonial history is full of such examples. She also insists that Latin American translation studies must work on the full loop of translatio studiorum and include the other direction of this flow, the *history of translation*, and through that history the impact of indigenous Mesoamerican intellectual production on other cultures, colonizing or otherwise. Her example is the complex transmission history of the fabled Mayan sacred text *Popol Vuh*, from its K'iche' oral form extant in the pre-Conquista era through a complex series of transcriptions, translations, and interpretations since its first graphemic "capturing" in 1524, and further to its influence on European and American cultural spaces, all the way to its "return" to today's Guatemala in its most recent, massively detailed, and also phonetic form.

Pulido's essay argues that translatio studiorum is the necessary research link between Latin America's historiography and its sense of identity, and Olga Behar's essay exemplifies her point well. Her account of the work involved in preparing a book on the combat strategies of the Colombian state against the Revolutionary Armed Forces of Colombia (FARC) guerilla, which subsequently came to be used as documentation in a war crimes trial, begins with a distinction she makes between stable, official, literal/exact translation (including what traditionally is called "simultaneous interpretation") and "interpreting," by which she means a kind of immersion into the lifeworld of the speaker, to the point of gaining his or her fundamental trust, overcoming the gap of otherness that incommensurable languages create. The scenario of vernacular comfort, the ability to grasp and convey a speaker's sometimes obscure or private sense so as to represent him or her adequately in his or her absence, is of course the ethical contract on which such "understanding" rests. What Behar's account reminds us of is the fragility and instability of the media involved in all mediation, a fact that conventional reliance on "equivalency" cannot adequately describe.

The larger argument, about positionality as a factor in translation, also makes itself visible in Elizabeth Drame's discussion of (among other things) asymmetries in terminology when a colonial language is used as a tool of social engineering. Drame parses the meliorative terminology (what she calls "person-first" language) of the social legislature of Senegal, written (and, Drame implies, *conceived*) in French. This new Western (English and French) legislative vocabulary has aimed to dispense with the "ableist bias" of older terminology in English and French, as well as in Wolof and other regional languages, by creating a separation between a person's identity and his or her ability to perform certain tasks. Under the discursive surface of such approach, Drame finds, however, a bias reflecting cultural ideas about personhood and independence, ideas that are—in her argument—in contrast with the realities of a society infinitely more grounded in interdependency than the Western social ideal for people with disabilities.

For all their differences, these three essays (Pulido, Behar, Drame) give a concrete shape to the condition of, in Sakai's terms again, heterolinguality and to the dynamic, even volatile, nature of translatorial practice—its positionality, its *eventfulness*, to use Liu's (and before that Baxtin's) term. In common, they reflect the asymptotic nature of the relationship between the clear and established nomenclatures of formal, written, grammatical language and the real conditions of speech, the vernacular, of language in its mutable, *working* form.

This position evolves to its logical conclusion in Suzanne Jill Levine's essay, which glosses phases of her long and distinguished career as a translator of Latin American fiction, in particular her uniquely dynamic collaboration in the early

1970s—during that first boom of translation studies in the United States—with Julio Cortázar on his formal, witty masterpiece *Tres tristes tigres*. Partly out of a political impulse, that of feminism, partly as an effect of her working temperament, Levine has ever since vigorously resisted the (literary) translator's secondariness and emphatically insists on—flaunts, even—the role of a rewriter, a cocreator.

In direct correlation with this expansive reach of "translation," scholars in translation studies have recently argued that, having undergone a full "cultural turn," the field is ready to be renamed "post-translation studies."[8] A next challenge to the discipline will surely be in accommodating the ever-more-expansive centrifugal movement of the vaunted "cultural turn," on the one hand, and, on the other, making room for the protocols of machinic translation in all their manifestations, from industrial to epistemological (AI)—protocols that directly confront post-translation studies' devotion to the instability and proliferation of meaning with the return of its repressed: the ghost of demonstrable equivalency.

NOTES

1. "Industrial" translation, known as localization, was the area of sophisticated theoretical work on translation as a distributed practice and the attendant idea of *value* in Anthony Pym, *The Moving Text: Localization, Translation, and Distribution* (Amsterdam: Benjamins, 2004).
2. See, for example, Yonghui Wu et al., "Google's Neural Machine Translation System: Bridging the Gap between Human and Machine Translation" (2016), https://arxiv.org/abs/1609.08144v2.
3. For a discussion of the relationship between equivalency and identity, see, for instance, the introduction to Ivana Hostová, ed., *Identity and Translation Trouble* (Newcastle upon Tyne: Cambridge Scholars, 2017). Douglas Robinson speculates on the surge of the field's "cultural turn" as a direct response to what he calls machine translation's "cenobitic," nonhermeneutic bent. See Robinson, *What Is Translation? Centrifugal Theories, Critical Interventions* (Kent, Ohio: Kent State University Press, 1997), 186–191.
4. Edwin Gentzler, foreword to Robinson, *What Is Translation?*, xii.
5. The more rigorous, systematic, semiologically grounded development of the discipline is in this chronology delegated to Europe, especially to regions such as the Low Countries and Eastern Europe, where a history of interest in structuralism had created a hospitable intellectual environment. See Edwin Gentzler, "Translation without Borders," *Translation: A Transdisciplinary Journal*, http://translation.fusp.it/articles/translation-without-borders, accessed July 18, 2018.
6. Edwin Gentzler, *Contemporary Translation Theories* (New York: Routledge, 1993); Michael Cronin, *Translation in the Digital Age* (New York: Routledge, 2013), 85.
7. Douglas Robinson identifies the work of Liu together with that of Sakai as forming a nucleus of another revisionist "turn" of translation studies. See his *Critical Translation Studies* (New York: Routledge, 2017).
8. Edwin Gentzler, *Translation and Rewriting in the Age of Post-translation Studies* (New York: Routledge, 2017). In the foreword, Susan Bassnett, a doyenne of the academic field, fully endorses Gentzler's view. And scholars like Michael Cronin and Douglas Robinson have, in their different ways, deployed translation in the strict interlingual sense as a kind of epistemological crowbar to demonstrate its core transformative processes present in, say, ecology and medicine.

PART 1 NEW PERSPECTIVES ON TRANSLATION

1 • THE EVENTFULNESS OF TRANSLATION

Temporality, Difference, and Competing Universals

LYDIA H. LIU

Imagine a poem fluttering down in the sky and somehow falling into your hands. You might think that this imaginary scenario would come from a surrealist movie, but I am referring to neither surrealist fantasy nor a writer's delirium. It is related to one of the scandals of translation in modern history. The scandal gripped my attention when I first learned that the U.S. Central Intelligence Agency prepared a Russian translation of T. S. Eliot's poem *Four Quartets* and airdropped it onto the territory of the Soviet Union during the Cold War.[1] This minor escapade quickly passed into oblivion, but the worldwide promotion of postwar modernist art and literature by the CIA and the IRD (the Information Research Department of the British Foreign Office) appears singularly effective in hindsight, so effective that Frances Stonor Saunders, who conducted research in the CIA's archives, came to the conclusion that the West won the Cold War mainly by conquering the world of arts and letters with weapons of the mind, rather than through the arms race or the economic sanctions that are generally considered responsible for the downfall of the socialist bloc.

Although critics may agree or disagree with Saunders's analysis, they need not accept her conclusion to notice a few striking consequences. One of them is that the majority of CIA- backed artists and writers—and there is a long list of them—have made their way into the modernist literary and artistic canon of the West and have systematically been translated as "world literature" around the world, where, for instance, George Orwell's works are read in more languages than Mikhail Sholokhov's novels, even though Sholokhov, in the candid opinion of a literary scholar such as myself, is by far a better writer. And as we turn to twentieth-century poets, T. S. Eliot is perhaps taught in more languages of the world than are Pablo Neruda, Nâzım Hikmet, and Bei Dao combined. It seems that the bets that the CIA placed on Eliot, Orwell, Abstract Expressionists, and other writers or artists whom they favored—airborne or subterranean—have handsomely paid off. Critics sometimes attribute this success to the sophisticated taste and foresight of CIA and IRD covert operators and their collaborators. There may be some truth in this analysis, but taste or aesthetic judgment is often mystifying. Taste cannot explain, for example, the remarkable coincidence whereby many of the writers blacklisted by Senator McCarthy and disfavored by the CIA on nonartistic grounds during the Cold War have subsequently been marginalized in contemporary literary studies or dropped out of the canon altogether after World War II.[2] Why does aesthetic judgment take a backseat when it comes to excluding certain writers from the literary canon, but plays a decisive role when it comes to including certain other writers? Is the making of the literary canon fundamentally political? Or is this merely a case of politics interfering with literature? What role, if any, does global politics play in the struggle over literary productions and their chances of survival in the modern world?[3] Can such political questions throw fresh light on some of the blind spots in the field of translation studies?

These questions have prompted my study of translation as a political problem. The more I learn about the cultural politics of the Cold War, the less I feel inclined to treat global politics as outside interference. Rather than close off the boundaries of literature and politics and render them external to each other, I propose that we, first, examine the dynamic interplay of forces and circumstances that precipitate the act of translation as an act of inclusion and exclusion. Such forces and circumstances are not so much external to translation as prior to any translator's determination of texts to be translated, a determination excluding other works. The study of these processes can help illuminate the meaning of the political more clearly than an examination of the intentions of writers and translators, or their idiosyncratic tastes.

Second, there is a formidable obstacle we must confront if we decide to undertake this line of investigation in translation studies. The obstacle, which often stands in the way of our understanding of the political, is the familiar mental image of translation as a process of verbal communication, linguistic reciprocity, or equivalences, or an issue of commensurability or incommensurability. It is almost as if the promise of meaning or its withdrawal among languages were the only possible thing—blessing or catastrophe—that could happen to the act of translation.[4] I have critiqued these logocentric assumptions in translation studies elsewhere and will not reiterate my position here. To do so would draw us through another round of critiques of linguistics, philology, the philosophy of language, and cultural anthropology, which would draw us too far afield. I should mention briefly, though, that when I proposed the idea of translingual practices many years ago, I was trying to grapple with epistemological issues about how we study translation and address conceptual pitfalls in philological approaches.[5] One question I came very close to asking but did not ask in the mid-1990s was this: Can the eventfulness of translation itself be thought? This question, as it now seems to me, may lead to a more promising approach to the study of translation than either the communication model or the biblical model.[6] And in the context of my chapter in this volume, the question allows me to develop a new critical method for discerning and analyzing the political in regard to translation.

The reason I urge us to develop new methods for analyzing translation is because the problem of translation not only troubles the study of language, literature, philosophy, and cultural anthropology but also cuts across other disciplines and fields. In molecular biology, for example, the idea of translation is ubiquitous and appears in the guise of a metaphor—unquestioned and undertheorized—used to conceptualize the biochemical processes of DNA and RNA. The mobility of this metaphor in the hands of scientists and social scientists has greatly outpaced our ability to think clearly about translation, much less come up with a method to analyze its discursive behavior across the disciplines. In short, translation is no more just a linguistic matter than linguistic differences can be reduced to cultural differences. I believe we have reached the point when the eventfulness of translation itself must be interrogated.[7]

In the first section below, I introduce my methodological reflections and develop some ideas about the multiple temporalities of translation in what I call *differentially distributed discursive practices across languages*. This analysis leads to a discussion of universalism and cultural difference in the second section, which is focused on the multilingual making of one of the best-known documents of the postwar period: the Universal Declaration of Human Rights (hereafter UDHR) of the United Nations. Here I examine P. C. Chang's contribution as vice-chair on the Drafting Committee of the UDHR document—which also included chair Eleanor Roosevelt and other members—and analyze his philosophical contestation of parochial universalism at the UN in 1947–1948. I turn next to a remarkable vision of competing universalisms with a focus on Afro-Asian Writers Conferences and their translation projects in the 1950s. The third section shows how some of these projects were organized and pursued in response to the postwar geopolitics of that time. I conclude with some final reflections on translation and literary diplomacy and internationalism in the Cold War.

DISCURSIVE MOBILITY

In light of my initial question—Can the eventfulness of translation be thought?—I would say yes, but not until we begin by rethinking the relationship among text, interpretation, and event. If all acts of translation—and, by extension, all textual work—are mediated by temporality and spatiality, do all translated texts qualify as events? The answer hinges on how the idea of "event" is defined or philosophically worked out, but that is not the task of this chapter.[8] Instead of indulging in exercises of definition that belong elsewhere, I choose to focus on the multiplicity of differentially distributed discursive fields as the site—in terms of both spatiality and mobility—of any translated text and explore their temporalities as instances of events. For no event worthy of the name—as naming is always part of the process—could possibly exist outside of the discursive practices that organize it and make it emerge as such, much less the event of translation, which always presupposes the multiplicity of discursive fields across different languages. The first step toward a fruitful understanding of the eventfulness of translation, therefore, is to develop a conceptual framework for analyzing the interplay of temporality and discursive practices across languages.

Before we contemplate the possibility of such a framework, we must address yet another potential objection: What is to be achieved through the proposed study of eventfulness of translation? Why not be content with our old philological methods? Is it not sufficient to analyze, say, a word-for-word rendering of a poem from English to Russian or the case of a mismatched verb in translated text? I would not rule out the value of this kind of philological work so long as it does not limit our understanding of how a work of translation is brought into being in the first place, and why one writer is deemed more worthy of translation into foreign languages than other writers. As a matter of fact, T. S. Eliot found himself compelled to address these issues when he accepted the Nobel Prize in Literature. In his acceptance speech at the Nobel Banquet in Stockholm in 1948, Eliot stated,

> If this were simply the recognition of merit, or of the fact that an author's reputation has passed the boundaries of his own country and his own language, we could say that hardly any one of us at any time is, more than others, worthy of being so distinguished. But I find in the Nobel Award something more and something different from such recognition. It seems to me more the election of an individual, chosen from time to time from one nation or another, and selected by something like an act of grace, to fill a peculiar role and to become a peculiar symbol. A ceremony takes place, by which a man is suddenly endowed with some function which he did not fill before. So the question is not whether he was worthy to be so singled out, but whether he can perform the function which you have assigned to him: the function of serving as a representative, so far as any man can be, of something of far greater importance than the value of what he himself has written.[9]

Eliot's disavowal of his unique accomplishment as a poet may have been motivated by real modesty, but it simultaneously touches on the truth of what it means to "fill a peculiar role and to become a peculiar symbol" or to "perform a function" and serve "as a representative." And of what is he a representative? When Eliot's *Four Quartets* leapt over the spatial, linguistic, and ideological divide of the

Cold War to fall from the sky—let's hope not directly into a river—the Russian translation was probably taken by covert operators to represent good poetry from the Free World as opposed to the dogma of socialist realism. In that case, the poet could do very little about the idiosyncratic decisions of those operators who instrumentalized his work.

It is interesting that Eliot was keenly aware of his own passivity when it comes to being selected, being endowed, being singled out, and being assigned by others and so on. To emphasize his passive role is not to extricate him from the complicity with the CIA but to point out that, in spite of himself, Eliot's name and his poetry do indeed float around like a symbol. Perhaps more mobile and airborne than other symbols, but nevertheless a symbol, often outside of his control but which he must live up to. And live up to it he did. Furthermore, the symbol called T. S. Eliot is assigned to function in a multiplicity of languages and discursive fields that inevitably mark a literary work for translation and international distribution. This discursive marking, I emphasize, holds out the potential of turning a symbol into an event, or an event into a symbol, back and forth.

In that sense, the question as to which translated or translatable text qualifies as an event depends very much on the ways we analyze the temporality and spatiality of its discursive mobility, hence its historicity. To bring the eventfulness of translation into critical view, one must stop thinking about translation as a volitional act of matching words or building equivalences of meanings between languages; rather we should start by taking it as a precarious wager that enables the discursive mobility of a text or a symbol, for better or for worse. The wager releases the multiplicity of the text and opens it to an uncertain future, more often than not an uncertain political future. The confluence of forces that enable the discursive mobility of a text, or those forces that can mobilize the energy of translators, or cause a poem to be airdropped from the sky, should give us the first clue about the role of the political in translation.

TRANSLATION AS EVENT

This is something I have learned from my previous study of the nineteenth-century Chinese translation of Henry Wheaton's *Elements of International Law* by American missionary W.A.P. Martin and his Chinese collaborators. In *The Clash of Empires*, I analyzed the military and political conflicts of the Second Opium War to understand who determined the selection of Wheaton's text and how its translation *Wangguo gongfa* (literally, "Public law of multifarious countries") was brought to fruition in 1863–1864.[10] Reflecting upon the temporalities of this translation and its dissemination, I was immediately struck by its peculiar eventfulness and realized that this translated text was by no means a singular event; I saw at least a triple event at the moment of its creation. And what do I mean by the triple event of the *Wangguo gongfa*?

The first and immediate event was the creation of the Chinese text itself, a textual event that required a great deal of negotiation and compromise between the Chinese translators and the American missionary. Words and their meanings were made up, suspended, substituted, or banished in the course of translation. Next comes the diplomatic event. As a matter of fact, the textual and diplomatic events became inextricably entangled before there was even a translated text. For example, the act of discursive marking in regard to which text of international law ought to be selected and which excluded from translation mirrored the diplomatic conflicts among the imperial powers in China. The timely interventions made by American ministers William B. Reed and Anson Burlingame and by Sir Robert Hart—the second British inspector-general of the Imperial Maritime Custom Service of the Qing—all played into the hands of Prince Gong and his Foreign Office *Zongli yamen* who agreed to sponsor the translation project. Even more interesting is the third aspect of this happening, which I have called the epistemological event because the historical unfolding of the *Wangguo gongfa* was predicated on a certain view of the global that was yet to come. That process requires a somewhat different temporality—spanning the late Qing through the Republican era, up to our own time—before a geopolitical consciousness could emerge among the Chinese elite. I attribute the rise of so-called global (and subsequently national) consciousness in East Asia to this triple event. In that sense, the multiple temporalities of the *Wangguo gongfa* vastly complicate our understanding of translation and its historicity. These temporalities were thoroughly embedded in the precarious wager I suggested earlier. Through the discursive mobility of the *Wangguo gongfa*, the wager in the realm of international politics unleashed the linguistic multiplicity of Wheaton's text from English to Chinese and then from Chinese to Japanese and so on, opening it to an uncertain political future. That future, in hindsight, converged in the Japanese annexation of Korea, Taiwan, Manchuria, and other colonial enterprises, all worked out in the legal terms of *Wangguo gongfa* or *Bankoku kōhō* (Japanese for "international law").

But what about the role of cultural differences in translation? Aren't cultural differences more central to the work of translation than the problems of temporality and spatiality? And do those differences matter? My answer is yes, they do matter, but not more and not less than the universalist aspirations that inspire any acts of translation or epistemological crossings through languages in the first place. As I argued elsewhere, universalism thrives on difference. It does not negate difference so much as absorb it into its familiar orbit of antithesis and dialectic.[11] The situated articulation of cultural difference has been embedded in the universalizing processes of past and present all along, and it is these processes that determine what counts as difference and why it should matter. Such processes can tell us a great deal about how cultural differences are differentially distributed through the event called translation and how these differences undergo discursive markings—inclusion, exclusion, comparison, cutting, abstraction, etc.—before they appear as such from the vantage point of the universal. Indeed, it is the struggle over the universal where the political asserts itself persistently with respect to cultural differences. As we turn our attention to the twentieth century, what could be more universal than the claims of the Universal Declaration of Human Rights?

COMPETING UNIVERSALS

The UN Commission on Human Rights got off to a troubled start in the spring of 1947. John P. Humphrey (1905–1995), the first director of the UN Secretariat's Division on Human Rights, recalls that the chairman of the Human Rights Commission, Eleanor Roosevelt, undertook the task of formulating a preliminary draft international bill of human rights, working with elected vice-chairman Peng-chun Chang (1892–1957) and the rapporteur Charles Habib Malik (1906–1987) with the assistance of the secretariat. On Sunday, February 17, 1947, Mrs. Roosevelt invited Chang, Malik, and Humphrey to meet in her Washington Square apartment for tea and to discuss the preparation of the first draft of the UDHR by the secretariat. Humphrey recorded a snippet of their conversation:

> There was a good deal of talk, but we were getting nowhere. Then, after still another cup of tea, Chang suggested that I put my other duties aside for six months and study Chinese philosophy, after which I might be able to prepare a text for the Committee. This was his way of saying that Western influences might be too great, and he was looking at Malik as he spoke. He had already, in the Commission, urged the importance of historical perspective. There was some more discussion mainly of a philosophical character, Mrs. Roosevelt saying little and continuing to pour tea.[12]

This seems to be the uncertain first moment of what would become several years of conversation and intellectual debates, leading to the birth of the International Bill of Human Rights in three landmark documents: the UDHR (1948), the International Covenant on Civil and Political Rights (1966), and the International Covenant on Economic, Social and Cultural Rights (1966).

Malik, a Lebanese Christian and Thomist philosopher, had studied philosophy in Europe before World War II, working briefly with Heidegger, and then completed his doctoral degree in philosophy at Harvard University. Malik was a man of strong convictions, and his Christian personalism was the main fount of his universalism, but his lifelong passion was anticommunism.[13] By contrast, Chang was a secular humanist, musician, and man of letters. Educated in China and the United States, he was thoroughly bilingual and bicultural.[14] Chang and Malik had different upbringings and were steeped in very different intellectual traditions, but they both joined the UN as scholar-diplomats who hailed from the non-Western world and saw themselves as bridges between East and West. They were followed by other non-Western members of the eighteen-member UN Commission on Human Rights, including Filipino diplomat Carlos Romulo, Indian feminist educator Hansa Mehta, and Latin American delegates who made important contributions to the conceptualization of the International Bill of Human Rights.[15]

Chang resolved to refashion the idea of "human rights" into a universal principle—more universal than ever before—and he envisioned the ground of that universalism somewhere between classical Chinese thought and the European Enlightenment. Upon his election as vice-chairman of the UN Human Rights Commission, he fought to reclaim the meeting ground between those radically different philosophical traditions. Records of the complicated processes of drafting the declaration suggest that Chang engaged in a relentless negotiation of competing universals between Chinese and European philosophical traditions. His method involved translingual reworking of ideas across these traditions—a constant back-and-forth—to open up the universal ground for human rights. And he did so by crossing the conceptual threshold of linguistic differences in the face of an old conundrum of incommensurability: Does the idea of the "human" in English mean the same thing in a language that does not share its linguistic roots or philosophical traditions? On the one hand, Chang took a pragmatic approach to the question of cultural difference and incommensurability in order to bring about consensus among member states on the Human Rights Commission; on the other—and more interestingly from a philosophical point of view—he made a wager of commensurability through a mode of intellectual persuasion and translation that required an unwavering commitment to his vision of universalism, a universalism of human rights.[16]

The numerous interventions Chang made in the drafting of UDHR illustrate this process very well. Article 1, for example, reads, "All human beings are born free and equal in dignity and rights. They are endowed with reason and conscience and should act towards one another in a spirit of brotherhood." This statement is deceptively straightforward; in actuality, the words on printed page are the outcome of one of the most contentious debates on the Third Committee concerning God and religion. In what is known as the Geneva draft, which was produced by the Second Session of the Commission on Human Rights in meetings that took place in Geneva between December 2 and December 17, 1947, the draft article states, "All men are born free and equal in dignity and rights. They are endowed *by nature* with reason and conscience and should act towards one another like brothers."[17] The phrase "by nature" in the Geneva draft was introduced by a Filipino delegate as a deistic reference to natural law.[18] Whereas Lebanese philosopher Charles Malik wanted to substitute the words "by their Creator" for "by nature," other delegates tried to introduce similar references to God in the UDHR.[19] Johannes Morsink's study shows that when the Third Committee began its meeting in the fall of 1948, two amendments were proposed to insert overt references to God in Article 1. The Brazilian delegation proposed to start the second sentence of Article 1 thus: "*Created in the image and likeness of God,* they are endowed with reason and conscience." The Dutch delegation came up with a similar assertion of religious faith: "Whereas recognition of the inherent dignity and of the equal and inalienable rights of all members of the human family, *based on man's divine origin and immortal destiny,* is the foundation of freedom, justice and peace in the world." These amendments led to intense debates. In the end, neither of the amendments was voted upon, although the Third Committee did vote to remove "by nature" from Article 1 (by a vote of twenty-six to four, with nine abstentions).[20]

Mary Ann Glendon has noted that on this occasion it was Chang who carried the majority by reminding everyone that the declaration was designed to be universally applicable.[21] His intervention and reasoning were essential to the decision of the Third Committee to remove the phrase "by nature" from the Geneva draft. Chang's argument was that the Chinese "population had ideals and traditions different from that of the Christian West. Yet . . . the Chinese representative would refrain from proposing that mention of them should be made in the declaration. He hoped his colleagues would show equal consideration and withdraw some of the amendments to Article 1 that raised metaphysical problems. For Western civilization, too, the time for religious intolerance was over."[22] The first line of Article 1, he suggested, should refer neither to nature nor to God. Those who believed in God could still find the idea of God in the strong assertions that all human beings are born free and equal and endowed with reason and conscience, but others should be allowed to interpret the language differently. Mrs. Roosevelt was clearly persuaded by his argument, for she adopted the same language when she had to explain to her American audience why the declaration contained no reference to the Creator.[23]

Chang urged the Third Committee not to indulge in metaphysical arguments and succeeded in sparing the committee from having to vote on theological questions. He asked the committee, rather than debating human nature again, to build on the work of eighteenth-century European philosophers. Morsink speculates that the motivation behind Chang's support for the deletion of "by nature" was that some delegates understood the phrase as underscoring a materialistic rather than a spiritual or even humanistic conception of human nature.[24] I am inclined to think that Chang's argument is remarkably consistent with what he had termed the "aspiration for a new humanism."[25] His universalist vision seeks even to overcome the conceptual opposition between the religious and the secular, and between the spiritual and the material.

That vision emerged early on in one of the most interesting and precarious interventions Chang made to the Cassin draft of the UDHR. The Cassin draft was based on the first draft of the declaration, which was written by Humphrey of the secretariat. Article 1 of the Cassin draft was very different from the final version.

It states, "All men, being members of one family, are free, possess equal dignity and rights, and shall regard each other as brothers."[26] In June 1947, when French delegate René Cassin presented this draft to the Drafting Committee, the group revised the language of Article 1 to read, "All men are brothers. Being endowed with reason and members of one family, they are free and equal in dignity and rights." In the course of that discussion, Chang proposed that Article 1 should include another concept as an essential human attribute next to "reason." He then came up with a literal translation of the concept he had in mind, called *ren* 仁, as "two-man-mindedness."[27] Drawing implicitly on classical Chinese sources, Chang glossed this written character as a composite of the radical for "human" 人 and the written character for the number "two" 二. Interpreting *ren* as "two-man-mindedness" through his epigraphic analysis of the discrete parts of the written character, Chang sought to transform the concept of "human" for human rights by regrounding that idea in the originary plurality of humanity, rather than in the concept of the individual.

Unfortunately, no equivalent of this important classical Confucian concept could be found in English or French to help Chang explicate its meaning, which has deep roots in the millennia-long philosophical tradition in China. Confucian tradition, in my view, has produced an overly abundant discourse on the concept of "human," its ethical being, and so on, but had almost nothing to say about "rights" until the second half of the nineteenth century.[28] Chang, straddling both traditions, found himself in a strange, precarious situation of having to use the words "sympathy" and "consciousness of his fellow men" to convey what he had in mind.[29] His effort misfired, and it certainly failed to impress Cassin, Mrs. Roosevelt, and the other members of the drafting committee, who accepted Chang's proposal but agreed to let the word "conscience" translate the idea of *ren*. "Conscience" was added to the word "reason" to make the second line of Article 1 read, "They are endowed with reason and conscience." With great insight, Glendon writes, "That unhappy word choice not only obscured Chang's meaning, but gave 'conscience' a far from obvious sense, quite different from its normal usage in phrases such as 'freedom of conscience.'"[30] Not surprisingly, the metropolitan languages were not about to surrender themselves to the Confucian term to produce a novel concept in English or French, missing a good opportunity to reimagine what it means to be "human" in other terms.[31]

As we turn to the Chinese version of the UDHR prepared by the United Nations, we discover that the Confucian concept has worked its way back into that document through the use of another term: *liangxin*.[32] The word *liangxin* 良心 is made up of two written characters: the character *liang* for "innate goodness" and the character *xin* for the "mind/heart." This translation openly takes the place of "conscience" and interprets the English word back into Chang's classical term *ren*, which articulates a more fundamental sense of what makes a human being moral than the idea of "conscience."[33] The word *liangxin* is associated with *ren* in

Confucian moral philosophy, denoting the empathetic endowment of the human psyche toward another human being prior to the formation of individual conscience. In the Chinese version of the UDHR, Chang's original explication of *ren* as "two-men-mindedness"—though lost in the English and French texts—is reasserted through an associated concept.[34]

I have discussed only one of numerous textual examples to be gleaned in the multilingual making of that historic document. In fact, a large number of languages besides Mandarin and classical Chinese contributed to the making of the UDHR, and these languages opened the document to the radical multiplicity and translingual plurality of the philosophies and cultures of the world, first in its moment of genesis and then in subsequent translations. If we lend an ear to the plurality of voices and substitutions across numerous multilingual editions of this document, we are bound to encounter other temporalities and universalisms that are waiting to be rediscovered and mobilized for the benefit of future politics. The fact that Chang's pluralist vision of the universal "human" fails to register in the texts of hegemonic metropolitan languages and philosophical traditions suggests that it will take more than individual scholar-diplomats, no matter how resourceful they are, to overcome the tremendous odds of East-West or South-North disparity in the arbitration of moral discourse.

Less than a decade after the UN adopted the UDHR, however, self-determination or national independence movements swept across the globe. Suddenly, an extraordinary opportunity emerged as the peoples of Asia and Africa began to stage their competing universals worldwide. After the 1955 Bandung Conference, a number of worldwide events played a critical role in the episode of Afro-Asian solidarity to which we now turn.

GEOPOLITICS OF TRANSLATION

I began to develop an interest in Afro-Asian Writers Conferences while researching the origins of the literary journal *Shijie wenxue* (World literature), which began publication in the People's Republic of China in 1959.[35] As I read Chinese translations of poets and writers from around the world in past issues of this journal, the Nigerian novelist Chinua Achebe's name immediately caught my attention. Selected chapters from his *Things Fall Apart* (1958) were printed in the February 1963 issue, so the novel was available in Chinese translation long before it became known to the mainstream readership of the West, and certainly long before Achebe's works were relegated to so-called Anglophone literature. I was struck by the fact that Achebe had been recognized as an Afro-Asian writer in China, Egypt, India, the Soviet Union, and other countries before he became a postcolonial Anglophone (African) writer, as he is currently known and taught in English departments of American academia and elsewhere. There is a world of difference between these two types of recognition. To my mind, the difference lies mainly in the forgotten history of post-Bandung Afro-Asian writers' interactions and solidarity between 1958 and 1970. A great deal of this history's politics lies in the work of translation.

The Afro-Asian Writer's Conferences were an offshoot of the newly formed Afro-Asian People's Solidarity Organization, which had been inspired by the Bandung Conference and met in Cairo on December 26, 1957.[36] The first Afro-Asian Writer's Conference took place in Tashkent, Uzbekistan, in Soviet Central Asia in October 1958. Asian and African delegates and Western observers flew in from all directions and landed in the new airport of Tashkent. Noting the arrival of these airborne poets and novelists, one journalist observed, "We had come to meet the writers of Asia and Africa, gathering for the first time. A new airport; a smiling reception committee; a drive along avenues of acacia and poplar hung with coloured lamps and banners lettered in Chinese, Arabic, and Hindi."[37] The conference was attended by leading writers of thirty-six countries, including renowned Turkish poet Nâzım Hikmet, Yashpal, Mulk Raj Anand, and Tarasankar Bandyopadhyay of India, Ananta Toer Pramoedya of Indonesia, Burma's U Kyaw Lin Hyun, Cambodia's Ly Theam Teng, Vietnam's Pham Huy Thong, Afro-American writer W.E.B. Du Bois, and Mao Dun and Zhou Yang, who led a delegation of twenty-one members from China.

Interestingly, W.E.B. Du Bois and his wife Shirley were invited to Tashkent as the honored guests of the first Afro-Asian conference in October 1958. Long deemed a dangerous radical in the eyes of the U.S. government, Du Bois drew the only standing ovation to an individual from the Asian and African authors at the conference. According to historian Gerald Horne, "In an informal discussion of African unification problems with writers from British Nigeria, Madagascar, Ghana, Somaliland, Senegal, and Angola, Du Bois told them: 'a socialist Africa was inevitable.'"[38] Such was the optimism of the Tashkent Conference.

Still, the Third-World delegates represented a broad spectrum of literary and political persuasions. They came together not to debate about their national or political priorities but to discuss an agenda that concerned them all. First, what role would the development of literatures and cultures in different Asian and African countries play in the progress of mankind, for national independence, against colonialism, or for peace and freedom throughout the world? Many writers commented on how colonialism had destroyed traditional cultural ties between Asia and Africa. Efua Theodora Sutherland, representing the Ghana Society of Writers, saw that occasion as "a step towards the reunification of the disrupted soul of mankind." She remarked, "It is up to us to seek practical ways and means of strengthening our cultural links. There is a need to channel to our continent some of your best literary contributions. We need to know the works of Asian and African writers, to be in touch with the wider horizon which those works represent, and which have hitherto been unavailable in our country."[39] Her enthusiasm was widely shared among conference participants, who agreed that a Permanent Bureau of Afro-Asian Writers should be set up for the purpose of maintaining future interaction and activities with headquarters located in Ceylon (present-day Sri Lanka).[40]

Unlike the scholar-diplomat P. C. Chang who staged a lone battle at the UN to recast the moral concept of "human" on the basis of plurality (*ren*, "two-human-mindedness") before granting universal validity to the concept of human rights, the Asian and African writers pursued a much more ambitious course of action. They mounted a full range of activities, forming international alliances, setting up transnational institutions, and creating journals to educate themselves and one another through translations and conversation. In the following decades, for example, the bureau coordinated numerous meetings, translations, and publications. There were, no doubt, attempts made by the Soviet Union and China to set the political agenda, for the purpose of either pushing the world revolution or undermining each other when the relationship between Kremlin and Beijing deteriorated. But as in the case of the Afro-Asian People's Solidarity Organization over the years, these attempts often met with resistance from the United Arab Republic (Egypt), India, and other Third-World countries.[41] Clearly, no one wanted a Soviet front organization. Egypt and India played a central role in the Permanent Bureau. After the second Afro-Asian Writers Conference in Cairo, the bureau started a quarterly called *Lotus*, which was published in Arabic, English, and French, and launched a prize for African and Asian literature—named the Lotus Prize—to honor distinguished poets and writers from Asia and Africa. Novelists and poets awarded this prize include Chinua Achebe from Nigeria, Ousmane Sembène from Senegal, Ngugi wa Thiong'o from Kenya, Malek Haddad from Algeria, and Mahmoud Darwish from Palestine.

Mulk Raj Anand was the leader of the Indian delegation to the second Afro-Asian Writers Conference in 1962. In his Cairo speech, he elaborated a new humanism as follows:

> Our literatures and arts are thus the weapons of a new concept of man—that the suppressed, the disinherited and the insulted of Asia and Africa can rise to live, in brotherhood with other men, but in the enjoyment of freedom and equality and justice, as more truly human beings, individuals, entering from object history, into the great history when there will be no war, but when love will rule the world, enabling man to bring the whole of nature under self-conscious control for the uses of happiness, as against despair.[42]

Interestingly, Anand invoked Garcia Lorca's poem "Ode to Walt Whitman" to express the sentiment of the socially engaged writers from Asia and Africa:

> I want the strong air of the most profound night
> to remove flowers and words from the arch where you sleep,

and a black child to announce to the gold-craving whites
the arrival of the reign of the ear of corn.[43]

Anand states that the mission of the writer is to "act as the conscience of the people aware of their pain. To have a creative vision of all that affords joy in life, to release the vital rhythms in the personality, to make man more human, to seek apperceptions of freedom from all forms of slavery and to give this freedom to other people throughout the world—in fact to awaken men to the love of liberty, which brings life and more life."[44] This call for freedom was not empty rhetoric but was echoed by writers from the socialist bloc as well as from the newly independent nations of Asia and Africa. To those who had intimate knowledge of slavery and racial and economic exploitation under colonialism, liberty had a specific meaning: it meant decolonization, national liberation, and world peace in the spirit of the Bandung Conference.

The Afro-Asian Writers Conference in Tashkent made a tremendous impact on China. Almost immediately, the journal *Yiwen* (Translations), which used to feature predominantly Soviet and Western authors, began to shift focus and publish works by Iranian, Iraqi, Egyptian, and Mozambican writers. In January 1959, the journal was renamed *Shijie wenxue* (World literature) and began to devote its bimonthly issues to a systematic translation of Afro-Asian writers, African American writers and, later, Latin American writers. By 1962, more than 380 titles from over thirty Asia and African countries had been printed in its pages. Irene Eber's survey indicates that by 1965, Afro-Asian and Latin American writers began to outnumber Western authors. The October 1964 issue, specifically dedicated to black literature, included African writers as well as Afro-American writers, such as W.E.B. Du Bois and Margaret Walker.[45]

Following the Tashkent Conference, the Chinese Writers Union extended invitations to their Afro-Asian friends, and over the years, many of them visited China more than once. The great Indonesian writer Pramoedya Ananta Toer made his second trip to China following the Tashkent Conference. His interactions with Ding Ling, Mao Dun, Guo Moruo, Zhou Yang, and other Chinese writers were frequent and helped transform his ideas about a writer's responsibility toward society. Hong Liu's study suggests that Pramoedya's contact with the Chinese delegation and the Chinese embassy dates back as early as the 1955 Bandung Conference. After that event, he began to follow the works of Chinese writers and came to admire the social prestige enjoyed by socialist writers in the PRC, "where literature is considered to be one of the political and economic forces" and where writers were paid generously for their publications, in stark contrast to conditions in Indonesia.[46]

Pramoedya regarded Mao Dun and Lu Xun as the foremost writers of modern China; he published some portions of Lu Xun's short story collection *Diary of a Madman* (*Catatan Orang Gila*) as well as one of Ding Ling's long articles, "Life and Creative Writing." Perhaps more than anyone else in Indonesia, Pramoedya took the socialist credo of "living with peasants and workers" to heart and fervently believed that writers should go into social life and live with the people. He himself "went down" to the countryside of the Banten area to investigate the lives of peasants and miners.

CONCLUDING REMARKS

I began my essay by raising some new questions about translation and its relationship to the political. My approach has been to work through the ideas of event, temporality, difference, and competing universals as a conceptual alternative to the familiar model of linguistic communication or the theological model with which we are all familiar in translation studies. The alternative method I have proposed involves analyzing the multiple temporalities of translation in differentially distributed discursive practices across languages. To bring such a method to bear on concrete analyses of the eventfulness of translation, I have taken the reader through the nineteenth-century translation of *Elements of International Law* in Chinese, the post–World War II multilingual fashioning of the Universal Declaration of Human Rights with a focus on P. C. Chang's contribution, and the Afro-Asian writers' translation projects during the Cold War.

And as I bring my discussion to a close, Benedict Anderson's observation on Pramoedya has come back to haunt me. Being a great admirer of Pramoedya, Anderson communicated with the Indonesian writer on numerous occasions. One afternoon, as I was reading Anderson's reflections on Pramoedya in *Language and Power*, I was struck by his remark: "More broadly, Pramoedya gave me an inkling of how one might fruitfully link the shapes of literature with the political imagination."[47] What could he have meant by the political imagination?

This question has led me to speculate about whether Anderson's personal correspondence with the Indonesian writer ever brought up the Afro-Asian Conference in Tashkent, where Pramoedya had been the leader of the Indonesian delegation. I wonder further if Anderson was aware of Pramoedya's extensive interactions with Mao Dun and Ding Ling, and of his published translation of the Chinese writers. In his own manner, Anderson was translating Pramoedya for the English-speaking audience, as the latter had enabled the translation of Lu Xun for his Indonesian audience. This unexpected trajectory of translations inspires me to look to the future itself as the preserve of multiple temporalities. I am hopeful that the legacies of the Afro-Asian Writers Conferences—their political imagination, their encouragement to think differently about the future of universalism, their ambitious, collective translation projects, and their reinvention of world literature—will live on through the temporalities of potential translations to come.

NOTES

This essay appeared first in the journal *translation: a transdisciplinary journal* as part of a special issue guest-edited by Naoki Sakai and Sandro Mezzadra, no.4 (Spring 2014): 147–170. I thank the editor Siri Nergaard for the permission to reprint my piece in the current volume.

1. Frances Stonor Saunders, *The Cultural Cold War: The CIA and the World of Arts and Letters* (New York: New Press, 2001), 248.

2. Robert Justin Goldstein, *Political Repression in Modern America: From 1870 to 1976* (Urbana: University of Illinois Press, 2001); on blacklisting in the United Kingdom, see Mark Hollingsworth and Richard Norton-Taylor, *Blacklist: The Inside Story of Political Vetting* (London: Hogarth, 1988).

3. Most scholars of literature who are familiar with the work of Fredric Jameson and Pierre Bourdieu would probably concur that canon formation is political. I find Bourdieu's notion of the literary field useful in a national setting but rather limited for thinking across national borders, especially when it comes to international politics in cultural life.

4. Although more sophisticated than other theorists, Walter Benjamin's conception of translation in "The Task of the Translator" ultimately endorses this manner of reasoning. In his notion of Pure Language, translation holds out a promise of meaning in messianic time, if not in secular temporality. See my critique in the introduction to *Translingual Practice: Literature, National Culture, and Translated Modernity, China 1900–1936* (Stanford: Stanford University Press, 1995).

5. See Liu, *Translingual Practice,* chap. 1.

6. The story of the Tower of Babel has heretofore dominated our framing of translation as a theoretical problem. I am doubtful that an endless rehashing or deconstruction of this biblical story can get us anywhere closer to a better understanding. For earlier critiques of the biblical story, see George Steiner, *After Babel: Aspects of Language and Translation* (Oxford: Oxford University Press, 1978); Paul de Man, "Conclusions: Walter Benjamin's 'Task of the Translator,'" in *Resistance to Theory* (Minneapolis: University of Minnesota Press, 1986), 73–105; and Jacques Derrida, "Les Tours de Babel," in *Difference in Translation,* trans. and ed. Graham F. Joseph (London: Cornwell University Press, 1985), 165–208.

7. In recent decades, new approaches have been developed here and there to open up the field beyond established translation studies. See Naoki Sakai, *Translation and Subjectivity* (Minneapolis: University of Minnesota Press, 1997).

8. I assume that the reader is familiar with Alain Badiou's rigorous philosophical work on the subject. See his *Being and Event,* trans. Oliver Feltham (New York: Continuum, 2005) and *Logics of Worlds: Being and Event,* vol. 2, trans. Alberto Toscano (New York: Continuum, 2009).

9. T. S. Eliot, "Banquet Speech" (Stockholm, December 10, 1948), http://www.nobelprize.org/nobel_prizes/literature/laureates/1948/eliot-speech.html.

10. Lydia H. Liu, *The Clash of Empires: The Invention of China in Modern World Making* (Cambridge, Mass.: Harvard University Press, 2006), chap. 4.

11. Lydia H. Liu, "Introduction," in *Tokens of Exchange: The Problem of Translation in Global Circulations,* ed. Liu (Durham, N.C.: Duke University Press, 1999), 2–12.

12. John P. Humphrey, *Human Rights and the United Nations: A Great Adventure* (Dobbs Ferry, N.Y.: Transnational, 1984), 29.

13. Malik was Edward Said's uncle, who married the first cousin of Said's mother. Said's reminiscences show some mixed feelings about Malik's politics and personality. See Edward Said, *Out of Place: A Memoir* (New York: Vintage, 2000).

14. P. C. Chang (or Zhang Pengchun, in the pinyin romanization system) was born on April 22, 1892, in Tianjin. He was the younger brother of P. L. Chang (Zhang Boling), who was the

founder of Nankai University and one of the most preeminent educators in the Republic of China. Both brothers studied at Columbia University. For Chang's life, see Cui Guoliang and Cui Hong, eds., *Zhang Pengchun lun jiaoyu yu xiju yishu* [P.C. Chang on education and theatrical arts] (Tianjin: Nankai daxue chubanshe, 2003), 615–710.

15. Mary Ann Glendon, *A World Made New: Eleanor Roosevelt and the Universal Declaration of Human Rights* (New York: Random House, 2002); see also Johannes Morsink, *The Universal Declaration of Human Rights: Origins, Drafting and Intent* (Philadelphia: University of Pennsylvania Press, 1999), 245–248.

16. For a critical study of the universalism of human rights, see my article "Shadows of Universalism: The Untold Story of Human Rights Around 1948," *Critical Inquiry* 40 (Summer 2014): 385–417.

17. Glendon, *World Made New*, 289, emphasis added.

18. The same theological reference also framed the language of the Virginia Declaration of Rights (1776) and the American Declaration of Independence (1776) as well as numerous other documents on the rights of men that had been promulgated before World War II and served as templates for the UDHR.

19. Glendon, *World Made New,* 89.

20. Morsink, *Universal Declaration of Human Rights,* 287.

21. Glendon, *World Made New*, 146.

22. Third Committee, Ninety-Sixth Meeting, October 7, 1948, 98; Ninety-Eighth Meeting, October 9, 1948, 114.

23. Glendon, *World Made New*, 147.

24. Morsink, *Universal Declaration of Human Rights,* 287.

25. Sumner B. Twiss, "Confucian Contributions to the Universal Declaration of Human Rights: A Historical and Philosophical Perspective," in *The World's Religions after September 11: Volume 2 Religion and Human Rights,* ed. Arvind Sharma (Westport, Conn.: Praeger, 2009), 110.

26. Glendon, "The 'Cassin Draft,'" in *World Made New*, 276.

27. Chang's epigraphic reading was derived from the *Shuowen jiezi* (25–220 CE), the first dictionary of Chinese written characters compiled by the Han dynasty scholar Xu Shen.

28. The language of "rights" and "human rights," like "sovereignty," was first introduced to China through the 1864 translation of Wheaton's *Elements of International Law*, discussed above.

29. Commission on Human Rights, Drafting Committee, First Session, Summary Record of the Eighth Meeting at Lake Success, New York, on Tuesday, 17 June 1947 at 2:30 p.m., E/CN.4/AC.1/SR.8.

30. Glendon, *World Made New*, 67–68.

31. I use the word "surrender" in Gayatri Chakravorty Spivak's sense. In "The Politics of Translation," she argues that the translator must "surrender to the [original] text." See Spivak, *Outside the Teaching Machine* (London: Routledge, 1993), 179–200.

32. http://www.un.org/zh/documents/udhr/.

33. The notion of *liangxin* was elaborated by ancient Chinese philosopher Mencius (ca. 372–ca. 289 BCE) to explicate Confucius's concept *ren*, and was subsequently developed by Song dynasty philosophers for the Neo-Confucian theory of moral personhood. In *Mencius*, *ren* or *renyi* and *liangxin* are both mentioned in a passage from "Gaozi I." Mencius is quoted as saying, "Can it be asserted that the mind of any man is not formed by *ren* and *yi* [justice]? The way in which a man loses his *liangxin* [innate goodness] is like the way in which the trees are denuded by axes and bills." The Neo-Confucian scholar of the Song dynasty Zhu Xi (1130–1200) explicates the notion *liangxin* as the "nature of kind-mindedness."

34. The official languages at the United Nations were initially English and French, but Russian, Chinese, and a couple of other languages were soon added to the list of official languages,

rendering the linguistic landscape extremely variegated. As for the Chinese version of the UDHR, I have not been able to determine whether Chang himself was involved in the translation. The substitution of *liangxin* for *ren* may be due to the facts that the Chinese translation of "conscience" as *liangxin* was an established usage and that this bisyllabic word had an obvious appeal to modern Chinese speakers.

35. The journal was originally called *Yiwen* (*Translations*) when it was founded in 1953 and changed its name to *Shijie wenxue* in 1959 after the first Afro-Asian Writers Conference in Tashkent in 1958.

36. On the history of the Afro-Asian People's Solidarity Organization and China's role in it, see Charles Neuhauser, *Third World Politics: China and the Afro-Asian People's Solidarity Organization 1957–1967* (Cambridge, Mass.: Harvard University Press, 1968).

37. Ralph Parker, "The Afro-Asian Writers' Conference," *Meanjin Quarterly* 18 (April 1959): 107–111. For the day-to-day events, see the diaries of Guo Xiaochuan, who served on the preparatory committee of the Tashkent Conference in *Guo Xiaochuan quanji* [Complete works of Guo Xiaochuan], vol. 9 (Guilin: Guangqi shifan daxue chubanshe, 2000). See also Shūichi Katō's reminiscence of his representation of Japan on the same preparatory committee in *A Sheep's Song: A Writer's Reminiscences of Japan and the World* (Berkeley: University of California Press, 1999).

38. See Gerald Horne, *Black and Red: W. E. B. Du Bois and the Afro-American Response to the Cold War, 1944–1963* (Albany: State University of New York Press, 1985), 321.

39. As quoted in Ralph Parker, "Afro-Asian Writers' Conference," 109.

40. The headquarters moved to the city of Cairo after a few years.

41. On that history, see David H. Shinn and Joshua Eisenman, *China and Africa: A Century of Engagement* (Philadelphia: University of Pennsylvania Press, 2012), 60–61. See also Bruce D. Larkin's *China and Africa: 1949–1970: The Foreign Policy of the People's Republic of China* (Berkeley: University of California Press, 1971).

42. Neena Arora, *The Novels of Mulk Raj Anand: A Study of His Hero* (New Delhi: Atlantic, 2007), 17–18.

43. I substitute here a translation of this poem by Stephen Spender and J. L. Gili in Francisco Garcia Lorca and Donald Allen, eds., *The Selected Poems of Federico Garcia Lorca* (New York: New Directions, 1995), 135.

44. Arora, *Novels of Mulk Raj Anand*, 18.

45. Irene Eber, "Western Literature in Chinese Translation, 1949–1979," *Asian and African Studies* 3, no. 1 (1994): 34–54.

46. Hong Liu, "Pramoedya Ananta Toer and China: The Transformation of a Cultural Intellectual," *Indonesia* 61 (April 1996): 124.

47. Benedict R. O'G. Anderson, *Language and Power: Exploring Political Cultures in Indonesia* (Ithaca, N.Y.: Cornell University Press, 1990), 10.

2 • THE TRANSLATION OF PROCESS

JOHN CAYLEY

Let's agree to call the operative aggregation of material culture and technology *technics*. Language making and, in particular, aesthetic language making, across all natural languages, is always and of necessity implicated, historically and specifically, with applicable technics, obvious examples being the material culture of the book and technologies of print. Technics are co-constitutive of linguistic artifacts and are compositionally significant for language makers. In all of what follows, readers should take such statements as applying, even-handedly, to what one may characterize as "productive" and "receptive" manifestations of linguistic practice as a whole, in the present context: writing and reading. However, the following arguments should also be read in the light of grammatology. What I say about writing, in the abstract, may be applied to speaking (vocal inscription); when I discuss reading, in terms of a philosophy of language, this may be taken to apply to hearing-understanding. Distinctions made between writing/reading, on the one hand, and speaking/hearing, on the other, should be understood, precisely, with respect to technics. They are not pertinent to the *linguistic ontology* of a particular artifact.

It's important for me to set out my understanding of these terms at the outset for at least two reasons. Practices of translation require us to give more or less equal consideration to linguistic "reception" and "production." The translator is both reader and writer. So is the original writer, of course, but translation's insistence on some kind of equivalence or regular relationship between what is read and what is written in the processes of translation brings home the requirement to give due consideration to the technics of both reception and production. A translation represents a reading; then, both subsequently and concurrently, it becomes a piece of writing that makes this reading manifest in a form, the distinguishing characteristic of which—as translation—is that it should be in a natural language different from the language of the reading. However, what I am calling the *technics* of the reading (and writing) in one language and the *technics* of writing (and reading) in another need not be distinguished in the same way or even with any direct reference to the ways in which the *languages* are distinguished.

My second explicit reason for setting out certain terms in the way that I have concerns the technics of reading and writing in their contemporary, historical moment. Since the mid-1990s there has been a bewildering proliferation of devices and platforms for the support of linguistic practices. The advent of the Mosaic Netscape web browser in 1994, for instance, is a relatively recent milestone. We still read and write, but we do so differently, and we do so differently, in large measure, due to contemporary differences in what I call technics. Moreover, the concurrent proliferation and popularization of user-programmable devices that are implicated in the reception and production of language have led to what are, arguably, entirely novel reconfigurations of technics and language in terms of ownership and control with respect to both production and reception. With new technologies and with a wild diversity of material cultural forms, the contemporary writer may bring technics into play as an aspect of composition to an extent and with effects that would have been all but inconceivable in the first half of the twentieth century. A number of writers have composed work in precisely this manner, and, in the academic world, there is a well-established field, usually referred to as electronic or digital literature, that is devoted to the theory and critique of such practices of aesthetic language making.[1] The reception—the reading—of any work in this field must, clearly, make specific, particular, and interpretively significant reference to any and all technics that have been deployed in the processes of its composition and dissemination.

As a reader and writer of aesthetic language of this stamp, implicated with technics that are no longer even "new," I have direct, personal experience of these circumstances. Since well before the mid-1990s I have used a variety of hardware and software systems and platforms to make chiefly poetic work for which I claim, explicitly, the compositional significance of specific technologies and material cultural supports. Moreover, I have deployed technics in my work to the extent that a considerable proportion of what I have made—from the late 1980s up until the mid-2000s—is currently unreadable, not because its compositional principles are inherently opaque, but because certain specific technologies in which I chose to express these principles have become, effectively, obsolete. Now, let us say that I believed that one or other work from this period and in this condition was deserving of translation into a natural language other than English. At the very least, there would have to be some attempt to engineer, technically, a reading of the work that would form some part of the reading that is an initial and fundamental process in what might then become a conventional practice of translation. My point is that this reading-as-(re-)engineering, this reading as an address to specific technics, is simply an ineluctable aspect of reading itself, of all reading. As we acknowledged at the outset: writing is implicated with technics; reading is implicated with technics. Translation, as requiring—explicitly and in practice—both reception and production, confronts the problematic interrelationship of language and technics in a doubled sense, facing both ways on the horizon of two (or more) natural languages. When proposed as translatable or otherwise made subject to translation, language making that engages with technics explicitly and that makes a plausible claim as to its compositional and therefore interpretive significance, realizes these redoubled circumstances in actual technologies and specific material cultural forms. A translator must, at least, work with technics to read the work and, when passing on to the productive phase of translation, must, at least, consider whether to realize a corresponding technics associated with the host language to which the translation is addressed.[2]

Theorists, critics, and practitioners of digital literatures have recently begun to engage with the problems of translation in actual practices specific to their media.[3] Linguistically applicable technics associated with networked and programmable media have been deployed throughout most of the distinct language communities in the developed and developing world for some decades now. Certain readers and writers in these communities have subscribed to the project of digital literature and have made linguistic artifacts within their own languages, innovating and experimenting while, occasionally, sharing technics that cross natural linguistic horizons. Even in less specialist circumstances, nearly all of us encounter multilingual web sites, for example. Conventional translation addresses the content of these web pages where the technics of, essentially, literary print culture are embedded within the historically more recent technics of hypertext. As an aspect of an encompassing practice of translation, however, the interlingual translation of hypertextual technics is the kind of problem that software engineers characterize as "trivial." The technology and material culture of hypertext is more or less "the same"—or at least isomorphic—across natural languages, particularly languages with similar, alphabetic, systems of graphic inscription.

Not all technics that may be applied to the composition and delivery of linguistic artifacts will have as little effect as hypertext on the linguistic forms—exemplified, on the web, by "pages" of text—that are characteristic of literary print culture. In fact, of course, hypertext does "break" or transform the typical dynamics (or traversal functions) of the textuality with which we are most familiar in the culture of reading.[4] How and when one moves on in one's reading changes from "turning the page" to "clicking through" and this is not necessarily a "trivial" change, especially if it is considered an aspect of textual dynamics with some potential for compositional and interpretive traction. Computational technics can clearly offer us a time-based, dynamic textuality, including one that is not (entirely) in the reader's control. If a screen presents us with text page by page, little may have changed in our culture of reading; but if a screen presents a literary artifact sentence by sentence, this may have appreciable stylistic implications in literary critical terms. If a text is presented phrase by phrase—in fragments shorter and less "complete" than the sentence—then grammatical considerations gain purchase on our processes of reading, and we may experience interruptions of grammatical and stylistic expectations.

A change in textual temporality and dynamics that is a function of technics is merely one of an indeterminate and large number of circumstances that might, potentially, affect the culture of reading. My point is that if any such change affecting reading at the level of natural linguistic structure has grammatical consequences, this will have consequential effects for the type of reading that is constitutive of translation. Specifically, in my example, if a translator must read a dynamic text phrase by phrase and encounters grammatical interruption or dissonance (in English say), then how and when should the translator encapsulate or resolve this interruption or dissonance and translate it for a language (French, for example) that has a distinct grammar and therefore a distinct experience of grammatical interruption and dissonance?

This is precisely the kind of problem that brings us to consideration of a "translation of process." In the example above, to experience, while reading in one language, a grammatical interruption or dissonance, and then to resolve, reproduce, or discount this experience by means of expression in another natural language—that is, to translate—would be to involve a translation of process. By "process" I mean, in the case of the writer, chiefly: a compositional engagement with technics that reconfigures or reforms the linguistic artifact in such a way as to enable readings that are significantly or affectively distinct. When it comes to the translator, there is, first, an encounter with language and with process through the kind of charged and directed reading that the translator undertakes, and then an obligation, somehow, to incorporate any process that may have been encountered in the actual production of a translation. Semantic and lexical incommensurabilities and niceties plague the adequacy of conventional—print literary—translation, often highlighting those areas of practice that allow us to distinguish better translation from worse. The technics of these processes are encapsulated within the forms and institutions of print literacy. When less internalized technics transform or deform linguistic artifacts so as to allow distinct readings, processes are exposed. When readings break rules or conventions, the exposure is startling. When translation is the linguistic practice that concerns us, technics-as-process applied, however aesthetically, in one language, will usually—and certainly if not "translated"—lead to rule breaking in another, typically at the level of grammar. Attending carefully to certain translations should, therefore, serve as a good way to expose and elaborate the role of process in linguistic reception and production generally.

This is the intention of the second part of this chapter: to attend carefully to a number of literary artifacts for which process has been compositionally significant and affective, and which have also been subject to published translation in at least one other language. The chosen artifacts will not, however, be examples of work that apply contemporary, digital, programmable, networked, or computational technics. The first part, however, outlines a series of rubrics that have emerged from my own practice and field of study, and my reflection on that work. Specifically, I have in mind examples I regard as instances of language art in which process is—to use a pointed, skeuomorphic metaphor—literalized, and also, at least partially, inscribed in or as actual programs, programs which, although machine-addressed, may also be human-readable and so provide material interpretive context for any actual text-to-be-read.[5] I have discussed and "attended carefully" to my own work in an essay from 2015.[6] It is from that study that I extract a number of rubrics that may be thought of as *conditions and contexts of non-correspondence,* that is, conditions or contexts that tend to induce or bring to light potential *dissonances of significance and affect.*

When attending to work with which I was associated as maker or collaborative maker, I first noted two variable properties that are arguably attributable to all texts—and perhaps all aesthetic artifacts—and that are associated with the moral rights that are sometimes accounted for in copyright law:

- Integrity
- Association

If these properties of a text are uncertain, indeterminate, or complex, this may prove to be a function of process—the application of technics—and it will certainly problematize and ramify any further application of process to the linguistic artifact, one such further potentially applicable process being, of course, translation.

I then noted two more variable properties that might, optionally, be attributed to a linguistic artifact as a function of its composition:

- Conceptualism
- Algorithm

Arguably, it is only in the recent history of literary criticism that "Conceptual Writing"—conceptualism in literature and language art—has come to be acknowledged as a significant category.[7] Conceptual understandings of linguistic form, however, may be discovered and articulated in most self-conscious aesthetic linguistic practice, as when certain prosodic formalisms are associated with conceptions of "the lyric" such that, for example, English quatrains with short lines are accounted lyrical, and the poet may fill this prosodic form in order that in itself—conceptually—a poem expresses "lyric." Justified by a concept—whether this is in terms of contemporary allegorical abstraction or because of traditional formal associations—the writer composes in the lights or within the constraints of a linguistically transformative process. Conceptualism brings process to the fore with respect to composition and dissemination.

Naming my fourth rubric "algorithm" was a function of its context in the earlier essay. Writing in programmable media literalizes process as algorithm. In the present context "algorithm" might be understood as regular procedure without any need for the constituents of this procedure (e.g., structured lists of operations) to have been explicitly recorded (e.g., as a program) and addressed to an actual generative machine. Or, to simplify, we might simply replace this rubric with "process" itself or, rather,

- Explicit process

In any case, the authors of certain linguistic artifacts will acknowledge explicitly that they have used processes, regular procedures associated with applicable technics, over and above those processes that are conventionally internalized, for the composition of certain works. When this property is discovered in a linguistic artifact, there may be consequences for many aspects of linguistic form: style, grammar, punctuation, orthography, and any or all facets of poetics in general. When the work is translated, further ineluctable consequences ensue.

The activities associated with language—writing and reading in grammatological terms—are human activities that help to define us, in the most fundamental sense, as what we are, collectively and individually. And yet, typically and for the most part, these activities unfold—*without impugning our humanity*—encapsulated within *singular* instances of particular natural languages. Monolingualism does not render anyone a lesser human, at least not qualitatively.[8] Those activities that are integral to our full animality—how we move, for instance—are materially *the same* across all human communities, whereas our linguistic activities are not. We translate in order to try and reestablish this "sameness" across linguistically distinct human communities, to reintegrate our definitive cultural practices of language with an understanding that this should be shared by all who share our species-being. But there is no *requirement* to translate for us to be fully realized as human persons or language makers.

Translation is, therefore, a special and privileged process—privileged with regard to a global humanist project designed to share something that we feel obliged, but not required, to share—a process that may be applied to linguistic artifacts, *optionally*. In the domain of language, it is, I would argue, a model for all process, in senses for which I am developing the use of this word. Once applied, notice that translation immediately invokes substantive complication under all of the rubrics outlined above:

- Integrity: The work of the source or, preferably, "guest" language is appropriated and "doubled" in the target or, preferably, "host" language. What are the relations between the two linguistic artifacts? The morally and legally pertinent relations? Are these artifacts now parts of some greater integral whole which is perhaps capable of impugning the "integrity" of the "original"?

- Association: There is at least one other writer in the mix. How should the other writers be acknowledged? With which constituents of the linguistic manifold should they be associated? Does the translator, for example, "own" a right of association with her reading of the work that she is hosting? With the hosted double?
- Conceptualism: What is the thinking on translation—individual or collective—within the host linguistic culture, or as underlying the translator's particular project?
- Explicit process: Can we articulate any of these processes of translation? Recursively, with respect to processes that are implicated in linguistic composition as a whole?

In the earlier essay, I went on to identify three more rubrics categorizing significant and affective linguistic phenomena that are brought into relief when linguistic artifacts composed with respect to process are confronted further with special processes of translation. What do I mean by "brought into relief"? We have established what is already intuitive: that process will transform, reform, or deform the linguistic artifacts to which it is applied. If, however, after the fact, we are simply presented with a text-to-be-read in our own language, within our monolingualism, with no explicit statement of process, and if questions of integrity, association, and concept are considered as resolved, then the work presents itself to us as, simply, an original linguistic artifact, more or less strange. We might translate it, conventionally, as such. If we did so, it seems intuitively likely both that any actual process that had been involved during its composition in our own language will have been concealed or removed in the version we make, or host, and also that any "strangeness" that our conventional translation may evoke in the host language will have nothing to do with any "strangeness" that we experienced during our guest, or translator's, reading.

In practice, the translator works to bring into relief any and all appreciable "strangeness" or peculiarities of form that are readable in the object of her attention. The translator works to recover the processes of composition, both internalized and explicit, with respect to the text. Typically, the translator is also a guest in what I am designating as the guest language (commonly, the "original" or "source" language). Their "first" language is, typically, the host. Having discovered, or having been informed of significant and affective process in the guest language, the translator learns to articulate corresponding processes in her own, the host language, often performing, to achieve this, as a kind of expert in the expressive potentialities of the host. She may not be an expert or artist in any other articulable sense, but one may reasonably expect the translator to be conversant with the grammars of both guest and host languages. If one thinks of grammar and syntax as being processes operating distinctly in distinct natural languages, then the way of regarding translation attempted here and what it "brings into relief" may become easier to express. Within a system, processes may interfere with the operation of other, separately motivated processes. Prosody interferes with grammar and brings grammar "into relief." All this is to say that grammar plays a crucial role in highlighting what I call procedurally induced significant and affective dissonance across languages. The remaining rubrics provide a simple categorization of these dissonances:

- Procedurally induced local dissonance: differences of natural linguistic form, typically grammatical, that are local to host and guest languages, some part of their local linguistic systems, and that may be remarked comparatively
- Procedurally induced global dissonance: differences of contextual and referential relation between particular languages—host or guest—and linguistic culture, globally considered[9]

The final rubric is simply a bald fact:

- Procedurally induced natural linguistic noncorrespondence or divergence: in host and guest versions despite their being proposed as correspondent, subsequent to practices of translation that are attentive to process, both receptively and productively

In the following second part of this chapter, I examine particular examples of aesthetic linguistic artifacts composed with reference to processes either that have already been made explicit by their authors or that can, quite easily, be inferred and made explicit by readers (the fourth self-referential, if not redundant, rubric). The guest texts for all of these examples have been subjected to translation; the results have been published in at least one host language and are thus, to an extent, authorized, valued. Such critically appreciative readings as I undertake below will generate statements in terms of all the other rubrics that I have outlined (with one possible exception), highlighting the translation of process and its effectiveness in expressing important problematics with respect to integrity and association (first and second rubrics), and bringing generative concepts for linguistic art (third rubric) into relief. This last includes bringing conceptualism to the practice of translation as linguistic art. I will be able to remark the notable characteristics and features of these texts—those that will provoke my critical statements—due to my inevitable, productive encounters with, as I see it, procedurally induced dissonances of significance and affect (fifth rubric), and with natural linguistic non-correspondence (seventh rubric). In traditional scholarship any appreciation of how linguistic processes in distinct natural languages relate to the differences in their contextual and referential resources globally (sixth rubric) extends beyond the horizon of the brief close readings undertaken here.[10]

There seems to be no clearly expressible conclusion to this writing. Given that any theoretical statements or considerations on offer have already been set out in this first part of the essay, if there were a conclusion, I would place it here. I prefer to state clearly what I may not have argued effectively but hope to have persuasively expressed. Reading and writing necessarily involve and generate process—processes at all levels of linguistic form and structure. When and if we translate, we translate processes of language. Any and all practices of translation constitute a special process that is particularly revealing of the vital role that process assumes in language and its arts.

Not only has it been conceivable for writers to make explicit process a generative impetus for their compositions, but I believe it can be shown that different writers have adopted distinctly different modes of authorial agency with respect to process. Such differences are exemplified in works by the first two authors and their translators to be read here. For writers in the tradition of the OuLiPo (Ouvroir de littérature potentielle, or "workshop of potential literature") such as Georges Perec, process is typically expressed as constraint. The constraint may be arbitrary, and thus entail a certain relationship with chance, the aleatory, but OuLiPian work often seems to be resolved as constraint overcome by mastery. For writers in the tradition of John Cage, in contrast, there is an acknowledged submission to chance and its effects, orchestrated by procedure and by the preparation of instruments—which, here, I take to include linguistic instruments—that preclude the possibility of their ever being mastered.

Comparing the opening pages of Perec's *La Disparition* (Box 2.1) with one of its English translations, *A Void*, by Gilbert Adair (Box 2.2), we immediately find evidence of the relationship of OuLiPian writers with process-as-constraint.[11] Famously, *La Disparition* is a lipogrammatic novel composed without the use of words in French that contain the letter "e." Its Anglo-translation as *A Void* also avoids this vital symbol. Both Perec and Adair work hard to build artifacts in language that present their readers, despite constraint, with a novel possessing character, plot, ideas, and the development of all such constituents. Adair takes on and "translates," literally, the process underlying Perec's voluntary, willful, and pointed constraint. He follows Perec's writing remarkably closely, but comparison of the work immediately reveals procedurally induced local and global dissonance, as well as natural linguistic non-correspondence, helping to exemplify what I intend by distinguishing these rubrics.

I use procedurally induced natural linguistic non-correspondence to refer to divergences between the language of the untranslated guest, and the language of the host translation that would not have been apparent—that would have been translated differently—if the translation of process were not taking place. "Anton

BOX 2.1

Qui, d'abord, a l'air d'un roman jadis fait où il s'agissait d'un individu qui dormait tout son saoul

Anton Voyl n'arrivait pas à dormir. Il alluma. Son Jaz marquait minuit vingt. Il poussa un profond soupir, s'assit dans son lit, s'appuyant sur son polochon. Il prit un roman, il l'ouvrit, il lut; mais il n'y saisissait qu'un imbroglio confus, il butait à tout instant sur un mot dont il ignorait la signification.

Il abandonna son roman sur son lit. Il alla à son lavabo; il mouilla un gant qu'il passa sur son front, sur son cou.

Son pouls battait trop fort. Il avait chaud. Il ouvrit son vasistas, scruta la nuit. Il faisait doux. Un bruit indistinct montait du faubourg. Un carillon, plus lourd qu'un glas, plus sourd qu'un tocsin, plus profond qu'un bourdon, non loin, sonna trois coups. Du canal Saint-Martin, un clapotis plaintif signalait un chaland qui passait.

Sur l'abattant du vasistas, un animal au thorax indigo, à l'aiguillon safran, ni un cafard, ni un charançon, mais plutôt un artison, s'avançait, traînant un brin d'alfa. Il s'approacha, voulant l'aplatir d'un coup vif, mais l'animal prit son vol, disparaissant dans la nuit avant qu'il ait pu l'assaillir.

Voyl n'arrivait pas à dormir. Il alluma." If we are not translating process, this might be rendered, "Anton Voyl was unable to sleep. He lit up." Adair works with process and writes, "Incurably insomniac, Anton Vowl turns on a light." We already have too much to say about this initial fragment of the novel. Even in terms of actual material, graphic representation—perceptible as punctuation conventions that are shared by the languages in question—there is natural linguistic divergence that contrasts with a correspondence in my "conventional" rendering. There are two periods in the French, one in Adair's English, where the turning on of an electric light—if this is, indeed what Voyl or Vowl does—is the consequence of an incurable condition rather than, for all we know at this stage, an exceptional nocturnal circumstance. A whole first sentence in French is collapsed into a descriptive phrase that may be read adverbially in relation to the much more concrete English illumination. There is also the spelling of Anton's last name in Adair's version, where what is again a materially, graphically perceptible difference, the substitution of "w" for "y," allows for the translation of an absence, the missing "e"s, which would be less remarkable for an English reader, or perhaps not perceptible at all for a reader having no French or who did not

BOX 2.2

Which at first calls to mind a probably familiar story of a drunk man waking up with his brain in a whirl

Incurably insomniac, Anton Vowl turns on a light. According to his watch, it's only 12.20. With a loud and languorous sigh, Vowl sits up, stuffs a pillow at his back, draws his quilt up around his chin, picks up his whodunit and idly scans a paragraph or two; but, judging its plot impossibly difficult to follow in his condition, its vocabulary too whimsically multisyllabic for comfort, throws it away in disgust.

Padding into his bathroom, Vowl dabs at his brow and throat with a damp cloth.

It's a soft, warm night and his blood is racing through his body. An indistinct murmur wafts up to his third-floor flat. Far off, a church clock starts chiming—a chiming as mournful as a last post, as an air-raid alarm, as an SOS signal from a sinking ship. And, in his own vicinity, a faint lapping sound informs him that a small craft is at that instant navigating a narrow canal.

Crawling across his windowsill is a tiny animal, indigo and saffron in colour, not a cockroach, not a blowfly, but a kind of wasp, laboriously dragging a sugar crumb along with it. Hoping to crush it with a casual blow, Vowl lifts up his right hand; but it abruptly flaps its wings, flying off without giving its assailant an opportunity to do it any harm.

(yet) know that the protagonist, Voyl, is francophone. If not for process, Vowl would surely be Voyl in most translations.

To an extent, the rubric of non-correspondence is a catch-all for instances or an aggregation of effects that are produced by the interrelation of languages and productive or receptive processes. I intend it to refer to differences that are more or less evident, such as graphically marked differences (punctuation, spelling) or the clear addition or removal of language in the host without a corresponding textually inscribed cause in the untranslated guest (addition here: "incurably"; removal of: "n'arrivait pas à"). The translation of process often generates non-correspondence of this kind without this divergence being, *necessarily,* directly related to the process. In this case, for example, the collapse of two periods into one has no bearing on the language containing "e," and neither does the substitution of "w" for "y" *directly.* The non-correspondent additions and removals that I have suggested are made with reference to the process—since its rule must be followed by Adair—but the choice of precisely what to add or what to remove is not directly related to the process and will tend, in fact, to refer more closely to conventional processes of translation where meaning, style, and tone are to the fore, however expressed, and however procedurally inflected.

Procedurally induced local dissonance relates, by contrast, to differences between untranslated guest and host translation that are inscribed more or less systematically according to the local circumstances of each language. Both Perec and Adair intend to master novel writing and translating, respectively, without using the most common letter in their languages, and this happens to be "e" for both French and English. The exact relative frequency of "e" and its distribution throughout the vocabularies of French and English is, however, different for the two languages and, for such frequent letters, this will be particularly significant—during composition—when it comes to any special orthography that is indicative of grammar or found among the languages' "closed class" words. Just one example of hundreds: in French a lipogram in "e" disallows an entirely different set of personal and possessive pronouns than is the case for its English counterpart. Procedurally induced effects will be consequent on linguistic circumstances that are "local" to the languages in question, systematically requiring different grammar and word choice so long as process is translated predominately. Another example of the consequences of procedurally induced local dissonance across our texts: Perec sets out in *passé simple* (it's handy that literary writing can dispense with the *passé composé*), while Adair chooses to use the historical present (since avoiding "ed" would cause difficulties).

Procedurally induced global dissonance is a function of the manner in which the languages of guest and host relate differently to linguistic practices as a whole, across all of whatever we may know, globally, concerning human language. Perhaps the clearest example relating to Perec's lipogrammatic novel concerns our global linguistic understanding of "most frequent letter" across languages. In translations of *La Disparition* into certain other languages, the lipogrammatic procedure is retained and applied, but a different letter has been avoided. In the Spanish of *El secuestro* there are no "a"s.[12] The property of "most frequent letter" in an alphabetic system of inscription is, of course, local to particular languages, and lipogrammatic effects on grammar or word choice may be also considered local (and dissonant with respect to the untranslated guest, as above). At the same time, these differences may also have global consequences for the differentiated significance and affect of the work as a whole, so long as we accept, for example, that, from the perspective of English readers regarding various languages globally, a text without "e"s will be affectively and significantly different from a text without "a"s. Such global differences might be shared and appreciated even across linguistic horizons, from other linguistic perspectives, if we believe, for instance, that the actual sounds or the linguistic "musics" associated with these graphemes have some kind of affective or significant consistency. Linguistically implicated consistencies like this are notoriously difficult to establish and, in any case, procedurally induced global dissonance in guest-host translation is really only relevant to translinguistic cultural politics, or translingual practice in Lydia Liu's terms.[13]

In the practice of literary criticism generally, and in the course of our subsequent readings here, procedurally induced global dissonance is not addressed. It is, nonetheless, worth some elaboration here because it highlights historically novel circumstances for linguistic practice, including translation. At the outset, this chapter dealt with computationally rendered versions of linguistic process, and now it is concluding with processes more generally expressed, without instantiations in networked and programmable media. The existence of these media, however, has inaugurated an era in which global differences of language practices can be significantly and affectively appreciated by any author or reader with network access, although not without implications for translingual cultural politics. For any appreciation of global differences, as for questions of linguistic musicality across languages, common reference points and contexts must be established. This is precisely what is provided by network access to linguistic references, contexts, corpora, and so on. Google Translate, for example, works differently for different languages because, on the network, languages in this context have different corpora and references available to their practitioners and to the systems of Google Translate itself. For the programmatic generation or manipulation of any particular natural language, in the context of the network, this means that procedurally induced global dissonance will obtain when the same process, for example, is applied to different languages that have different relationships globally to corpora and references on the net. In the current era of big data, these differences amount to differences of quality in linguistic production and reception that are a function of the quantity of data that are available for the analysis of different languages. For the moment, big data on global (U.S.) English predominates, with troubling consequences.

When Adair translated and composed *A Void*, most of the dissonances between his own text and that of his untranslated guest were configured locally and separately by his own knowledge and mastery of the French and especially of its English host. Today, insofar as Adair might now make reference to networked linguistic resources, he might also be able to discover and perhaps even to exploit correspondences and dissonances that are determined by those differences between French and English that are made perceptible and appreciable to us, globally, by the network, although they would be induced by procedure just as they are in literary practice.

None of the purported "dissonances" that we have already discussed or will go on to examine would exist at all if the host translations were not composed. As we have suggested before, translation might be considered as both the model and the generator of receptive and productive linguistic process as a whole. The process of translation must be under way before the translation of process can begin. If no explicit process can be read into the untranslated guest, there will still be dissonances between guest and host, both local and global, with perhaps even some marked natural linguistic non-correspondence in the case of many translations. These dissonances are induced by the processes of translation itself, since even translation translates actual processes of writing. In what follows, we briefly read a few more examples of linguistic artifacts that have been composed in the light of explicit process while we entertain the theory that these writings are also proposed, simply, as exemplifications of writing itself within the framework of particular technics. The translation of process exposes the processes of translation and writing as process.

The mesostics of John Cage, his "writings through," are quite well known. A text is "prepared" as an orthographic instrument by searching through it for the letters—most frequently—of a proper name, that of a hero of the avant-garde, or occasionally some special word. The letter need not be acrostic—at the *beginning* of a piece of language, usually a line—but it may be: by chance. It need only be "mesostic," allowing its discovery, by chance operation, anywhere—at any arbitrary point in a word that is then positioned more or less in a *middle*, on a central vertical axis for lines thereby raggedly ranged both left and right and rendered poetic through the process itself or by the writer's subsequent adjustments. In the texts and translations figured as examples and translated examples of this process, the proper name is that of Christian Wolff (Boxes 2.3 and 2.4).[14]

Wonderful translations by Carol Richards work Cage's process into French, preserving an easily verifiable—as we match the spelling letters—process perfectly. This generates local dissonance in an exemplary manner, since, as for "e," the distribution of letters across English and French vocabularies is distinct. "aCross" begins both of the figured sections of Cage's "Songs for C.W." For the first translation, Richards discovers a root common to both languages spawning English "cross" and French "croisant," with shared orthography including "c." She exploits this to light on the required mesostic letter and to justify a grammatical transformation, strengthening Cage's preposition into a verbal form that tends to actualize and temporalize what could be read simply as situation in the untranslated guest. In the second figured section, "across" is rendered by the prepositional "à travers," which does not contain a "c" (local dissonance), so this time Richards moves a conventionally translated "cette" for "this" to the first line of the host version, ironically introducing a form of natural linguistic non-correspondence—of the lineation, the poetic punctuation of the linguistic artifact—while maintaining conventional translation standards—"á travers cette" is perfectly good for "across this" (whereas "croisant" is interpretive)—and satisfying the strictures of her translation of process.

Once again, richly wrought text enables us to discuss many fascinating niceties of composition and reading with reference to the translation of process, even

BOX 2.3

aCross
Hope
gReet we
deeplIer

Simply
Turn
It
to Play it

it souNds

When
i lOve

we Leap

and ever aFter

ever Fine

---

aCross
tHis land
and actIon
Severed
aT
drInk
plAy
souNd

When and read
sOund is
Leg

Few
and Find

in the first few words of our examples. Although it would be perfectly possible, and might even prove literary-critically engaging and satisfying, these are not the kinds of readings that I would like to undertake here. Instead, I'd like to make a couple of more general remarks before continuing to an entirely new and separate example.

The most materially perceptible difference—a natural linguistic non-correspondence in my terms—relates to the "shapes" of untranslated guest compared with their host translations. The mesostic central axes correspond and line breaks, as if between verses or verse fragments, are respected, but length of line and disposition and amount of language on either side of the mesostic letter

BOX 2.4

Croisant
l'Hespoir
nous accueilleRons
mIeux

il Suffit
de le Tourner
pour qu'Il
mArche

il résoNe

quWand
j'adOre
nous nous éLançons

juqu'à la Fin des temps
parFaits

à travers Cette
terre Héritée
se tRouvent
le soliel et l'actIon
rompuS
au Temps
à boIre
A jouer
à soNs

quWand et lu
le sOn est
L'appui

Force de peu
et Fouille

(*Traduit de l' américain par Carol Richards*)

varies greatly. When there is correspondence, we assume this is a matter of chance. This shaping, a phrasal and potentially rhythmic shaping, of the untranslated guest is, however, an important aspect of its poetics, regardless of its generation by chance operations. In fact, this non-correspondence, driven by the local dissonance of letter distribution in the two languages, may also be read as a *good* translation of the chance operations (process) to which Cage subjects his literary art, that is, in the Fluxus manner that contrasts, as I suggested above, with an OuLiPian mastery of constraint. If the phrases of the Cage mesostic fall where the letters make them fall, the same procedurally induced subjection to mesostic chance arranges the host translation's phrases. When we realize that what this also allows, if not empowers the translator to do, is precisely the kind of conventional interpretative translation that proceeds from some combination of the common sense and poetics in one language into the common sense and poetics in another. If one arranged the Cage texts and their Richards translations in prose-like paragraphs—breaking more than one aspect of the process and its translation (even the mesostic letters would still be present)—Richards would read as fine literary translation, in my view, that is, as very fine conventional translation.[15]

This is an interesting insight, once more interpretively collapsing translation that is complicated by a translation of (explicit) process to translation and writing as we know it, while recognizing that they always already, more or less implicitly, involve processes that are conscious, significant, and affective. Nonetheless, we must push back on behalf of process and critique the extent to which Richards—whether consciously or unconsciously or as constrained by institutional habit—has been faithful in the translation of Cage's process. Two points of divergence: for the major part of his mesostic work, it is clear that Cage started with texts from which the language for the mesostic was selected. While I have been unable to ascertain the status of any supply text that Cage may have used as the text-read-through to create his "Songs for C.W."—original to him or otherwise—Richards does not, as far as I know, begin either with this supply text—in the language of the guest—or with a (conventional) translation of this text. It might be argued that for a faithful translation of Cage's process, a prior translation of the source text, the text to be read through, is called for, thereby constraining the language of the eventual translation. Second, by some lights, the mesostics of the untranslated guests in our examples and those of the host are different. In the untranslated guest, the language between one mesostic letter and another does not contain any other instance of the next mesostic letter that is about to be punctuated as axis-forming.[16] In Richards's texts these conditions do occur. Her translation of the process is not "literal" in this sense. Here we can see how close reading of a translation of process might have a bearing on our critical reading, as a whole, of a literary artifact and its translation. In this case, I would argue that Richards's translations are excellent and any critique associated with a lack of "faithfulness" to process is of minor consequence. For other kinds of process-intensive work, however, such inattention could well prove aesthetically and hermeneutically damaging. For writing generated by algorithm, appreciation of the algorithm is clearly vital, and full, detailed translation of such an algorithm, making it operative in the host, would be crucial to translating the guest into a generative linguistic engine in the host.

After its initial publication in 1966, a version of Nanni Balestrini's novel *Tristano* was translated into French by Jacqueline Risset and brought out in 1972.[17] Actually, what was published in 1966, and then translated by Risset, was only one possible instantiation of a combinatorial work, the supply texts of which are able to generate a vast number of possible novella-length books all bearing the title *Tristano*. It was only in 2007 that print publication—in Italian—of Balestrini's novel, as it was conceived, can be said to have begun.[18] Print-on-demand technology had made it viable to manufacture—successively, serially—actual instances of *Tristano* in, effectively, unique printed copies. In 2014, the London publisher Verso, as part of an effort coordinated with the Italian publisher, brought out Mike Harakis's English translation.[19]

Balestrini composed thirty paragraph-sized fragments for each of the ten chapters of *Tristano*. As its author, as part of the process of composition, he then proposed to intervene at the point of publication with two operations: the selection and ordering of only twenty from the thirty possible fragments for each chapter; and the random presentation of the chapters themselves. With no other constraint—and discounting the random arrangement of chapters—the number of possible unique permutations for selections from this number of elements has twenty-five digits.[20] If there are further authorial constraints reducing this theoretical number, these are unclear. When Balestrini published the single Italian version with Feltrinelli in 1966, he published a single star from this galaxy. This was a galaxy whose necessarily constrained significance and affect the author might have grasped, though it would be literally impossible for Balestrini to ever explore each star by visiting, that is, reading. He comprehends only the composition of the elements that make up these stars but cannot possibly comprehend more than a tiny, tiny set of instances having specific arrangements of his paragraphs.

When such elements are not atoms of language, like letters, when they are paragraph sized—and full of interpretable sense—this combinatorial math of selection and permutation works on us strangely. Balestrini wrote for the form he conceived, in an abstract style with a few abstracted, self-reflective characters in a few abstracted locations, these characters getting nowhere in particular while indulging in abstracted, if mildly erotic, romantic entanglements and psychosexual musings. As presented, the book is readable and, if they are aware of its procedural composition, its readers may be ready to believe that the arrangement of chapters and paragraphs, the absence of an indeterminate third of the book-behind-the-book, does not matter or, rather, that this is one of the statements it makes.[21] "This is life," says the book, and some readers might argue that this is life *toute simple*: that both the style and form of *Tristano* are as expressive of a certain experience of human life as the next novel.

Briefly here, in this context, our concern is translation of process with respect to *Tristano*. It is clear that the conventional translation of one instance of the novel is not a translation of the work, not even a "complete" translation, although such a translation—of which Jacqueline Risset's 1972 is one—might well serve as the translation of a particular experience of the work from, say, Italian into French. Harakis proceeded by translating all of the source fragments of Balestrini's artifact and Verso arranged for the publication of instances according to the author's generative algorithms.[22] Paradoxically, it seems, a translation of the kind undertaken by Harakis and actualized by his publisher, a translation that makes natural linguistic correspondence between any Italian copy and any English copy humanly impossible—this is a "better" translation of the work and also one that is easily conceived by human readers even if a literal comprehension of the novel's potentiality is precluded. A mathematical, computational sublime lurks in the background of Balestrini's project. Does it redeem or enhance the banalities and abstractions of the novels that we can read? Balestrini went ahead and published in 1966 and a fine French translator associated with Tel Quel took the time to translate a version of this single speck of light from Balestrini's project. The technics of print precluded any realization of the author's overarching intention. By 2007 this was no longer a problem, and further publication of the process on the network as a dynamic process would be "trivial" as the technologists put it.

It may seem a little unfair, now, to turn to an example of recent contemporary literary practice that falls squarely within the purview of conceptual writing, but Caroline Bergvall's "VIA: 48 Dante Variations" has received considerable attention and is widely regarded as an elegant poetic gesture. Moreover, it is composed, almost entirely, from language that has been generated by translation: conventional, if literary, translation. Bergvall does not compose this language itself. Her linguistic artistry is all in the collection and arrangement of these fragments of language. Bergvall found and recorded all of the forty-seven English translations of the initial tercet of Dante's *Divine Comedy* that were held by the British Library and published before May 2000 "exactly 700 years after the date fixed by Dante for the start of the Comedy's journey."[23] She then ordered them alphabetically, numbered them, and added brief translator surname and date attributions. The forty-eighth variation, Bergvall explains in an introduction to the piece's appearance in *Fig* (2005), was a sonification generated from Bergvall's vocal reading of the forty-seven translations, by her collaborator, Ciarán Maher.[24] Performances of the piece by Bergvall, live and recorded, include vocalizations of the attributions, but not the numbers.

Recently "VIA" has been translated into Polish by poet and scholar Katarzyna Szymanska.[25] To make her translation, Szymanska assembled the twenty existing Polish translations of Dante's opening lines and then added her own translation of the tercet, constraining her version to begin with the last letter of the Polish alphabet so as to set this verse at the conclusion of her translation as a kind of signature.[26] What concerns us in this context is the fact of natural linguistic noncorrespondence between Bergvall's "VIA," as untranslated guest, and Szymanska's host language version, which was made, and could theoretically be remade, without any reference to Bergvall's English. Dante's Italian, of course, underlies all of these tercets, with their various historically situated conventionalities of translation bewilderingly in play. To disturb us in the middle of our way through literature and literary translation, Bergvall puts the outset of Dante's journey through a model process of translation diachronically and also demonstrates how each of the generated English versions is strangely divorced—non-correspondent from conventional perspectives—from all its others. In one of the world's major, though certainly not global natural languages, Szymanska then takes the next conceptual step, and shows how a translation of process can perfectly render an artifact of language without any need to reference the actual, materially expressed, constituent language of an untranslated guest. These paradoxical circumstances have, I believe, a bearing on the production and reception of language generally, suggesting, through extreme example, that the role of process in language making and translation is, to put it simply, underplayed.

We come, finally, to a reading of Canadian poet Lisa Robertson's *Cinema of the Present*, and its translation by Pascal Poyet, *Cinéma du présent*.[27] In the production of the manuscript for this long poem, Robertson's already complex—even when intuitive—poetic processes of composition are further complicated by a simple explicit process, one which any translator would be compelled to confront. Robertson was, moreover, directly involved with the French translation and this is evidenced even in the original publication of the English edition. That book includes "Present: An Index / by Pascal Poyet," an alphabetized list of words that Poyet discovered in his reading of Robertson's text.[28] This index and list is also a composition of verse-lines and a work of its own, in response to *Cinema of the Present*. In draft notes for a reading performance of "An Index," Poyet explains that he was seeking and grouping words like the characters of a novelistic text.[29] They were assembled in trios to first reflect and then exceed the dual, folded, interlaced repetition-structure of Robertson's poem, with the third terms foreclosing any collapse into reductive binaries. Poyet's list presents three English words from *Cinema of the Present*, comma-separated, per line and index item. There are no page or line references back into Robertson's text.

Although it lacks page and line references, "Present: An Index" highlights the chief characteristic of the simple explicit process that Robertson has applied to her writing: alphabetization. Tellingly, the index also exhibits an initial, expressive "glitch" in alphabetic ordering. At the very beginning of "An Index," "Again, again, again." precedes the second entry, "Absolutely, totally, love." This is the only "error" of order in the index and it is telling because it signals the fact that Robertson's use of alphabetization is also deliberately unsettled. There are a number of places in the English poem where the alphabetic order is deliberately "broken" and Poyet's version reflects this.

As overarching compositional process, Robertson wrote, line-by-line and as they came to her, the verses of approximately half of what is printed as *Cinema of the Present*. However, she did not write linearly, as if each line "followed" the one last written. She wrote complete verse-line periods that were conceived as inserted into the middle of the accumulating text.[30] Once this text was composed she took further steps to baffle its default poetics as linear poetic sequence, in pursuit of a *duration of the present.*[31] She took these same lines and alphabetized them. Having done so, she interleaved the lines-as-written with the lines-as-alphabetized, and set the ordered lines in italics. This was not, however, the final gesture in her processes of composition since there is clear evidence of subsequent manipulation, whatever the degree of authorial or writerly intention. Robertson, like Cage, submitted her work to arbitrary process and then also continued to act, making adjustments in response, although not necessarily to master the text, in the OuLiPian manner.

For an unsettling start to our own actual reading, we note that there is at least one additional italicized line, since the text begins and ends with a line thus formatted. This means that all the lines of the poem-as-written in a series of "presents" are framed by alphabetized lines. For this reader, there is a suggestion of the cinematic frame in this formalism. The inscriptions of (once) present (re-presented) moments are framed in the text and in the memory by rhythmic structures composed from these moments. Pairs of italicized lines form a "gate" like the projector's gate that captures each frame of film for projection, with displaced repetition—albeit on an entirely different scale—and conjure a flickering which resolves itself, as we watch and read, into an apparently fluid poetic motion, while hinting at moiré patterns of significant and affective interference.

Then we notice that the italicized text ends with "*Now only time is wild.*"—wildly out of order. The preceding three italicized lines begin "*With . . . // What . . . // What . . .*" and follow, rather than precede, an important long section beginning with "*You . . .*" or variants like "You'd . . ." and finally "Yours . . ." although the last italicized line in this section reprises an initial "*You . . .*" Nonetheless, overall, the order of alphabetization holds for the poem's lines in italics such that we may rely on it to discover where else a particular line occurs. Or, returning to Poyet's index, we can look for lines that also begin with the initial words of his "Index" entries. If we do this, we discover that hardly any of the ordered lines begin with Poyet's head words. The disordered "Again, again, again." leads to "*Again you consider the sumptuous wreckage of the present.*"—a line that we may read, again, again, again, as a highly significant comment on Robertson's project as a whole. Poyet's head words, however, are nouns, and few nouns, other than pronouns, initiate Robertson's lines; as I go through "An Index," I note that "You, yourself, beginner." will lead to many lines beginning "You . . ." but between "Again, again, again." and "Index, information, irony." only "Funny, cosmic, humble." refers me to an actual line in the italicized order: "*Funny, cosmic and humble.*"

In Poyet's "Remarques sur *Cinéma du present,*" apart from citing and discussing Robertson's concerns with the "enduring present" temporalities of thinking and reading, and their instantiation/representation in or as folded, interlaced, recurrent poetic form, Poyet also quotes a stated intention that Robertson shared from her notes toward the poem, "I want to build the pronoun *she*."[32] The question of pronouns, their address, and their role in the generation and modulation of subjectivities—this is one of the focal themes in Robertson's long poem. She wrote in large part to build her feminine pronoun, and this in dialog with herself and with the work of linguist and linguistic philosopher Émile Benveniste. In the event, however, although she began the actual writing in the third person, she shifted her thinking and her writing so as to engage these complex questions by way of the second person, *you*, replacing, at one point, all occurrences of "she" in her initial work, while retaining "her" when this was necessary or commodious.

For the practice of translation, pronouns provide an important grammatical locus at one of the many liminal, shared horizons between natural languages. When we pass over from one language to another at the point of pronouns, procedurally induced local dissonance is very likely to arise, simply from those processes necessary for translation as such. Differences in the ways that English and French treat pronouns and the dissonances that emerge are conceptually important for Robertson's text regardless of any other explicit processes that have been used to generate or order the poem and its translation. French has two second-person pronouns and it also requires agreements, expressed in terms of gender, that call for commitments on the part of the translator and their text. Poyet chooses to translate Robertson's "you" with a "tutoiement," the familiar second person (the pronoun, presumably, with which one would address oneself) and also insists that all agreements referring to or from a "you/tu" should be feminine. He argues eloquently that the French translation, as it were, instantiates and articulates certain processes of thinking that Robertson passed through as she composed and yet chose to leave inexplicit or ambiguous in her adoption of the English second person. For Poyet, "*Elle* disparaît presque complètement du texte anglais . . . pour réapparaître partout diffus(e) dans les accords du texte français," actualizing, linguistically, what in English remains a speculative, poetic, thought-realized construction of the feminine pronoun.[33] Gender is paramount for the interpretation of these processes in the poem but we should remark, in passing, that Poyet's French forecloses the literal, grammatical plurality that "you" in English allows, such that any plurality of address that the text might demand from its French "tutoiement" must, in a complementary manner, be performed as speculation or as thought, rather than remaining within the literal gift of English grammar.

The choice of pronoun, furthermore, provides a significant way into our reading of alphabetization in *Cinema of the Present* since so many of the verse-lines begin with the text's most common pronoun and, local linguistic difference generates a dissonance in terms of position in the alphabet. "You" begins with its penultimate letter and "tu" does not. "Vous" would more nearly have approximated the position of "you" but more significant and affective considerations, in Poyet's estimation, overruled this alphabetic consideration. Nonetheless, "t" is still relatively late in the alphabet. The (re)ordering system provides not only a mechanism for the arbitrary disposition of repeated lines—their "mere" return or recall so as to problematize reading/thinking temporality and a present-without-duration—it also establishes longer passages and movements in the work, most notably the longest such section toward its conclusion in either language where either "tu" or "you" and their morphological variants begin so many lines. For this section of the work to have been promoted to much earlier in the alphabetic order might have been a serious problem. Note, moreover, that the alphabetic order of the main subject case form of the second-person pronouns and their contractions/variations differ in English and French: "you, you'd, you'll, you're, you've, your, yours," uninterrupted by non-pronomial forms versus "ta, tes, toi, ton, tu" with "telle, testaments, totalement, tourbillons, tout, toute" *interrupting* the procession of verse-lines that are pronoun-led in French. Given the significance of these pronouns to the interpretative content of the work, there remain points of potential intervention for which the full relative expressive possibilities of host and guest text may not have been and might still be addressed. Importantly, as a concluding reflection on my arguments in this chapter, such interventions would be addressed, clearly, in terms of differential *translations of process*, and would be unambiguously implicated with the original interpretative content of the guest.

Further examples demonstrating this principle can be pointed to, all within the scope of the simple explicit process of alphabetization in *Cinema of the Present*. In English many question words, notoriously, begin with "wh-" and so a significant passage of the poem, held together by "wh-" questions, closely precedes its "you" section. In Poyet's French, the passage with interlaced lines beginning "qu-" is a little shorter and differently displaced while the corresponding passages retain the same relative order. The question of "wh-" question words is significant in that Robertson breaks alphabetization following the poem's long "you"-and-variants passage, after a final, properly alphabetized "Yours . . ." line—with the important italicized line "*You seem to remember.*" The next begins "With . . ." which is followed by two "What . . ." questions, remotely mirroring in a kind of miniature the disposition that precedes the "you" passage. The French cannot or does not achieve this degree of nicety with respect to its quasi-arbitrarily constrained ordering and its final break down. Between the "tu" passage and the order-breaking lines—the final ten lines, both roman and italic, are all finely and, in the common sense, "conventionally" translated by Poyet—there intervenes a properly ordered passage of verse-lines beginning, in particular, "Un . . ." and "Une . . ."

Let us consider one final example of a procedurally induced local dissonance that was explicitly addressed and ameliorated by Poyet in consultation with Robertson. In the English, toward the very beginning of *Cinema of the Present*, there is a striking passage of interlaced italic lines all beginning with "A gate (made) of. . . ." French, "une porte," initially, would have sited this passage at the end of the book between the "tu" passage and the poem's final lines. Both Poyet and Robertson read the "gates" as a way of entry, helping to balance the long passage of pronomial address toward the book's conclusion. They agreed to prefix these nominal-phrase lines with "à" rendering them prepositional and adverbial, but thus repositioning the gates and preserving a large-scale structural arc and symmetry of the English poem, including the pronomial "high point" (*un point d'orgue*). ". . . tous les *tu* au féminin disséminés dans le texte, précédés des *ta, toi* et *ton* pour qu'ils soient eux aussi à l'initiale, de façon spectaculaire et symétriquement aux portes qui nous y ont fait accéder au cours des premières pages. . . ."[34] Not only does the process of translation itself serve to bring out many aspects of a larger complex, coauthored text which is generated by its practices, it would be difficult to find a finer example of how the translation of process—even one as simple and as arbitrary as alphabetization across English and French—may be able to form and articulate the significance and affect of aesthetic language.

NOTES

1. The most important academically oriented organization devoted to the field is the Electronic Literature Organization (ELO, http://eliterature.org), also a major sponsor and contributor to the Consortium on Electronic Literature (CELL, http://cellproject.net). The field's best knowledge base and research starting point is the ELMCIP (Electronic Literature as a Model of Creativity and Innovation in Practice) Electronic Literature Knowledge Base (http://elmcip.net/knowledgebase).
2. In this essay and generally, I prefer to use the "guest" and "host" terminology advocated by Lydia Liu with regard to translation, where the guest language is what is usually referred to as the "original" or "source" and the host language is the "target." Lydia H. Liu, *Translingual Practice: Literature, National Culture, and Translated Modernity, China 1900–1937* (Stanford: Stanford University Press, 1995).
3. This is far from a complete survey. The ELO (http://eliterature.org) works hard to promote the practice of digital literature in languages other than English with its 2013 and subsequent conferences having this as a main theme (http://chercherletexte.org/en/). There are associated centers of related activity in Norway (http://elmcip.net and http://www.uib.no/en/rg/electronicliterature/90332/decentering-global-electronic-literature), Spain (http://www.hermeneia.net), Portugal (http://po-ex.net), Poland (http://techsty.art.pl), Canada (http://nt2.uqam.ca and http://revuebleuorange.org), and France (http://hypermedia.univ-paris8.fr, http://www.labex-arts-h2h.fr and http://paragraphe.info), with many other writers and scholars from across and beyond Europe taking part. A European eLiterature collection was produced in 2013 (http://www.eliteraturecollection.eu/collection/). The author's paper on the speculative translation of one of his own collaborative pieces (John Cayley, "Beginning with 'The Image' in *How It Is* When Translating Certain Processes of Digital Language Art," *Electronic Book Review* [2015], http://www.electronicbookreview.com/thread/electropoetics/howitis) was delivered at a 2013 conference in Paris on "Translating E-Literature," the proceedings of which are published online as Arnaud Regnauld and Yves Abrioux, "Translating E-Literature = Traduire la littérature numérique," *Traduire la littérature numérique*, http://www.bibliotheque-numerique-paris8.fr/fre/ref/168448/COLN11/. The author's "Untranslatability and Readability" (*Critical Multilingualism Studies* 3, no. 1 [2015]: 70–89) also makes some further reference to related questions. "The Trope Tank," directed by Nick Montfort of MIT's Comparative Media Studies | Writing department, initiated their Renderings project in 2014,

and the following is quoted from their website (http://www.nickm.com/trope_tank/renderings/): "The Renderings project locates digital literary work from around the world and translates it into English. This process involves close attention to the computational aspects of the work—along with the concern for language that has been developed over centuries by literary translators. The project also sometimes entails porting earlier work to contemporary platforms and making such computational work available on the Web." The first phase of actual Renderings (thirteen works in six languages) has been published in Fordham University's literary journal *Cura* (http://curamag.com/issues/2014/11/30/renderings).

4. "Traversal function," as a term for the way a literary artifact presents its text and the relation of this presentation to temporality (typically), is from Espen Aarseth, *Cybertext: Perspectives on Ergodic Literature* (Baltimore: Johns Hopkins University Press, 1997), which remains a standard reference for the analysis of textuality having affordances that are enabled by programmable digital media.

5. John Cayley, "The Code Is Not the Text (Unless It Is the Text)," *Electronic Book Review* (2002), http://electronicbookreview.com/essay/the-code-is-not-the-text-unless-it-is-the-text/.

6. Cayley, "Beginning with 'The Image.'"

7. References to contemporary literary conceptualism are given in Cayley, "Beginning with 'The Image.'"

8. One of the striking arguments of Jacques Derrida's *Monolingualism of the Other* is that human persons may become monolingual in a language that is not, in personal historical terms, their own (Jacques Derrida, *Monolingualism of the Other; or, The Prosthesis of Origin*, Cultural Memory in the Present, trans. Patrick Mensah, ed. Mieke Bal and Hent de Vreis [Paris: Éditions Galilée, 1996]). These remarks raise further complications of macro- and microlinguistic history, the fact that statements about language are complicated by diachronic and synchronic perspectives. Nonetheless, it seems to be phenomenologically the case that at any (synchronic) moment during the (diachronic) course of reading and writing, one can only ever be acting within a particular, singular language.

9. I have made slight adjustments to the terminology for these rubrics as compared with my earlier essay on the translation of digital language art and especially algorithm-intensive linguistic artifacts (Cayley, "Beginning with 'The Image'"). I have replaced "algorithm" with "explicit process" (which is easier to apply more broadly) and have then ordered, more logically, the qualifiers for the two types of dissonance, replacing "algorithmically" with "procedurally induced."

10. Real-time network access to archival and referential resources for linguistic practice has quietly revolutionized reading and writing. The internet, as itself a site for such practice, is indexed by a number of search engines that have rendered it, effectively, a living multilingual corpus. Discussion of this revolution is far beyond the scope of this essay. Suffice it, here, to point out that, for the first time, historically, the network allows both scholars and practitioners to have some direct sense, for example, of the differential access and comparative comprehensiveness of archival and referential resources *across* distinct natural languages. Whereas, previously, it would have been very difficult to make any kind of authoritative or even anecdotal statements concerning what I call "procedurally induced global dissonance," it is now plausible to address these effects critically, as I have begun to do in a previous essay when discussing the translation of generative processes as applied in English and, by contrast, in French (Cayley, "Beginning with 'The Image'").

11. Georges Perec, *La disparition, Collection L'Imaginaire* (Paris: Denoël, 1969); Georges Perec, *A Void*, trans. Gilbert Adair (London: Harvill, 1995).

12. Georges Perec, *El Secuestro*, trans. Marisol Arbués, Mercè Burrel, Marc Parayre, Hermès Salceda, and Regina Vega (Paris: Editions Denoël, 1969).

13. Liu, *Translingual Practice.*
14. The discussion here refers to John Cage, "Songs for C.W.," *Ex Tempore* 3, no. 2 (Fall/Winter): 17–23, and John Cage, "Songs for C.W.," *Revue d'Esthetique Nouvelle série,* nos. 13–15 (1987–1988). The 1987–1988 issue of *Revue d'Esthetique,* devoted to Cage's work and containing these French translations of the artist's "Songs for C.W.," has much else of interest, including other mesostics in translation and both English and French versions of "Untitled," which reads through the word "SILENCE" (John Cage, "Untitled, " *Revue d'Esthetique Nouvelle série,* nos. 13–15 [1987–1988]: 543). The untranslated English of this piece is John Cage, "Untitled," in *X: Writings '79–'82* (Middletown, Conn.: Wesleyan University Press, 1983), 117; see in the same volume Cage, "James Joyce, Marcel Duchamp, Erik Satie: An Alphabet," 53–101, which is translated for the *Revue.*
15. In the current case study reading, I wanted to highlight the (re)shaping of the guest and host texts in terms of mesostic-driven lineation, but did not address the spectacular disruption to orthography, in both the figured translations, represented by "quWand" for French *quand* = "when." This substitution is a function of a procedurally induced local dissonance since the frequency of "w" in French, essential to the name "Wolff," is far, far lower than its frequency in English. The dissonance here extends to the introduction of a "misspelt" word, with what would be called a "double-u" in English that plausibly hides itself as a more or less unsounded "différance" in the French and definitely evokes the deconstructive translingual pun. All this also harkens back to Perec's letter-driven constraints and forward to the question of English-French alphabetization in Robertson's *Cinema of the Present,* for which the position in the alphabetic order of English "w"-question words and their French equivalents, in any translation, is an issue that is, to an extent, taken up in this essay's final close readings.
16. This procedural distinction may be appreciated in purely formal terms but was also explicitly recognized by Cage, according to this Wikipedia article, https://en.wikipedia.org/wiki/Mesostic, citing Cage's assistant, Andrew Culver. Here, the untranslated guest form of mesostic was referred to as "one-hundred-percent mesostic," whereas those in Richards's versions would be "fifty-percent" mesostic.
17. Nanni Balestrini, *Tristano: romanzo, I Narratori de Feltrinelli* (Milan: Feltrinelli, 1966); Nanni Balestrini, *Tristan,* trans. Jacqueline Risset, *Tel Quel* (Paris: Éditions du Seuil, 1972).
18. Nanni Balestrini, *Tristano, LM3665 copia unica, romanzo multiplo* (Rome: DeriveApprodi, 2007).
19. Nanni Balestrini, *Tristano: A Novel,* trans. Mike Harakis (London: Verso, 2014).
20. "The number of ways twenty things can be selected from a group of thirty things and arranged in different orders is 30!/(30–20)!, which is a number with 25 digits: about 73.1 septillion, or just over 240 times the number of stars in the observable universe. And that's before we take into account that there are ten such chapters, themselves ordered randomly." Martin Wakefield's letter to the *London Review of Books* 36, no. 16 (August 21, 2014).
21. As others who have attempted this have remarked (see Thomas Jones, "Short Cuts," *London Review of Books* 36, no. 11 [2014]: 25), making any kind of reading that compares the original 1966 publication with anything other than Risset's conventional translation (this has the kind of natural linguistic correspondence we expect) is bewildering and, frankly, seems pointless, particularly when we recall that the chances of there being any substantive correspondence between any copies of any of the uniquely printed editions in any language are infinitesimal (if not impossible: the 0–9,999 copies that may eventually be issued by DeriveApprodi could, theoretically, exclude those permutations calculated for Verso's copies that commence with number 10,000). Nonetheless, here are a few notes intended to give some sense of the scale of the problem with regard to, as it were, correspondent readings. I own #10,330 and #10,544 in the Verso edition of Harakis's translation. The primo capitolo of the 1966 text is chapter 2 in

#10,330 and chapter 10 in #10,544. The two English versions have a total of seventeen of the twenty fragments in 1966's chapter 1, whereas Balestrini composed thirty possible for each chapter, including this one. #10,330 has seven fragments not included in 1966; #10,544 has eight, some of which are also in #10,330. Thomas Jones's letter to the *London Review of Books* of June 5, 2014, reports, "I have number 5121 in Italian [the 2007 DeriveApprodi edition], and number 10,603 in Mike Harakis's English. . . . Chapter 10 in copy no. 10,603 corresponds to Chapter 8 in copy no. 5121. They have ten paragraphs in common. So I happen to have all 30 paragraphs of that chapter, distributed across two books in a completely different order in each."

22. With the proviso that, in the original Italian text, punctuation of the fragments within chapters differs from that in the 1972 Italian edition and the English translation. For the 1966 publication Balestrini or his publisher ran pairs of the selectable fragments together to form ten longer typographic paragraphs or sections for each chapter. The later Italian and the English translation break all twenty fragments per chapter into blank-line separated paragraphs. Risset's translation corresponds with the original Italian edition with respect to this point.

23. Caroline Bergvall, *Fig: Goan Atom 2* (Cambridge: Salt, 2005), 64.

24. Ibid., 63–71. Bergvall also explains that, in the version for the first publication of the piece—the "Transluccinacion" issue *of Chain* (Fall 2003)—she added a forty-eighth translation of the tercet but removed it later so as to adhere to the seven-hundred-year rule. The title to Szymanska's republication and translation into Polish (details below) refers to the forty-eighth and twenty-second "variations," but this is also because Szymanska considers the entirety of each set of Dante translations to be a variation. For Bergvall (*Fig*, 64), the sonification by Maher based on her vocalized readings brings the collated variations, materially, together into a unitary, countable artifact. This, by the way, makes for a highly complex situation with regard to our rubrics of integrity and association. Szymanska's Polish translation of "VIA" contains her own new translation of the Dante into Polish and then also forms a constituent part of her translation of "VIA," which is also a twenty-second "variation," which is what exactly: a part of her translation? the "signature" of a new work of conceptual writing in Polish? The first thirty-six variations are printed in the following anthology: Craig Douglas Dworkin and Kenneth Goldsmith, *Against Expression: An Anthology of Conceptual Writing* (Evanston, Ill.: Northwestern University Press, 2011), 81–86; a publication on the Poetry Foundation website has "all" forty-seven (http://www.poetryfoundation.org/poem/245738).

25. Caroline Bergvall and Katarzyna Szymanska, "Via: 48 Dante Variations/Via: 22 wariacje na temat Dantego," *Ha!art* 50, Numer konceptualny = Conceptual Issue (2015): 17–21. I have not traced all the translations of "VIA" that have been made. Szymanska kindly referred me to an online interview with Bergvall (Caroline Bergvall and Eva Heisler, "Propelled to the Edges of a Language's Freedom, and to the Depths of Its Collective Traumas," www.asymptotejournal.com/visual/eva-heisler-caroline-bergvall-propelled-to-the-edges-of-a-languages-freedom/), where she speaks of the pleasure she has taken when considering the approaches of poets and scholars who have asked her about translating this piece. She mentions explicitly Szymanska's version and one in Portuguese. "In this respect, I have really enjoyed the way poets have approached me to translate my piece 'VIA (48 Dante Translations),' seemingly untranslatable. Yet I have made the process so transparent that they are invariably happy to generate a new text based on their culture's own history with Dante. I do specify the musical quality of the Bach fugue variations so that they bear in mind the alphabetic quality of the selection but that's all. Most recently VIA has been translated for a Polish anthology as well as for a Portuguese project, following these guidelines."

In the same section of this interview, as she is being questioned about a remark in her introduction to Caroline Bergvall, Laynie Browne, Teresa Carmody, and Vanessa Place, eds., *I'll Drown My Book: Conceptual Writing by Women* (Los Angeles: Les Figues Press, 2012), on translating practices that are "along the line of structure, rather than verbal correspondence," Bergvall responds in a manner that is in accord with my arguments here. "It seems to me very silly to wish to translate the language from instruction- or template-based pieces. Especially if there's been no other editing or writing than accepting the material and reorganizing it. Best to utilize the process itself to generate a text in the arrival language and, in this sense, reframe the translation process."

26. Katarzyna Szymanska, "Caroline Bergvall: Poezja przekładem pisana = Caroline Bergvall: Poetry Written with Translation," *Ha!art* 50 Numer konceptualny = Conceptual Issue (2015): 23–27. Readers may find the following remarks by Szymanska of some interest, kindly supplied to the author in an email of October 21, 2015:

> [T]he title reads: VIA: 22 wariacje na temat Dantego [VIA: 22 Variations on Dante]. I collected the opening lines of all existing translations of Inferno in Polish (20 versions) and added my own one (21st version: Szymanska, 2015) treating it as the translator's signature. In order to keep it at the very end of the series while simultaneously staying with the alphabetical order of the original, I needed to make sure my final terza rima starts with the last letter of Polish alphabet, Ż (diacritic: Z with a dot above).
>
> Now, the shape of my tiny Polish addition is important for the entire chain for two reasons:
>
> Firstly, Slavic languages signal the speaker's gender in past tenses more explicitly than English. As a consequence of that, two women translators in Polish renderings (Świderska 1947, Kuciak 1989) ended up expressing their sense of being lost using masculine forms. I decided to keep these forms without editing them. In doing so, I try to suggest that the artistic language of women poets/translators has always been dictated by writing/translating men, even in expressing emotions/writing about being lost in life etc. (I guess that this device might be interesting for scholars working on Women's Studies/Feminism). And as a counterbalance to that tendency, I used feminine forms in my own final version; not only because of being a woman myself, but also since what I actually "translated" was Caroline Bergvall's 48th private reading, i.e. another woman's variation.
>
> Secondly, all 20 versions in Polish are either old or were intentionally rendered archaic. Sadly, Polish translation practice differs from the amazing Anglo-Saxon tradition of modernising and playing with the language of the classics. My version was in a sense supposed to dissent from the earlier stylistic patina, and sound transparent and modern. I hoped it would give a new lease of life to Polish Dante and appear as something valid nowadays, that is a sincere statement of someone living in 2015.

27. Lisa Robertson, *Cinema of the Present* (Toronto: Coach House Books, 2014); Lisa Robertson, *Cinéma du présent*, trans. Pascal Poyet (Clamecy dans la Nièvre: Théatre Typographique, 2014).

28. Robertson, *Cinema of the Present*, 108–109.

29. Documentary notes by Poyet, in English, attached to a personal email communication from Lisa Robertson, November 11, 2014.

30. "Lisa Robertson n'a suivi d'autre contrainte pour écrire phrase après phrase *Cinéma du present* que de ne jamais ajouter la nouvelle phrase à la dernière, mais de faire grandir le texte par le milieu." Pascal Poyet, "Remarques sur *Cinéma du présent* de Lisa Robertson," in *Cinéma du présent* (Clamency dans la Nièvre: Théatre Typographique, 2014), 91.

31. Poyet refers this to Robertson's engagement with the thought of Hannah Arendt, who writes about Henri Bergson's "enduring present" (as the received translation has it) in Arendt, *The Life of the Mind* (New York: Mariner Books, 1981). "Duration of the present" is my own formulation and is intended to refer more directly to Bergson's thinking and, especially, to the much more complex and interesting treatment of reading and temporality in the first essay, in particular "Time in the codex" in *Nilling* 9–18 (Toronto: Bookthug, 2012). *Nilling* was composed during roughly the same period as *Cinema of the Present* (according to Poyet, "Remarques sur *Cinéma du présent* de Lisa Robertson," 87), and should be read as a vital companion text for any more thorough critical reading of Robertson's poem, one that is, sadly, beyond the scope of this essay.

32. Pascal Poyet, "Remarques sur *Cinéma du présent* de Lisa Robertson," 88.

33. Ibid., 89.

34. Ibid., 94.

3 • WHO'S IT FOR?

Toward a Rhetoric of Translation

RUSSELL SCOTT VALENTINO

Identifying the rhetorical features of any manner of communication requires stereotyped forms of expression. To understand what they are being told, and especially to be persuaded by it, people need to recognize a novel situation as a variation on a theme with which they are already familiar. Rhetorical theorists since Aristotle have known this. They call these canned formulas *topoi,* or places. When the occasions are typical enough they are called *commonplaces.* Surprisingly, the form of communication called *translation* offers fertile ground for rhetorical exploration, not least because when it comes to translation, people have been repeating themselves for millennia. If their repetitions have often appeared new and, to use a medieval commonplace, "never seen before," it is largely because of the skillful variations in which they have been expressed and the changing circumstances of a changing world, which tend to make each generation think or—perhaps more accurately—feel that it has discovered, if not created, something altogether new, rather than learned something that people before them knew, too.

The truth is that, outside of certain technical spheres, about which I shall have more to say below, translation has changed very little over the centuries. It is characterized today, as it has ever been, by the need for careful study of a foreign language and culture, by a thorough understanding of the text from which a translation is derived, and by skillful manipulation of the receiving culture's language and expressive modes. Obviously, this is not an exhaustive definition of the activity of translation. In fact the wide variety of translation commonplaces may derive in part from an inscrutable quality that, like the figure of the translator, who shifts between cultures, appearing to belong to and speak for one or the other from one moment to the next, makes it difficult to say what translation *is.* In other words, we keep trying and keep failing to adequately describe it, and each failure invites still more attempts, covering the same or similar ground, approaching but never quite reaching the inscrutable center.

When I claim that people have been repeating themselves, I do not mean to say that all conversations about translation are identical. The fact that translation from one language to another is embedded within ideas about the distinguishability of languages from one another, and that these ideas change from time to time and place to place, makes such a claim untenable in any but the most abstract sense. "A language is a dialect with an army and a navy," quipped the linguist Max Weinreich, and this thought—expressed, significantly, in Yiddish—points to the conditions of power upon which translation always rests.[1] Our understanding of the clear demarcations among languages, especially as markers of national affiliations, is not only relatively new, it is relatively contestable, depending on the nation and the time.[2] To borrow a formulation from Mikhail Bakhtin, national languages are always projects that, if not worked at, have a tendency to bleed into other languages, drift, and innovate and mix.[3] Making them solid requires consistency, rules, grammar, teachers of grammar, schools, dictionaries, newspapers, and standard ways of editing, and it is upon this apparently solid foundation that translation rests. Translation marks the boundary between the point where one nationally recognized language stops and another begins. Translation validates a language with its own sovereignty.

Most claims that begin with the words "translation is like" fall somewhere amid a network of commonplaces that surrounds an inscrutable center and rests upon conditions of power. These commonplaces often appear as sparkling lights blinking on and off, luring us toward them according to our proclivities, interests, and politics. Thus translation as intercultural exchange flickers on a green tower while translation as art glows red in the café *en face*. Translation as performance has its own top-floor marquee, while outside the basement below, translation as midwifery hangs its lantern. The betrayer burns a black lamp, hidden behind an Italian dictionary. The hijacker's bulbs are bright, multicolored, broadcast over a loud speaker. The cannibal watches from the jungle across the avenue, eyes bright. The wires crisscross, the power flows from the inscrutable source.

Exploring the discrete commonplaces of translation discourse in English is likely to take the form of short excursions into the rhetorics of accuracy, violence, equivalency, communication, loss, and mimesis. Instead of indulging in any of these micro-explorations, this essay tests more general waters in an attempt to situate the rhetoric of translation amid a variety of discursive and disciplinary trajectories, particularly in relation to teaching and learning.

The wide divide between practice and theory has its own points of rhetorical interest, as does the divergence between the relatively new field of translation studies as an offshoot of applied linguistics, on the one hand, and literary theory, on the other, particularly in its comparatively inflected modes. There is a parallel to this divide, however, in the fact that contemporary translation practice might also be understood as an offshoot of foreign language instruction, literary history in the commentary and intervention mode (as in classics or philology), and creative writing. Each of these domains operates through commonplaces and assumptions about audience and effectiveness, using tropes that often contain complex unarticulated arguments that, once made explicit, help to define the interests and aims of their practitioners. More than this, they help to clarify what is at stake and how to measure the successes and failures of such differently marked approaches.

I must also contrast the pedagogical aspect of this project to what might otherwise look like a purely descriptive engagement, much as there was a pedagogical aspect to Wayne Booth's seminal study *The Rhetoric of Fiction*, which my title echoes.[4] Translators, historians of translation, teachers of literature and language, and theorists of translation and cross-cultural communication (the most likely audiences for this chapter) will see each of their approaches in clear demarcations along a spectrum that puts them into greater focus, helping to inform practice and clarify the often fraught language of what poet and translator Cole Swensen once characterized as "the blood sport of translation" across the entire range of these forms of writing.[5]

Rhetoric plies a middle ground, with enough theoretical gravitas, history, and connections to neighboring fields to constitute a field of its own, but also with grounding in real communication situations and handy concepts—like "kairos" (timeliness), "ethos" (character), and "lexis" (style)—that are highly applicable to translation. Such concepts have rarely been applied to the study of translation in a systematic manner, despite the fact that many translation studies approaches, from those of Lawrence Venuti and Susan Bassnett to those of David Damrosch and Emily Apter, have often operated within unstated rhetorical fields. To take a well-known example, the notion of the "translator's invisibility," which Venuti coined in the mid-1990s, is essentially a study in the rhetorical category of "ethos." When considered in this way, it becomes clear that invisibility can be deployed as part of an implicit argument, a means of moving an audience. The hidden claims of such an argument might be explicitly formulated so that the translation in question is an "authentic" replication of the original or, at least, of those aspects of the original that matter; it is implied that the author's words appear in English without intervention, if not magically, then at least with utmost faith and rigor. The translator's invisibility (or rather, silence) suggests that the original text has not been contaminated by some inscrutable third party (the translator). To test such an assumption, one can simply observe the degree to which such notions about authenticity and transparent communion with the source author are discarded the more visible the translator becomes, especially when the translator's own inventions are highlighted. The rhetorical positioning of the translator shifts, and she or he becomes an author, discarding the translator's cloak. The entire implied argument pivots on the fulcrum of the translator's ethos.

In a more global sense, however, I want to ask what a rhetoric of translation would actually look like. In some ways it would be a corrective to thinking of translation as a nonrhetorical activity, from an arts standpoint at one extreme or a technical standpoint at the other. These are in fact the two radical conceptions of translation in which this nonrhetorical aspect of translation most frequently appears. In the first case, translation is its own form of artistic expression, where a translator is inspired to create in the receiving culture's language and the creation stands as an artistic work in its own right, its success or failure dependent purely on its own aesthetic merits. At the other extreme lies a range of lexical items with exact equivalents, such as the word for the computer term "interface" or the term for a door hinge. These are technical usages that have limited and exact equivalents in other languages, at least on first glance. For "interface" and "hinge" also have figurative usages that make the exactness that we might initially perceive look rather more tenuous. Writing as a form of audience-free self-expression suggests a nonrhetorical act that contrasts with the production of technical equivalents for lexical items in another language. In the first case, it is as if the authorial role has completely taken over the ethos of the translator; this author is an English-language author writing in English, for the purpose of English—some poets refer to this self-positioning as "writing to the language." In the second case, the author seems to disappear completely, and the translator is a mere conduit. It does not matter who might fill that role; you always end up with the same word.

Both of these extreme cases are fascinating abstractions. To the extent that they might be realized, or attempted, in the practice of translation, they are also naïve and wrongheaded. For translations are always—whether conceived of as artistic or technical or anything in between—rhetorical acts, acts conditioned by considerations of the audience for whom they are imagined. And this is true not only at the global level—the level of why a text comes into being in English—but also at the level of every local decision made in creating the text, from paragraphing to discrete lexical items, commas, periods. And fragments. In this sense, there are as many different modes of translation, which means methods of creating it, reading it, engaging with it, and so on, as there are audiences for it, and there are many different conceivable audiences—from devoted religious readers to first-grade poetry explorers, historians, literature students in college survey courses, foreign language learners, critics, reviewers, and more. Whenever someone begins from that commonplace phrase "translation is," with its weak little copula verb no less, that person has an audience in mind, often unspecified, sometimes not even clear in her or his head, but always there to condition the aims of the translation, its existence, its manner of work, and, most importantly, any judgments that might be made about it. This fact, moreover, points to the major failing of all forms of automated translation, whether performed by means of a database like Google's or by some manner of machine or software: they do not act rhetorically. They are not sensitive to the specific conditions of an audience, not yet at least.

The rhetoric of translation, then, is corrective on the one hand, that is, to thinking of translation as nonrhetorical. On the other, considering translation through the prism of rhetoric can provide a bridge between highly theorized approaches, which look at translation and tend to place it within other domains, such as postcolonial studies, linguistics, or literary theory, and highly practice-oriented approaches, as in creative writing circles, which have tended historically to look at the theoretical pronouncements of their comrades in disciplines such as comparative literature or English and see little to nothing of use or interest to them. A rhetorical approach can sit squarely between these often opposing ways of engaging in translation and provide insight into each. It can translate the one for the other and vice versa.

Understanding how translation functions in a rhetorical frame of reference can be made clear by contrast to neighboring kinds of writing, those that might look similar on first consideration but whose distinctive differences point out the contours that surround and give translation its own distinctive shape. In the following sections, I treat three such neighboring domains in turn: foreign language learning, close reading, and creative writing. I use each to demonstrate how translation stands apart as a practice unto itself. Here I borrow an insight from Gilbert Highet's *Anatomy of Satire*, in which the contours of a genre come into focus by contrast with the kinds of writing that are closest to it but distinct from it, a little like a note becomes clear when an instrument is out of tune.[6]

TRANSLATION AND FOREIGN LANGUAGE TEACHING

The dominant foreign-language teaching methods in the United States over approximately the last thirty years do not, in principle, welcome translation. We are about a generation downwind of the great sea change in foreign language pedagogy that was marked by the emergence of the communicative method and oral proficiency standards in the 1980s. That framework positioned itself by contrast to a variety of other methods, perhaps none more polemically than the one known as "grammar/translation." Indeed, grammar/translation came to be an object of especial scorn for the early proponents of the new science of second language acquisition. Those who had adhered to grammar/translation were often criticized as unsystematic, ineffective teachers who actually did not speak the languages they taught very well. They were hiding their lack of fluency, so the criticism went, behind grammar rules and rote translation drills that did little but take up valuable class time. The use of translation in foreign-language teaching was equated with ineffective methodology used by poor speakers.

The rather consistent bias, in proficiency models of foreign language instruction, toward fluent speaking was especially evident in this early stage, and it lingers still. What I would like to emphasize is second language acquisition's methodological privileging not of speech per se, but of expressivity as a category of language experience, of language life. The very definition of proficiency in most second language models betrays such a bias. In the standard oral proficiency interview (OPI), a speaker is provided with a situation in which she or he is unlikely to know all the specific words that might pertain to that situation. For example, you are getting a haircut and you want to tell the stylist that you would like to shorten the bangs and thin the hair at the temples. The problem is designed with the assumption that the language learners being tested most likely will not know the words for "bangs," "temples," and "to thin"; their proficiency is measured by how well they are able to maneuver around their ignorance, that is, circumlocute. The assumption behind the test is that circumlocution is what native speakers do all the time, in the many situations where they do not know the precise vocabulary, for example, for that thing you stick under the horse's stomach or the little dealybob that holds the glass for a wristwatch. Circumlocution constitutes a metaspeech strategy of sorts that, when combined with a variety of language rudiments, enables superior speakers to communicate in just about any situation.

This is perhaps the smartest global strategy for foreign-language teaching that has ever been devised. It is flexible and testable. When you explain it to administrators, moreover, they are quick to see its virtues, especially when one stipulates the specific skills that an "intermediate mid" language user is supposed to be able to exhibit, for instance, in an exit interview. I will note only in passing here the considerable degree to which this approach has tended to alienate from the entire enterprise of foreign language instruction those who like to emphasize literature and ideas in their teaching. This is an important matter in the current, fragmented foreign language and literature environment of postsecondary education, but it lies outside my focus.

Instead, to the essentially expressivity-based method described above, where the teaching tools emphasize the verbalization of one's own thoughts and desires, translation highlights comprehension and expression in the writing of *someone else's* thoughts and desires. In practicing translation, one must pay especially close attention to what other people write and how they write it. If one does not know the words, one has to find them out, not find a way around them. In doing so, one discovers that that thing is likely a billet and the dealybob a bezel. In translation, circumlocution is almost never an option. Nor can one skip over what one does not understand, or stop paying attention when one doesn't agree. This adds an important dimension to translation that might be thought of as an aspect of morality.

Let me be clear that I am not advocating a return to grammar/translation in the teaching of modern foreign languages. On the contrary, rote drills are no more likely to cultivate the sort of translational sensibility I have in mind than is learning how to express one's wishes to a hairstylist. I wonder, however, if the pervasiveness of proficiency notions in foreign language education might stand in the way of a fuller engagement with language learning and language life, and this prompts me to ask the question: by marginalizing translation from the language teaching process, might we be depriving learners of an essentially empathic linguistic practice, like training musicians by focusing only on the solo? I have in mind the practice of serious literary translation rather than drills. Incorporating translation as practice into the teaching of language would create a hybrid method of sorts. What would students of such a method need in order to practice it proficiently?

They would have to have a solid grasp of a source language, its grammar and syntax, its sound possibilities, regionalisms, slang, and idioms—all from the period during which the source texts were written. They would need to have a thorough understanding of the genres of the works, their histories and variations, and the poetics of the periods in question, as well as closely neighboring genres—is this lampoon or parody? They would need to be able to identify literary, cultural, and historical allusions in a source text, which means they would have to have a sense of the author's range of knowledge and experience, too. Then—pivoting 180 degrees in the manner that translation commentators ironically describe as being "faithful"—they would need to know at least as much or more about the language tradition into which they were translating—its poetics and genres and sound possibilities and so on, in order best to engage an audience in that language. They would have to have a sense of rhetoric, of how to position themselves vis-à-vis their author; they would have to be able to write good dialogue, and differentiate one voice from another. They would need to discriminate among words of different registers, and find metaphors and sayings appropriate to language users of different ages and cultures: a twenty-year-old homeless man in a coastal resort, a sixty-year-old widow on an inland farm. And they would have to recall, in the midst of doing all this, that the words they were using were not merely an expression of what they might themselves want, or their own thoughts, at least not entirely their own.

TRANSLATION AND CLOSE READING

The teaching of literature is another key academic domain from which translation has been marginalized. In contrast to proficiency-oriented language teaching, here we are not one but rather two, or two and a half, generations removed from the great transformation, which was inaugurated by the New Critical and Formalist interventions in literary interpretation in the early twentieth century. Both New Critics and Formalists had a deep understanding of what it meant to engage translated literature because such literature had been an institutional norm of their own education. Writers like T. S. Eliot, James Joyce, Ezra Pound, and Vladimir Nabokov and critics like I. A. Richards, Viktor Shklovsky, and Georg Lukács were comfortable in multiple languages. More to the point, through their education and training, they were comfortable with the translation-fed dynamic of literary crossings, pairings, and mixings that continue to make works from the Modernist period so exciting. But their isolation of the text as an object of study unto itself and, more importantly, the manner in which their initial ideas became institutionalized by their students and their students' students in the teaching of literature in U.S. secondary and postsecondary education tended to exclude from an ideal literary analysis virtually all the questions that translators would normally grapple with—how a work was perceived by its original audience, how one's own potential rendering of it might match or not match the literary conventions of a target audience, what might be the cultural, political, or social need to translate the work, and a host of other extratextual considerations.

Translators sometimes like to say that translation is the closest form of reading, implying that it is a variety of close reading. It is not, and the ways in which translation is not close reading help to show what translation in fact *is*. Close reading is a New Critical method of analysis. Its particular bias does not lean, as in proficiency-based language instruction, toward prolix expressivity, where performance is measured largely by how well one can get around words one does not know in order to say what one wants. Instead, close reading showcases invention, marshaling a plethora of words, derived from but ultimately external to a text, in order to launch them at that text in the service of the "original" idea or "discovery" of the close reader. This is how you can get a five-hundred-page dissertation out of a dozen lyric poems. Apprentices to the method in freshman introductory courses have long been routinely encouraged to quote from a work but then "do things" with the quoted material, shape it into their own argument, control it as part of their critical explication. The analytic skills being taught have to do with unraveling the strands of the text under consideration in order to show how they ultimately cohere in a meaningful whole. Moreover, the exploration of the text takes place by means of a critical reflective apparatus that should ideally maintain its distance, and not, for instance, engage in naïve identification with characters, or any of the other typically unsophisticated reading practices of those who have not been properly schooled. The high Modernist bias in this approach should be evident. Such a lack of sophistication among his American students was a favorite target of Vladimir Nabokov's irony. He called us "minor readers" when we identified with the characters in books.[7] The point here is not about close reading per se but about the reliance on invention and critical distance by literary scholars and the manner in which these tend to push translation to one side—especially when it is practiced without additional words of explanation, without scholarly intervention.

In contrast to this New Critical inspired approach, I am wondering what a pedagogy that incorporated translation fundamentally in the teaching of literature might look like. I have in mind serious literary translation, of a variety of genres, of works from a variety of historical periods, in the service of creating English-language literature that might in the end find its way to readers. Of course what teachers emphasize would be different for different ages of students, and only at the very highest levels of instruction, at something like the translator apprentice stage, would one expect that students should have mastered all or most of the knowledge and skills needed to create a professional translation. But it can be used immediately in college-level literature courses, since canonized works typically have multiple translations available for exploration. As soon as multiple versions are available, they can become the basis of new, intralingual translations. And by far the richest source for finding multiple versions of literary works is among the ranks of interlingual translations, that is, in translations from other languages into English. There are many Dantes, Sapphos, Bashos, and Akhmatovas to choose from. These provide passage upon passage of multiple versions with different emphases, different stylistic choices, different interpretations and effects. Together they constitute an extraordinarily diverse and detailed subject for the analysis and discussion of literature. And obviously when approached through the framework of translating—that is, the creation of new writing in English—they can be used to extend analysis and discussion to writing more broadly.

One might take, for instance, the first paragraph of Dostoevsky's *Notes from Underground* as a point of departure. Students read five versions, discuss their differences, identify points at which they part ways (e.g., "wicked" vs. "spiteful" or "nasty"), and then create their own version, either selecting from those available or creating something altogether new. Along with their version, they might create a commentary about what they have done, indicating their audience (e.g., third graders, Twitter fanatics, lovers of Anthony Burgess's *A Clockwork Orange* or lolcat) and what stylistic effects they hoped to achieve by choosing X word over Y. This is a ratcheted-up version of intralingual translation, paraphrase on steroids, and an extremely compelling tool for getting students to understand literature in an active way, almost from the inside. It is also a way of getting them to see how translating works and how writing works.[8] It does this, moreover, from a standpoint that combines insider and outsider perspectives, eschewing unsophisticated identification but remaining close enough to encourage a sense of responsibility.

TRANSLATION AND CREATIVE WRITING

Isaiah Berlin once famously set out hedgehogs and foxes as categories of thinkers on the basis of a Greek fragment from the poet Archilochus: the fox knows many things but the hedgehog knows one big thing. "Taken figuratively," Berlin wrote, "the words can be made to yield a sense in which they mark one of the deepest differences which divide writers and thinkers, and, it may be, human beings in general. For there exists a great chasm between those, on one side, who relate everything to a single, central vision . . . and, on the other side, those who pursue many ends, often unrelated and even contradictory. . . . The first kind of intellectual personality belongs to the hedgehogs, the second to the foxes." And so Plato was, according to Berlin, rather a hedgehog and Aristotle rather a fox; Dante, Nietzsche, and Dostoevsky were clearly hedgehogish, while Shakespeare, Voltaire, and Joyce were all foxy.[9] But when Berlin turned to Lev Tolstoy and asked whether he was "a monist or a pluralist," whether his vision was "of one or of many," the question didn't seem to apply. It seemed to "breed more darkness than it [dispelled]." What sort of a thinker, Berlin asked, was the man whose work his essay was intended to explore? This was a terribly clever move for the start of an extended analysis of Tolstoy's philosophy of history, a subject that very likely required a bit of cleverness to engage his readers. When faced with the question of what Tolstoy was, Berlin turned his little intellectual personality game into a profound psychological tool: Lev Nikolaevich was, he suggested, by nature a fox, but a fox who believed in being a hedgehog, a fox who really wanted to be a hedgehog.

I borrow Berlin's gambit here partly because of the equivalently dry word "translation," which has a powerful way of turning people's eyes up into their foreheads whenever it's brought up (an effect I have likely compounded by combining "translation" with "rhetoric"), and partly because the activity of translation, like Berlin's enigmatic Tolstoy, does not fit comfortably in any of the categories one usually encounters in discussions of writing. On one side, theorists, critics, and practitioners of translation remind us that we read translations differently than we do non-translations,[10] and commentaries on the specific nature of translation practice, as opposed to the practice of fiction, poetry, or drama, are legion.[11] But another side suggests that we routinely forget about the fact of translation while we're reading; we read over or through it, thinking that we are somehow communing with the author through a magically or inspirationally channeled version of that author's voice in English.[12] Some on this other side would have us see translating as akin to dual authorship,[13] where translators and authors differ "in name alone,"[14] or where translation is a form of "rewriting" if not "pure writing."[15] The question of what sort of activity literary translation is vis-à-vis authorship does not seem wholly appropriate; it, too, seems to "breed more darkness than it dispels." Yet it is not lack of information that makes us pause. Translators, translation historians, and translation theorists have told us a great deal about the practice and its history in many different language traditions. Nor can translation be considered obscure in any usual sense of the term: you read the source text, look up the words you might not know, then start shaping lines in the receiving culture's language that correspond to the qualities you want to bring out. Why then does the question seem out of place? When asked what translating is in relation to authoring, what are we to say?

I do not intend to propose an answer to this question here, since doing so would require a systematic comparison of the activity of each. Instead, I shall limit myself to suggesting that the difficulty may be due, at least in part, to the fact that translators are not unaware of the problem and often obfuscate rather than clarify any clear demarcation between the two practices. In other words, just as Berlin's Tolstoy practiced being a hedgehog while really being a fox, so translators practice being authors, deploying the skills of authorship and, in effect, wearing the garments associated with authorship, without totally committing to being authors.

When pressed, they will step back, raising their hands, and say, "I'm not making this up!"

And this, in fact, is why translation is such a powerful tool for all writers and teachers of writing. It provides a means of continually sharpening our awareness of the possibilities of our own language, and in a much more engaging way than any sort of invented exercise—because the texts are real, the results can be published in their own right, and the focus on writing is especially, all-consumingly, performative. Translation thus opens avenues into experimentation with style and genre, especially styles and genres into which one might be less inclined to open avenues without translation's signposts. It also provides a model of stewardship and careful reading of another's words that authors with a good ear can turn to the development of character and dialogue. And it expands the now-pervasive workshop environment, lowering but not eliminating the problem of the wounded ego, by allowing everyone a constructive "out" that is *the source text.*

I have written elsewhere about the manner in which the creative writing workshop can be enhanced through the incorporation of translation.[16] Here I would like to point out some of the less frequently examined borders that serve to delineate translation as a form of creative writing.

Like the oft-employed free-writing exercise, translation, too, might be used as a productive means of getting through a patch of writer's block. But translating in this manner differs fundamentally from the sort of open-ended word generation that, no matter how self-important one might like to feel, often rings with a sort of hollowness that makes one question the point. No, this is something weighty from the start. We are translating—to return to a previous example—Dostoevsky, hating him, loving him, advocating for or fighting against, stylizing, ironizing, toning down, ratcheting up, making minute and poignant choices about how to shape and pace, but translating Dostoevsky. This idea shifts the ground beneath us, bringing with it both humility and responsibility.

The performance of style in translation, moreover, is a way of learning to manipulate style, and this in turn has an organic connection to reading and interpretation. John Nathan, the exemplary translator into English of works by Yukio Mishima and Kenzaburo Oe, has noted what he called "Jamesean moments" in the work of the Meiji Era Japanese novelist Natsume Sōseki.[17] Just when he noticed this in his reading—and there were historical reasons to support an assumption that Sōseki might have been influenced by Henry James—he was faced with a writing problem. Could he write prose like Henry James? Could he write prose that suggested the influence of Henry James? Could he write prose that suggested the influence of Henry James on an author who happened to have been writing in Japanese? The writing challenge is partly about reading with a good ear, partly about expression, and partly about the demonstration of style that evokes in an audience a desired effect.

Beyond stylistic practice, one might consider the manipulation of genre, and here, too, the placement of translation—near enough to touch but facing slightly askance—helps to define it. In contemporary writing and publishing circles, as opposed to those of literary history and theory, the term "genre" is rather loosely applied. On one hand, genres are the categories of the literary magazine, as in *poem, essay, story, review,* and so on. Once inside the slush of a category, these get closer to the language of literary historians, where a sonnet or a lyric essay might contrast to a ghazal or a flash fiction (and potentially get tossed into someone else's reading pile as a result). Distinctions like these become especially productive when contrasts and clashing expectations are deliberate, such as an epigraph that reads like an epitaph or a sestina on the Holocaust. Such distinctions apply to translation in exactly the same way and, also, not at all. In other words, translation is not a genre or a formal category, but it can stand in for, play the role of, assume the contours of any genre, any kind of text, just as translators can stand in for, play the role of, assume the contours of any kind of writer.

And yet translation is not parody. The moment one might begin to read a translator's work as if it were parody—as if this were some sort of Nabokovian play with roles—that would be when the translator lost all credibility as a translator. Translators cannot be tricksters; otherwise, how can they be trusted to convey what is in the source? Trust can be lost only once. Translation is its own kind of activity, its own practice, and this suggests, once again, how we read translations differently than we do other kinds of works, just as we treat translators differently than we do other kinds of writers.

Perhaps "form" is a better word than "genre" here. This is how W. S. Merwin discusses his work in the prefaces to his 2013 *Selected Translations*. In three poignant essays that contextualize and attempt to make sense of more than fifty years of rendering the voices of others, Merwin engages in an extended, searching analysis of his own practice, ending in a principled abandonment of formal consistency with the source. Embedded within this exploration is also a drama of poetic independence as played out in translation practice. Merwin seems to approach this practice with Pound, who once spoke to him "of the value of translation as a means of continually sharpening a writer's awareness of his own language."[18] But he also struggles over the next fifteen years to free himself from the idea, advanced by Pound and many others, that "fidelity in translating a poem should include an ambition to reproduce the original verse form."[19] By the end of this struggle, he notes, "I had come to consider the verse conventions of original poems as part of the original language, in which they had a history of associations like that of individual words—something impossible to suggest in English simply by repeating the forms."[20] Such a statement suggests that the translator is looking for something deeper than formal equivalency or what is sometimes loosely called equivalency of effect. Here translation clearly slips into authorship once more, or at least the garb of authorship, where one might try on, as has Merwin over the course of his career, a variety of national cuts and textures.

Maureen Freely discussed the relationship between her own fiction and her translations of the fictions of Orhan Pamuk at the 2013 annual conference of the American Literary Translators Association. At an early point in one of her projects, she said, the novel she had begun to write seemed to be going nowhere: "My characters were just standing there smoking and staring at me."[21] She turned to Pamuk's characters and they had a lot to say. Translating their words into English helped her hear what her own characters had to say, too. This is a direct relationship that might not apply to many people, since her novels happen to be set in Turkey, just like Pamuk's. But her example is illustrative in a more fundamental way. Even in the grip of expressive volubility, when the words are flowing out onto the page, the translator cannot stop listening. This is a lot like playing an instrument or singing a part in an ensemble. If you stop listening and focus on the sound of your own voice, you will lose track of what's happening around you, risking at least dissonance and possibly complete disconnection. When the listening aspect of translation diminishes, then I suspect the writing becomes something else and perhaps that is the moment when writers who have been hitching a ride with translation might want to go their own way. If indeed translation and authorship part ways when the author's hearing grows hard, this seems a much greater problem for authorship than it does for translation.

Even at the most mechanical level, in choosing punctuation or the markers to use for dialogue, translation provides an intensive, skill-based workshop, but one that is always characterized by expression filtered through listening. This is because other languages and other literatures weigh punctuation and mark speech differently, which means that every instance of a comma or capital letter, a splice, semicolon, or dash, becomes a decision about how to write in English, how to build a voice, create an image, contour a page. The stakes, moreover, are another author's lifeblood.

Whether they intend to or not, translators invariably end up being advocates for their works, so translating usually comes to entail trying to find the best, most effective way to make a character's and an author's voice compelling, to sell it and make it sing. This means, as I have tried to emphasize, listening carefully and writing skillfully. And as inevitable advocates, we care about our chosen works and the words in which we have chosen to express them and make them effective. But if someone says, "That's not working for me," or any of the myriad similar ways that critics use to say "I don't like what you've written," one can always look to the source, explain it in other words, and try together to make what one has written on its basis better. This can lead to an especially productive writing experience, one that is likely to build community, a rare occurrence in the world of creative writing. It can also help to show where one's own creative impulses might in fact differ from those of one's source author, where, in effect, a writer might choose to branch out from the source, taking a new direction.

We have probably all witnessed how public discussions of controversial topics can become so heated that constructive debate is no longer possible. One way of diffusing such emotional bombs is to focus on wording, style, accepted formulas, and the effects of such rhetorical features on an audience. For instance, rather than discussing the politics of the war on terrorism or No Child Left Behind, we can talk about the "war on terrorism" and "No Child Left Behind"—in other words, on how such arguments are put together, by means of what words, suggesting what things, relying on what assumptions, pushing what buttons. This in turn enables us to discuss the arguments and how we might understand and use them, without coming to blows in the process. In much the same way, many creative writing workshop participants have witnessed, or experienced for themselves, the deterioration of a writing community when personal stakes have overwhelmed everything else. People write what they care about, and if others don't like it, or if just about any of a million other possibilities come to pass, the results for a workshop, and perhaps for a career, can be tragic. Translation provides something of the same constructive misdirection as does focusing on the rhetoric of controversial public debate. You are still talking about the issues in such cases, but you raise everyone's awareness about the ways in which language affects how we shape them, make meaning from them, use them, and feel about them, and all this in fact makes it possible to talk about them. And so in the writing workshop, translation provides a constructive way to write and talk about writing that, like trying on someone else's garments, can lower the existential stakes, make it clear that we are all in some discomfort, all expressing thoughts that are ours but might have been another's, advocating for our words and for someone else's words, too, trying out authoring, in effect, in a manner that is one step removed from baring our souls.

The delicate play between one's own words and someone else's, which is what both inspires and limits translation, likewise can enable writing to flourish outside the usual narrow category of pure creation that authors have struggled with since at least the Romantic era. The performance of authorship can thus serve as a healthy corrective to the demons of authorship, encouraging the sort of responsibility and commitment to others that pure creation can sometimes eclipse.

TRANSLATION AS A MORAL PRACTICE

Let me conclude this discussion of translation's rhetorical contours by returning to the notion of morality introduced above. I have, many will have noticed, been dancing around the idea through this chapter. The expressive emphasis in foreign language pedagogy, the plethora of words aimed at a text in the service of an original reading in the New Critical mode, and the loss of listening that tends to characterize the weakest, least engaging forms of creative authorship—these are variations on a theme. The ground tilled by literary translation, which prepares another's written word and then attempts to nurture it in another culture, offers rich possibilities for very different ways of understanding all of these other kinds of writing. Moreover, I want to use the word "moral" in this context because, conceived in this manner, translation can be linked with the cultivation of character, both of an individual and of a society.

Literary translation plies a middle course between readerly identification, which is essentially mute, and distanced critical explication with its plethora of words. I have in mind translation as practice, a word I use in the manner proposed by Alasdair MacIntyre: a practice aims at the goods internal to its activities while extending human powers to "achieve excellence." "To enter into a practice," he writes, "is to enter into a relationship not only with its contemporary practitioners, but also with those who have preceded us in the practice, particularly those whose achievements extended the reach of the practice to its present point."[22] This view presupposes the subjection of one's understanding of a work to standards of the practice rather than privileging, as the dominant strain in Anglo-American critical explication has tended to do, one's own interpretive inventions.

To the extent that translators might engage in the ironizing techniques noted above that would highlight their own inventions over something else—call it truth, fidelity, or authenticity—their credibility suffers. Intention in this case is directed toward creating a translator's persona that is *telling the truth*, not *making things up*. Their challenge is similar not to that of the Modernist author but rather to that of the nineteenth-century Realist author, who might write something like, "I'm not a very good storyteller, so I'll just stick to the facts," or "I wish Mr. Newman had not thought such a thing but I would be lying to you if I pretended that he hadn't." The convention here is one of having no conventions. And though the specific conventions deployed might be different in different cases, and may not even look like conventions much of the time, their intent is palpable: "You can trust me," they proclaim. "I'm not making this up. I am telling the truth."

To ask the question, "the truth about what?" is to move onto another rhetorical plane, from which we can see the differing rhetorical position available to translators on one hand, and fiction writers and poets or critics and theorists on the other. This is the ground on which translators contrast most sharply with the writers who hold invention dearest. While it is true that "pure" creation often has plenty of real life in it, and just about any story might be described somehow as "based on actual events," the foreign language source text exists in a different category, on a different plane.

This difference and what it entails for the practice of translation is illustrated in a story often recounted about Lev Tolstoy's comment to Nikolai Strakhov on being asked to clarify a particular passage in *Anna Karenina*. "If I wanted to express in words," he wrote, "everything I planned to express through my novel, I would have to write anew from the beginning the very same novel I wrote."[23] In part this is sheer authorial orneriness. What I wish to point out, however, is how Tolstoy highlights the hollow ground under his creation, which does not exist anywhere except in the form in which he expressed it. Paraphrasing any portion of it means abstracting the events and characters it depicts as if they existed in some dimension other than the original text. Translators, by contrast, are only ever writing one version among many possibilities. Another person might come along and treat the same text differently tomorrow, and then another after that. Phenomenologists claim that thought is thought only when it is directed at something. In the same way we might make the distinction I am trying to suggest by seeing the common ontological nature of the source from which translations spring by contrast to the inventive weight that forms the ballast of the work of most other kinds of writing. Some might claim the distinction is overdrawn, and I do not wish to insist on it as a division. Like all distinctions, it is only as helpful as the point of view it offers for looking and comparing. Let me suggest, however, that the all too frequent impulse of translators to claim for themselves a status closer to that of the author mistakes the nature of their source, or is blind to it. The very concreteness of their subject puts them in a different category, offering them a different set of expressive resources and encouraging a different set of skills—skills of reading, writing, and communicating, if not of living as well.

NOTES

1. "A shprakh iz a dialekt mit an armey un flot." Weinreich attributed the phrase to a teacher from a Bronx high school who attended one of Weinreich's lectures between December 1943 and June of 1944. The earliest known published source for the phrase, in Yiddish, is Weinreich's "Der YIVO un di problemen fun undzer tsayt," *YIVO Bleter* 25, no. 1 (January–February 1945).

2. See, for instance, David Bellos, *Is That a Fish in Your Ear? Translation and the Meaning of Everything* (New York: Faber and Faber, 2011), 11–23.

3. This idea appears in various forms throughout Bakhtin's writings. Gary Saul Morson and Caryl Emerson have grouped it under the global Bakhtinian concepts of "unfinalizability" and "heteroglossia." For their discussion, with reference to several of Bakhtin's pronouncements, see *Mikhail Bakhtin: Creation of a Prosaics* (Stanford: Stanford University Press, 1990), 36–40, and 139–142.

4. Wayne C. Booth, *The Rhetoric of Fiction* (Chicago: University of Chicago Press, 1961).

5. In a personal communication.

6. Highet's use of this analytic technique is perhaps clearest where he distinguishes satire from its neighbors of invective, lampoon, comedy, and farce. See Gilbert Highet, *The Anatomy of Satire* (Princeton: Princeton University Press, 1962), 151–156.

7. Nabokov's opinion is typically explicit and categorical: to identify with a character in a book is "the worst thing a reader can do." See his "Good Readers and Good Writers," in *Lectures on Literature* (New York: Harvest Books, 1980), 4.

8. Translator-directors of dramatic works do this as a matter of course, selecting and shaping a new translation on the basis of several existing ones, inviting different emphases, nuances, settings, and so on, depending on one's intended audience and effects.

9. Berlin's 1950s lists are clearly marked by their lack of diversity.
10. Lawrence Venuti's short "How to Read a Translation" (http://wordswithoutborders.org/article/how-to-read-a-translation) points to the difference in reading practice, as does Eliot Weinberger's "Anonymous Sources" (http://iwp.uiowa.edu/91st/vol1-num1/anonymous-sources).
11. See, for instance, William Weaver's "The Process of Translation," in *The Craft of Translation*, ed. John Biguenet and Rainer Schulte (Chicago: University of Chicago Press, 1989), 117–124.
12. Lawrence Venuti famously finds fault with such simpatico assumptions in his *The Translator's Invisibility: A History of Translation* (New York: Routledge, 1995).
13. It is worth noting that Amazon.com currently lists nearly all translations as "by [author's name] and [translator's name]"; more substantively, the historical connection between poetry and translation was noted by Horace, who took translation as one aspect of the activity of the poet, a claim that rings true in the work of Anne Carson, Cole Swensen, W. S. Merwin, Charles Simic, Rosemarie Waldrop, and many other poets today.
14. Quoted in *The Art of Translation: Kornei Chukovsky's A High Art*, trans. and ed. Lauren G. Leighton (Knoxville: University of Tennessee Press, 1984), 18.
15. André Lefevere uses the concept of "rewriting" in his works on translation. See, for instance, *Translation, Rewriting, and the Manipulation of Literary Fame* (London: Routledge, 1992); Elizabeth Harris suggested the notion of translation as "pure writing" in a 2011 interview (http://www.iusbpreface.com/news/literary-translation-talk-held-at-iu-south-bend-1.2727633#.UzxnyFfjJJs). The concept formed the basis of a 2014 AWP panel featuring Harris and fellow translators Esther Allen, Susan Bernofsky, and Bill Johnston.
16. "Cross-Dressing for Workshop: or, The Uses of Translation in Creative Writing," https://www.awpwriter.org/magazine_media/writers_chronicle_view/3897/cross-dressing_for_workshop_or_the_uses_of_translation_in_creative_writing; and "On Three Cultures: Workshop, Review, Translation," http://mdash-ahb.org/the-translation-forum/3-on-three-cultures-workshop-review-translation/.
17. Nathan's comments were part of a translation seminar held at Indiana University on December 16, 2013.
18. W. S. Merwin, *Selected Translations: 1948–2011* (Port Townsend, Wash.: Copper Canyon Press, 2013), 12.
19. Ibid., 168.
20. Ibid., 169.
21. Maureen Freely, keynote lecture at the Nexus of Translation, American Literary Translators Association (ALTA) Conference, Bloomington, Ind., October 17, 2013.
22. Alasdair MacIntyre, *After Virtue*, 2nd ed. (Notre Dame: Notre Dame University Press, 1984), 194.
23. Quoted in Elisabeth Stenbock-Fermor, *The Architecture of Anna Karenina* (Lisse: Peter de Ridder Press, 1975), 14.

PART 2 TRANSLATION AT THE LIMITS OF THE NATION-STATE

4 • TRANSLATION AND IMAGE

On the Schematism of Co-figuration

NAOKI SAKAI

In this chapter, I am particularly interested to pursue the possibility of liberating translation from the curse bestowed on it by the view of translation organized around the model of communication, that is, the communication of a written text from one language to another. As an art or a *poietic* technology, translation grants us the possibility to examine anew social action in general; it offers us an invaluable gateway into an inquiry into sociality itself. Nevertheless, the modern and conventional view of translation has elided the potent sociality that suffuses it, through its collaboration with and substantialization of "national" and "ethnic" languages.

The argument regarding translation that I offer here tries to avoid a lapse into another systematic dichotomy of the differentiability (known as phonocentrism) of the written and the spoken. But this is not all. By "text" I do not imply the traditional view of the text that limits it to documents or books, nor do I adopt here the common dichotomy between the practical task of oral interpretation and the translation of scriptures, philosophy, and literature in writings. I do not accept the distinction between interpretation and translation precisely because I want to examine the operation of trope that permeates the translation situation, even while historicizing the traditional view of translation.

In studying translation, we must pay close attention not only to how troping operates, but also to how it malfunctions, for we cannot overlook an important aspect of translation, namely its poietic function, which serves to manufacture institutions and social relations through images, figures, or schemata. In this sense, translation is a sort of technology (*technê*) that transforms subjects by means of images. In view of translation as subjective technology, we need not only a transformation of the basic concepts, but also a recomposition of the tropes and figurations that we employ in order to devise shifts in the theory of translation.

Today we cannot take for granted the schematization of one language and another, a schematization that involves a spatial representation not only of imaginary figures but also of their relationship. When a language is represented as a figure in space, its relationship to another language is also represented spatially. As a result, it is most often assumed that one language is representable as external to another language. The schematization of a language thus gives rise to another presumption: that a language has a border, dividing its inside from its outside. But it is now necessary to examine this presumption, thanks to which the international juxtaposition of languages has been assumed as an indisputable verity, and which has dominated our general discussion of languages in the last two centuries. We must call into question this epistemic apparatus at work in our discussions of translation, according to which one language is represented spatially as external to and exclusive from another language. I have referred to this apparatus as the *modern regime of translation*, in which translation is represented through the strict distinction between the interior and exterior of a language. Integral to this apparatus is a modus operandi, or procedure of conduct, which I call "homolingual address." By this idiom, I want to suggest a certain manner of translational conduct in which a speaker or writer relates herself or himself to others in enunciation whereby the addresser adopts the position representative of an allegedly homogeneous language community and relates to the addressee or addressees, who are also representative of an equally homogeneous language society. It is important to note that homolingual address does not imply the social condition of conversation according to which both the addresser and the addressee supposedly belong to the same language community. They may well believe themselves to belong to different languages, yet can still address themselves homolingually.

In my view, we must historicize the curse of this modern regime of translation, in which the homolingual address is a widely accepted convention, but at the same time moving toward thinking about translation under the aegis of "heterolingual address."[1]

Homolingual address derives its legitimacy from the vision of the modern international world, and this vision projects the world as a forum for a juxtaposition of territorial state sovereignties as well as the reciprocal recognition of nation-states. Of course, the international world and the nation-state reinforce each other mutually and form a system of complicity. Consequently, central in the modern tropology of translation is the figure of "border," an image, an institution, or a geopolitical indicator that marks the spatial limit of one territorial and national sovereignty as well as—sometimes—the beginning of another, different national territory. The homolingual address—the modus operandi of translational enunciation within the modern regime of translation—is nothing but the consequence of a tropic exercise that maps the spatial configuration of the international world onto the locale of translational transaction.

The world accommodates one humanity, but a plurality of languages. It is generally upheld that precisely because of this plurality we are never able to evade translation. Our conception of translation is almost always premised on a specific way to conceive this plurality of languages. Not surprisingly, when we try to think through the unity of humanity as well as the inevitability of translation, we often resort to the fable of Babel. But do we have to assume this unity in plurality transhistorically? Can we not envisage discourses in which the thought of language is not captured in the formula of many in one? Are we not able to conceive of language in an alternative way?

In this context let me draw attention to the increasing significance of the problematic of "bordering" in knowledge production today.[2] This problematic has to be specifically denoted as one not of "border" but of "bordering," because what is at stake is more significant than the old problem of boundary, discrimination, and classification. At the same time that it recognizes the presence of borders, discriminatory regimes, and the paradigms of classification, this problematic sheds light on the processes of drawing a border, of instituting the terms of distinction in discrimination, and of inscribing a continuous space of the social against which a divide is introduced. In other words, the term "bordering" forces us to be attentive to the politics of border. The analytic of bordering requires us to simultaneously examine both the presence of a border and its drawing or inscription.

The modern regime of translation begins by taking for granted the very premise that one language is separate from another. It is postulated beyond dispute that deliberately and systematically one language is differentiated from another language by a definite border that is allegedly naturally given. The very contour of a language, according to which its organic unity is imagined, is given even when the conduct of translational enunciation, an instance where the very difference of one language and another is negotiated, is at issue. What is disavowed is the active and performative aspect of translation. The homolingual address completely overlooks what is thematically problematized in the act of translation: namely, in what sort of difference or discontinuity translation is expected to engage.

Translation intervenes in cultural difference or discontinuity in our social world. When one cannot understand what one's interlocutor wishes to say, express, or convey—that is, when one is at a loss in relation to some person one is engaged with in a social relation—one resorts to the act of translation. Only when there is an element of nonsense or incomprehensibility in the very locale where I am addressing my interlocutor while she is addressing me as her interlocutor is translation called for. In this locale of translational transaction, are we already and miraculously informed that the very incomprehensibility or nonsense is caused by the fact that, while I speak English, for instance, my interlocutor does not speak it? Is it because my language and her language are different that we are left in a situation of noncommunication? How can I know a priori that my experience of nonsense is already structured by the international configuration of borders in which one language is separated from another?

By now the fundamental weakness inherent in the modern regime of translation is obvious. The modern regime of translation always determines "difference" as a substantialized one between two individual entities, as a sort of gap between two individual—and indivisible—languages. It goes without saying that the homolingual address derives its legitimacy from a gullible acceptance of the conceptual economy—genus, species, and individuum—of classical logic or its modern derivative, the classification system of the Linnaean taxonomy.

Above all else, the difference at stake in translation is not reducible to diaphora or species difference: difference between two species, two particular languages, under the genus of language in general. It cannot be subsumed under the class of species differentiated by borders; it is not a border in stasis. Rather it is a bordering that is also performative and poietic; to translate is to inscribe a difference, to project an image of difference whereby two languages are constituted.

Accordingly as soon as the conduct of translation is viewed in terms of bordering, the constitutive order of the modern international world no longer appears natural; the concept of border-ing thus helps us to see that the modern regime of translation and the view of the international world taken for granted in that regime is no more than one among many possible ways of what Sandro Mezzadra and Brett Neilson have called *fabrica mundi* or the making of the world.[3] The world could have been mapped, projected, or institutionalized in manners other than that of the modern international world.

Indeed, it is in order to elucidate the differentiation of transnationality from nationality that I want to emphasize the problematic of border-ing in the first place. Most importantly, I want to reverse the order of apprehension in which transnationality is comprehended on the basis of nationality and to challenge the presumption that nationality is primary and transnationality is somewhat secondary or derivative. The transnational is apprehended as something that one creates by adding the prefix "trans-" to nationality. Unfortunately the word "transnational" retains a morphology that the "trans+national" obtains only after "national" is modified; "transnational" is thus subsumed to the "national," thereby misleadingly implying that the national is more fundamental or foundational than the transnational. Consequently the transnational is assumed to be derivative of the national. This widely accepted pattern of reasoning derives from our mental habit, according to which the adjectival "transnational" is attributed to an incident or situation uncontainable within one nationality. For example, an individual or group of people moves across the outer limits of one national territory into another, and such a movement is called "transnational." Or a company is incorporated in multiple national territories and manages projects mobilizing its employees of different nationalities living in different countries at the same time: such a company is called a "transnational" corporation. What I want to highlight, first, is the implicit presumption underlying the concept of nationality; nationality cannot make sense unless it is postulated against the horizon of *internationality.* Transnationality must thus not be confused with internationality. In order to assert the priority of transnationality to nationality, therefore, our first move is to delineate the semantics of transnationality as distinct from that of internationality.

One of the distinguishing characteristics of the modern world can be found in its internationality; the modernity of the modern world has manifested itself in the formation of the international world. Today transnationality is generally understood within the schema of the international world. By "schema," I mean a certain image or figure against the background of which our sense of nationality is apprehended. Yet it is important to underline that in some regions, such as East Asia, the international world did not prevail until the late nineteenth century. In this part of the globe, the international world was entirely new, and it took more than a century before East Asian states gave up the old tribute system and yielded to the new interstate diplomacy dictated by international law. In this regard, the international world was here a mark of colonial modernity. With the advent of the international world, the binary of the West and the Rest began to serve as the framework in which the colonial hierarchy of the globe was installed.

Of course, the international world is not exclusively a phenomenon of the twentieth century. Dividing the world into two contrasting areas, the West and the Rest, has been an institutionalized practice widely accepted in academia for a few centuries. This dichotomy may be traced as far back as the seventeenth century when the system of international laws was inaugurated with the Treaty of Westphalia in 1648. This peace treaty, subsequent to the Thirty Years' War, established the division of the two geopolitical areas. The first of these two areas would subsequently be regarded as "the international world" in which four principles were to be observed: (1) the sovereignty of the national state and its self-determination, (2) the legal equality among national states, (3) the reign of international laws among the states, and (4) the nonintervention of one state in the domestic affairs of another. The second was a geopolitical area excluded from the first, in which these four principles, including the reign of international laws, had no binding force. The first area would later be called the West, while the second area would be excluded from "the international world" and became literally "the Rest of the world," with its states and inhabitants subject to colonial violence.

Japan's colonization of Korea, for instance, was accomplished following the protocols of the international world. Many parts of the globe were also colonized, and the colonial subjugation of the Rest of the world was legitimated according to the system of international law. By the beginning of the twentieth century, the majority of the second area was transformed into colonies belonging to a few superpowers. Yet this pseudo-geographic designation of the West—pseudo-geographic because, in the final analysis, the West is not a geographic determinant—gained currency toward the end of the nineteenth century when the international world expanded to cover the entire surface of the earth as a consequence of three developments: first, colonial competition among the imperialist states; second, the emergence of the United States and Japan as modern imperial powers; and third and most importantly, the increasingly widespread anticolonial struggles for national self-determination. In this historical determination of the West, its distinction from the Rest of the world derived from the legacy of colonialisms.

In order for a colony to gain independence, the colonized people had to establish their own national sovereignty and gain recognition from other sovereignties. In other words, nationhood follows from and is a result of colonialism. As the number of nations being recognized in the international world increased, the presumptions of nationality and internationality were accepted as if these had been naturally given. As the schematic nature of the international world, given rise to as a consequence of *fabrica mundi*, was forgotten, both nationality and internationality were naturalized, as though the institutions marking the border of the national community—national territory, language, culture, and so forth—had continually existed for millennia.

One cannot overlook one key aspect of this process of nationality formation in the modern international world: it is not only an individual language in isolation but also the very relationship between one language and another that was fetishized and naturalized. The formation of a national language was always accompanied by a fetishization of the pairing of one language with another. Hence the image or figure of a national language was projected *co-figuratively* in the pairing of one figure with another. The question of how the relationship of one language to another should be represented played a decisive role in the creation of national identity via language. That is to say, in comprehending the international world, we cannot neglect the central role played by the *schematism of co-figuration* in the modern regime of translation.

It is at this juncture that the concept of transnationality must be reinvigorated and rejuvenated in order both to undermine the apparent naturalness of nationality and internationality and to disclose the very historicity of our presumptions about nationality, national community, national language, national culture, and ethnicity, which are more often than not associated with "the feeling of nationality." To historicize the schemata of the international world, the classical notion of nationality in British Liberalism is of decisive importance. According to John Stuart Mill, nationality entails that

> a portion of mankind are united among themselves by common sympathies which do not exist between them and any others—which make them co-operate with each other more willingly than with other people, desire to be under the same government, and desire that it should be government by themselves or a portion of

> themselves exclusively. This feeling of nationality may have been generated by various causes. Sometimes it is the effect of identity of race and descent. Community of language, and community of religion greatly contribute to it. Geographical limits are one of its causes. But the strongest of all is identity of political antecedents; the possession of a national history, and consequent community of recollections; collective pride and humiliation, pleasure and regret, connected with the same incidents in the past.[4]

In East Asia, it was arguably Fukuzawa Yukichi (1835–1901) who first systematically introduced the British discussion on nation and nationalism. Today he is remembered as one of the leading enlightenment intellectuals who advocated for the creation of the modern nation in Japan. In the early Meiji period, in the 1870s, he translated the English term "nationality" as *kokutai* (national body). In the Japanese Empire of the early twentieth century, the term "nationality" or "national body" had nearly acquired sacrosanctity, so that Fukuzawa's interpretation of the word "nationality" had to be publicly repressed. In his *Outline of the Theory of Civilization* (first published in 1873), Fukuzawa included Mill's explications of nationality and the "feeling of nationality" (*kokutai no jô*) almost verbatim in his exposition of *kokutai.*[5] For Fukuzawa, the project of creating the feeling of nationality among the inhabitants of the Japanese archipelago was an absolutely indispensable part of the construction of a nation-state. First of all, what must be acknowledged is that under the reign of the feudal government, there was an absence of the feeling of nationality among the multitude inhabiting the islands of Japan; there was no nation of Japan, no Japanese as a nationality. Therefore, the task of creating an unprecedented type of community called the "nation" had to be accomplished through the manufacture of the feeling of nationality.

Without being recognized as a sovereign state in the international world, however, people living in the Japanese archipelago would never constitute themselves as a nation or enter the modern international world. For Fukuzawa, the modernization of Japan, therefore, meant the creation of the institutional conditions for the feeling of nationality, without which people would never form a national community. Neither as individuals nor as a collectivity would the Japanese be able to become independent without the feeling of nationality.

In the late nineteenth and early twentieth centuries, nationalist intellectuals in East Asia and elsewhere in the Rest believed, almost without exception, that the introduction of nationality was an absolutely necessary condition without which peoples in the Rest of the world could not deal with colonial modernity. They understood that only by turning local masses into a people with nationality could they incite them to refuse their predicament of colonial subjugation and humiliation. It was, of course, imperative to institute the systems of industrial capitalism in their own countries and to educate the population so as to make it capable of thinking scientifically. This is to say, the fate of the nation could not be divorced from the project of modernization. Modernization necessitated the introduction of a new form of parliamentary government, industrial production facilities, national education, the system of national transportation, a national currency regulated by the national bank, a modern military built up with national universal conscription, and the spirit of scientific rationality guiding modern technology and production into a society. But any of these institutions necessary for the nation-building would be empty and useless if not accompanied by the feeling of nationality to bind people together as a nation, as a community of shared destiny. Nationalist intellectuals firmly believed that people under colonial domination would never be able to deal with the actuality of colonial modernity unless they formed a political community called "nation," a new political camaraderie shaped after the pattern of "fraternity" independent of the previous familial or tribal affiliations. They were convinced that unless the indigenous population first formed a nation, they would never be able to liberate themselves from the shackles of colonial subjugation.

However, let me note that the problematic that guides my inquiry in this chapter is entirely different from this nationalist concern. Rather, it is committed to the problem of how to emancipate our imagination from the internationality of the modern world, not through negation of the institutional presence of the nation-state itself but by problematizing the "feeling of nationality" permeating knowledge production in the humanities, particularly in area studies, and thereby projecting an alternative image of the transnational community. Suspending nationalist conviction, I refuse to view nationality as something given; instead I reverse the order of priority while never rejecting our struggle with colonial modernity.

Simply put, my starting point is that nationality is a restricted derivative of transnationality, and my guiding question is how the transnational, the foundational modality of sociality, is delimited, regulated, and restricted by the rules of the international world. It is in this context that I have to confront the issue of bordering in an implicit reference to translation.

In order to call the priority of nationality and the international world into question, we must first problematize the figure—image, trope, or schema—of the border. A border is primarily a matter of tropics as far as translation is concerned because the unity of a national or ethnic language as a schema is already accompanied by another schema for the unity of a different language; the unity of a language is possible only in the element of many in one. In order for there to be many, one unity must be distinguishable from another. In the representation of translation, therefore, one language has to be clearly and visibly distinguished from another. The unity of a language thus requires the postulation of a border in the tropics of translation.

The border cannot exist naturally; physical markers such as a river, a mountain range, a wall, and even a line on the ground become a border only when made to dictate a certain pattern of social action. In this respect, a border is always man-made and assumes human sociality. Only when people react to one another does a border come into being. Even if a border separates, discriminates, or distances one group from another, people must be in some social relation for a border to serve as a marker or representation of separation, discrimination, or distance. For separation or discrimination is nothing but a symptom of sociality. Therefore, a border is posterior to social relations, which may well be composed of an act of exclusion, discrimination, or rejection. At the beginning, there is an act of bordering. Only where people agree to observe a border can we talk about a border as an institution. Thus, bordering always precedes the border.

Prior to bordering, it is impossible to conceptualize the national border. Thus, the national territory is indeterminate prior to bordering. Similarly, it is impossible to determine a national language prior to bordering. So what is it that corresponds to this bordering as far as language is concerned? Of course, it is translation. What I want to put forth here is that, on the level of schematism or the practice of schemata, translation comes prior to the determination of language unities that it is usually understood to bridge. Conceptually, the relationship of languages must come before the unity of a language in isolation. Before the postulation of a national or ethnic language, there is translation, just as there is transnationality before nationality, as I have already indicated above.

So far I have deliberately avoided an explanation of what translation as an event or as a procedure is. Instead, I have discussed only how translation has been represented. This is indeed not unrelated to the truism that translation is recognized as necessary when we are at a loss, unable to comprehend what the interlocutor says or means to say, or do not know how to make ourselves understood. Almost without exception, the fables of translation, the most famous of which is the Tower of Babel, retrace an incident or disaster of noncommunication and nonsense. What I pursue in my preliminary investigation of translation beyond the conventional domain of the linguistic is an appreciation for this elementary event or experience of non-sense, even though the concept of event or experience may well be inadequate to describe the happening of non-sense. Instead of direct discussion of translation, I purposely begin my inquiry with how translation is represented.

Non-sense is unrepresentable. It cannot be represented since I, we, or one does not know what it is. Yet, it always designates a primordial locale of sociality, a starting point from which social relations are to be articulated. Let me tentatively define this locale of primordial sociality beyond representation in terms of "discontinuity."

At this stage we must acknowledge that, in the modern regime of translation, the representability of translation has not been critically examined. It has been taken for granted that translation is somewhat representable. Accordingly, the first moment to confront in my inquiry is how the very cause of translation, a happening of non-sense to which translation is supposedly a remedy, is represented, and how the incident of noncommunication is figured in the representation of translation. In the vast majority of cases, noncommunication is described as the presence of a gap or separation between one medium and another, one language and another. This is why the trope of bridging or filtration is so often used to comprehend the working of translation. Two distinct media or two unities of languages are already presupposed in this mobilization of the tropes of gap or filter.

The second moment in my inquiry is concerned with the topic of comparison. It may be summarized as an occasion where we are obliged to compare. Comparison takes place because the determination of *species difference* is needed. But to discern certain political complexity in the notion of the determination of species difference, let me instead ponder what is often referred to as *cultural difference,* and indeed two distinct approaches to cultural difference.

In the presence of a person who appears to be speaking, I can understand neither what she wants nor what she is meaning to do. Consequently I am at a loss. At such a point, some explanation as to why I or we are at a loss is demanded: reasoning may well provide a schematic explanation about some generalized experience of incommensurability, and the most popular explanation for such an occasion is that of cultural difference. Allegedly she and I are different. Supposedly, what she speaks is the Chinese language, whereas what I speak is English. Both belong to the general class of languages, but we cannot make ourselves understood by one another because the Chinese language is different from English.

Let me pause here momentarily since I do not think at all that the difference at stake in this instance can in due course be subsumed under the concept of species difference. What is at stake here is some difference, but it is not reducible to the conception of difference between Chinese as a particular language and English as another particular language, of difference that conforms to the conceptual economy of species and genus in the Aristotelian logic. The determination of the species difference is sometimes offered as a solution to the initial problem of our being at a loss, in response to the perplexity we come across in such a locale. Presumably language difference is a kind of species difference that purports to offer a clue as to why we are at a loss in a locale of incomprehension, perplexity, or helplessness. As I have argued elsewhere, however, the determination of the species difference leads us only to a confusionism.[6] And it is imperative to keep in mind that confusionism of this kind is almost always present in the term "cultural difference." Once again, let me stress that cultural difference prompting the conduct of translation is of different register than the language difference.

Language difference is supposed to cause a situation where we need to know why we are at a loss with one another. Language difference, already preliminarily determined as species difference, is a serious matter when we do not understand one another, when we cannot be confident in our directives for the immediate future. It is usually assumed that our sociability is grounded on some primordial communality, on our capacity to be immediately and instantaneously in a common sharing, such as through the same culture or language. It is alleged that language difference therefore causes our inability to share, to result in the absence of this communality. Normally—we presume, normalcy consists of this unwarranted assumption, asserted repeatedly in the homolingual address, that people do understand each other unless disrupted by some abnormal obstacle—we do not express our doubt about either the comprehensibility of our expressive behaviors or our ability to apprehend others' actions and expressions. The need for comparison occurs only on occasions where we are forced to become aware of different people, different beings. The encounter with cultural difference or discontinuity is thus interpreted as a meeting with one type or another of species difference.

The term "difference" becomes marked precisely because of this experience of "non-sense" (or simply "nonsense"), "being at a loss," or "being unable to make sense of the occasion," in short, of "being deprived of the world." The determination of species difference becomes something urgent and even desperately important, precisely because we are in the presence of others in *discontinuity*. Most often we talk of this encounter with discontinuity in terms of the "foreign," but it is significant that, initially, the foreign does not connote the outside or the external in a strictly spatial sense. Instead it is an outside of a given and familiar comprehensibility, an outside indicative of the non-sensical that evades the spatial alternative of either inside or outside. It is an outside but it cannot be accommodated in the spatial register of our thought.[7] The foreign acquires the status of the external or the outsider mainly through the modus operandi of the homolingual address, through an assumption that we are inside the common element—language, culture, or nationality—represented as an "inside," spatially delimited by borders. Only when the being-in-common is represented by a spatial figure of enclosure does the foreign gain the trope of the external-to or the outside-of the domain of domesticity or familiarity.[8] Yet, it is important to keep in mind that discontinuity is something incommensurate with the logic of location in spatial economy; it is discontinuous precisely because its location cannot be identified in the continuous expanse of space. At this stage, discontinuity cannot be represented as a relationship within a smooth continuous space. It is not because some person or people are different—in the sense of species difference—from me or us, that we are at a loss. On the contrary, it is because we are at a loss or unable to make sense in the first place that we attempt to determine this encounter with difference within the logical economy of species and genus. Are we to overlook the very difference between difference in the sense of "nonsense" or "being at a loss" and the species difference already regulated by the logical economy of species and genus?

Let us consider another situation in which we need to know how we are different from one another, why certain people are not subjugated to the imperatives or commands I normally obey or yield to, or why some of us are free from a set of proscriptions and others are not. We compare ourselves so as to find where we are situated vis-à-vis one another in a practical sense, in terms of what we must do. Comparison is indispensable precisely because we want to know how we are related to one another, who should lead among us, who should follow, who should work for whom among us, and so on. It is through the act of comparison that we comprehend the configuration of our subject positions, who we are in terms of socially determined relations: gender, commodity exchange, race, social rank, nationality, civilization, kinship, religious faith, cultural heritage, professional qualifications, pedagogic hierarchy, sexual orientation, academic expertise, and so forth. When we cannot locate ourselves in the configuration of subject positions, we are also at a loss or do not know how to act in accordance with others in a situation. On such occasions, we sense that something is different, and that we ought to behave in a manner that is different from the ways in which we are normally and normatively expected to. Yet, it is important to note that this sense of difference cannot be simply reduced to difference in the paradigm of the homologous and the heteronomous. As I have suggested throughout this chapter, this is of crucial importance to how we understand two different approaches to cultural difference.

In the context of our discussion of cultural difference, I would like to introduce this conceptual ambiguity of the individual into my understanding of the locus of comparison, of a place where we are articulated to one another in ways that I have called "heterolingual," in contrast to the homolingual address.[9]

It is with regard to these problematics concerning cultural difference that we must consider the task of how to reverse the conventional comprehension of translation that depends on the trope of translation as bridging between two separate languages or transferring a meaning between them. My inquiry here takes the form of a discursive analysis beyond the domain of the linguistic. Accordingly it involves the questions of figuration, schematism, mapping, and cartographic representation and the institution of strategic positions. In the conventional understanding of translation—elsewhere I characterized it as the schematism of co-figuration—the separation of two languages or the border between them is already presupposed.[10] In this order of reasoning, regulated by the trope of translation, I find one of the delimitations imposed by the presumptions of nationality and the international world. Nationality must be postulated prior to the process of the transnational transaction precisely because it cannot be conceptualized otherwise, just as national language must be assumed to exist prior to the process of translation because translation is programmed to be represented as bridging the gap between two separate languages. For this reason, the international world cannot but be predetermined as the juxtaposition of distinct nationalities that are external to one another. The economy of the international world thus excludes the potentiality of heterolingual address from the outset.[11] We have to guard against the static view of translation in which difference is substantialized; we should not yield to the reification of translation that denies it its potentiality to deterritorialize. Therefore, it is important to introduce the difference in and of language so that we can comprehend translation not in terms of the communication model of equivalence and exchange but as a form of political labor to create continuity at the elusive point of discontinuity in the social.

One may presume it possible to distinguish the type of translation according to the type of difference in or of the language to which translation is a response. To follow Roman Jakobson's famous typology of translation, one may refer to a project of overcoming incommensurability as a type of translation—interlingual translation—from one natural language to another. Or one may talk about an act of retelling or interpreting from one style or genre to another in the same language as an instance of translation: intralingual translation. Furthermore, one may cite an act of mapping from one semiotic system to another as a distinctive type of translation: intersemiotic translation. In this typology, however, the unity of a language has to be unproblematically presupposed. Were it not for this supposition, it would be hard to discuss a language that is different from the original language, in interlingual translation that takes place between languages external to one another. Neither would it be possible to designate the inside of a language or to refer to a language as the same in intralingual translation. Thus, we are forced to return to the question, "what difference?" In short, the sort of translation studies proposed by Jakobson was premised upon the homolingual address; it served as an endorsement of the modern regime of translation.

How do we recognize the identity of each language; that is, how do we presume that languages can be categorized in terms of one and many? Is language countable, like an apple or an orange, and unlike water? Is it not possible to think of language, for example, in terms of those grammars in which the distinction of the singular and the plural is irrelevant? What I am calling into question is the individual or indivisible unity of language, a certain positivity of discourse or historical a priori in terms of which we understand what is at issue whenever a different language or difference in language is at stake. How do we allow ourselves to tell one language from another, to represent language as a unity?

My answer to this question is that the unity of language is like Kant's regulative idea.[12] It organizes knowledge but is not empirically verifiable. The regulative idea does not concern itself with the possibility of experience; it is no more than a rule by which a search in the series of empirical data is prescribed. It does not guarantee empirically verifiable truth but, on the contrary, "forbidding [the search for truth] to bring it[self] to a close by treating anything at which it may arrive as absolutely unconditioned."[13] Therefore, the regulative idea gives only an "object in idea." It means only "a schema for which no object, not even a hypothetical one, is directly given."[14] The unity of language cannot be given in experience because it is nothing but a regulative idea, enabling us to comprehend related data about languages "in an indirect manner, in their systematic unity, by means of their relation to this idea."[15] It is not possible to know whether a particular language as a unity exists, but by subscribing to the idea of the unity of language, we can organize knowledge about languages in a modern, systematic, and scientific fashion.

To the extent that the unity of national language ultimately serves as a schema for nationality and offers a sense of national integration, the idea of the unity of language opens up a discourse to discuss not only the naturalized origin of an ethnic community, but also the entire imaginary associated with national language and culture. A language may be pure, authentic, hybridized, polluted, or corrupt, yet regardless of a particular assessment of it, the very possibility of praising, authenticating, complaining about, or deploring it is offered by the unity of that language as a regulative idea. However, the institution of the nation-state is, we all know, a relatively recent invention. Thus we are led to suspect that the idea of the unity of language as the schema for ethnic and national communality must also be a recent invention.

How should we understand the formula of many in one, the plurality of languages in one humanity, when the unity of language has to be understood as a regulative idea or schema for an object in idea? For Kant, a regulative idea is explicated with regard to the production of scientific knowledge; it ensures that the empirical inquiry of some scientific discipline will never reach any absolute truth and therefore is endless. Every scientific truth changes as we accumulate more empirical data. Kant also qualifies the regulative idea as a schema; that is, an image, design, outline, or figure not exclusively in the order of idea, but also in the order of the sensory.

From the postulate that the unity of national language is a regulative idea, it follows that this unity of national language enables us to organize various empirical data in a systematic manner so that we can continue to seek knowledge about the language. At the same time, it offers not an object in experience but rather an objective in praxis, toward which we aspire to regulate our uses of language. The principle is not only epistemic but also prescriptive. Hence it works in double registers: on the one hand, it determines epistemologically what is included or excluded in the database of a language, what is linguistic or extralinguistic, and what is proper to a particular language or not; while on the other hand, it indicates and projects what we must seek as our proper language, what we must avoid as heterogeneous to our language and reject as improper for it. The unity of a national language as a schema offers a norm for ethical judgment, and guides us in what is just or wrong for our language, what is in accord or discord with the propriety of the language. In everyday parlance, therefore, the word "grammar" connotes not only objective regularities observable in experience but also didactic norms that we must obey.

Of course, "translation" is a term with much broader connotations than the operation of transferring meaning from one national or ethnic language into another. But in this context, I am specifically concerned with the delimitation of translation according to the modern regime of translation by which the idea of the national language is put into practice. In other words, here I am concerned with how the very notion of translation has been impoverished by the modern regime of translation. Thus the representation of translation according to this regime of translation serves as a schema of co-figuration: only when translation is represented by the schematism of co-figuration does the putative unity of a national language as a regulative idea ensue. This schema allows us to imagine or represent what goes on in translation, to give to ourselves an image or representation of translation. Once imagined in this manner, translation is no longer a movement in potentiality. Its image or representation always contains two figures, which are necessarily accompanied by a spatial division in terms of border. Insofar as the representation or image of translation—not the act or enunciation of translation—is concerned, we are already implicated in the tropes and images of translation. As long as we represent translation to ourselves, it is not possible to evade this historically specific tropics of translation.

Translation takes various processes and forms as long as it is a political labor to overcome points of incommensurability in the social. This labor need not be confined to the specific regime of translation; it may well lie outside the modern regime of translation.

The modern is marked by the introduction of the schema of co-figuration, without which it is difficult to imagine a nation or ethnicity as a homogeneous sphere. As Antoine Berman has taught us about the intellectual history of translation and Romanticism in Germany, the economy of the foreign, that is, how the foreign must be allocated in the production of the domestic language, has played the decisive role in the poietic—and poetic—identification of the national language.[16] Without exception, the formation of a modern national language involves institutionalizations of translation according to the modern regime of translation.

Most conspicuously manifest in eighteenth-century movements such as Romanticism in Western Europe and *Kokugaku* (national studies) in Japan, intellectual and literary maneuvers to invent a national language mythically and poetically were closely associated with a spiritual construction of new identity, in terms of which national sovereignty was later naturalized. As Antonio Negri and Michael Hardt argue, it makes "the *relation* of sovereignty into a *thing* (often by naturalizing it) and thus weed[s] out every residue of social antagonism. The nation is a kind of ideological shortcut that attempts to free the concepts of sovereignty and modernity from the antagonism and crisis that define them."[17] This foundation for the legitimation of national and popular sovereignty was proffered as a "natural" language specific to the people, which ordinary people supposedly spoke in everyday life. This historical development of the valorization of ordinary people's language is generally referred to by literary historians as the emergence of the vernacular. The emphasis on ordinary and colloquial languages went with the reconception of translation and the schematism of co-figuration.

Modernity is usually characterized by the decline of the authority of universal languages: Latin, Sanskrit, classical Chinese, and so forth. Primarily, these classical languages are languages in which holy scriptures were written and were regarded as the source of authority and eternal verities. None of them was specifically associated with any ethnicity, nationality, or race. In this respect, each could enjoy the status of a universal language in the region of its domination. However, as soon as the regime of translation underwent a radical transformation and as national languages emerged as authentic media for ordinary peoples, the authority accorded to these universal classical languages collapsed.

In regard to the question of the relation between translation and discontinuity, I have so far explored how our commonsensical notion of translation is delimited by the schematism of the world (our representation of the world according to the schema of co-figuration) and conversely how the modern figure of the world as international (the world consisting of the basic units of the territorial national state sovereignty) is prescribed by our representation of translation as a communicative and international transfer of a message between a pair of ethnolinguistic unities.

The measure by which we are able to assess a language as a unity—again, I am talking not about phonetic systems, morphological units, or syntactic rules of a language but rather about language as *langue*—is given to us only at the locale where the limit of a language is marked, at the border where we come across a nonsense that forces us to do something in order to make sense of it. This occasion of making sense from nonsense, of doing something socially—acting toward foreigners, soliciting their response, seeking their confirmation—is generally called translation. The unity of a language is represented always in relation to another unity; it is given never in and of itself, but in relation to an other. One can hardly evade dialogic duality when determining the unity of a language; language as a unity almost always conjures up the copresence of another language, precisely because translation is not only a border-crossing but also, and primordially, an act of drawing a border, of bordering.

If the foreign is unambiguously incomprehensible, unknowable, and unfamiliar, it is impossible to talk about translation because translation simply cannot be done. If, on the other hand, the foreign is deemed to be comprehensible, knowable, and familiar, it is unnecessary to call for translation. Thus, the status of the foreign in translation must always be ambiguous. It is alien, but it is already in transition to something familiar. The foreign is simultaneously incomprehensible and comprehensible, unknowable and knowable, and unfamiliar and familiar. This foundational ambiguity of translation derives from the ambiguity of the positionality generally indexed by the peculiar presence of the translator. She is summoned only when two kinds of audiences are postulated with regard to the source text: one for whom the text is comprehensible, at least to some degree, and the other for whom it is incomprehensible. But it should never be naïvely presumed that these two audiences are differentiated along the border of ethnicity, nationality, or race. It is the task of the translator to ultimately determine the border of distinction. No border is given before the work of the translator, who inscribes the border itself. The translator's work lies in dealing with the difference between the two audiences. It is only insofar as comprehensibility is clearly and unambiguously distinct from incomprehensibility that the translator can be discerned from the non-translator without ambiguity in the conceptual economy of this determination of the foreign and the proper.

In this context, the notion of language is unavoidably figurative: it need not refer to any natural language of an ethnic or national community, such as German or Tagalog, since it is equally possible to have two kinds of audiences when the source text is a heavily technical document or an avant-garde literary piece. Language may refer to a set of vocabulary and expressions associated with a professional field or discipline, such as legal language; it may imply the style of graphic inscription or an unusual perceptual setting in which an artwork is installed. One may argue that these are examples of intralingual and intersemiotic translation, respectively, but they can be postulated only when they are in contradistinction to what Roman Jakobson called "translation proper." The propriety of translation presupposes the unity of a language; it is impossible unless one unity of language is posited as external to another, as if, already, languages were considered as countable. These figurative uses of translation illustrate how difficult it is to construe the locale of translation as a linking or bridging of two languages, two spatially marked domains. Here I want to stress, one more time, that translation is not only a border crossing but also and preliminarily an act of drawing a border, of bordering.

Considering the positionality of the translator, we can now approach the problematic of subjectivity. The internal split in the translator, which reflects the split between the translator and the addresser or between the translator and the addressee, and furthermore the actualizing split in the addresser and the addressee, demonstrates the way in which the subject constitutes itself.[18] This internal split in the translator is homologous to the fractured I, the temporality of "I speak," which necessarily introduces an irreparable distance between the speaking I and the I that is signified, between the subject of the enunciation and the subject of the enunciated. Yet in translation, the ambiguity in the personality of the translator marks the instability of the "we" as the subject, rather than the "I." This suggests a different attitude of address, which I have called heterolingual address and in which one addresses oneself as a foreigner to another foreigner.[19] Heterolingual address is an event, because translation never takes place in a smooth space; it is an address in discontinuity.

Rejected in monolingual address is the social character of translation, of an act performed at the locale of social transformation where new power relations are produced. Thus the study of translation will provide us with insights into how cartography and the schematism of co-figuration contribute to our critical analysis of social relations, premised not only on nationality and ethnicity but also on the differentialist identification of race, or the colonial difference and discriminatory constitution of the West.

Of course I cannot present an exhaustive account of how transnationality is prior to nationality, but I hope to have suggested how we might emancipate our imagination from the internationality of the modern world by problematizing the methodological nationalism that permeates knowledge production in the humanities, particularly in area studies, and thereby project an alternative image of the transnational community. By focusing on the tropics of translation, I refuse to view nationality as something given, and to seek in nationality the sole exit from colonial subjugation. Instead I choose to reverse the order of priority between the transnational and the national. Simply put, my starting point is that nationality is a restricted derivative of transnationality, and my guiding question is how the transnational, the foundational modality of sociality, is delimited, regulated, and restricted by the rules of the international world. It is in this context that I situate the issue of bordering as one of translation.

NOTES

1. See Naoki Sakai, "Introduction. Writing for Multiple Audiences and the Heterolingual Address," *Translation and Subjectivity: On "Japan" and Cultural Nationalism* (Minneapolis: University of Minnesota Press, 1997), 1–17.
2. I learned the term "bordering" from Sandro Mezzadra and Brett Neilson, "Border as Method; or, The Multiplication of Labor" (paper, Italian as Second Language—Citizenship, Language, and Translation conference, Rimini, February 4, 2008).
3. Sandro Mezzadra and Brett Neilson, *Border as Method; or, The Multiplication of Labor* (Durham, N.C.: Duke University Press, 2013), 23.
4. John Stuart Mill, *Utilitarianism: Liberty. Considerations on Representative Government* (1861; London: Dent, 1972), 391.
5. Fukuzawa Yukichi, *Bunmei ron no gairyaku* (Tokyo, Iwanami Shoten, 1937); or its translation, *An Outline of a Theory of Civilization*, trans. David Dilworth and G. Cameron Hurst (Tokyo: Sophia University Press, 1973).
6. See Sakai, *Translation and Subjectivity*, 1–17.
7. We must attribute the thought of "outside" that is neither inside nor outside to Maurice Blanchot's monumental work *The Space of Literature*, trans. Ann Smock (Lincoln: University of Nebraska Press, 1982). Indeed, I owe much to Michel Foucault's essay on Blanchot, *La pensée du dehors* (Paris: Fata morgana, 1986).
8. In regard to the concepts of being-in-common, communication, and communion, I owe much to Jean-Luc Nancy's essay "La communauté désoeuvrée," *Aléa*, vol. 1 (1983): 11–49. See Nancy, *The Inoperative Community*, ed. Peter Connor, trans. Peter Connor, Lisa Garbus, Michael Holland, and Simona Sawhney (Minneapolis: University of Minnesota Press, 1991), 1–42. Also

important is Nancy's essay "De l'être-en-commun," in *La communauté désoeuvrée* (Paris: Christian Bourgois Editeur, 2004), 199–234.

9. For the term "heterolingual," see my *Translation and Subjectivity*.

10. Ibid., 1–17, 41–71.

11. Ibid., 1–17.

12. Naoki Sakai, *Voices of the Past: The Status of Language in Eighteenth Century Japanese Discourse* (Ithaca, N.Y.: Cornell University Press, 1992), 326.

13. Immanuel Kant, *Critique of Pure Reason*, trans. Norman Kemp Smith (New York: St. Martin's, 1929), 450 [A 509; B 537].

14. Ibid., 550 [A 670; B 698], emphasis added.

15. Ibid., 550.

16. Antoine Berman, *The Experience of the Foreign: Culture and Translation in Romantic Germany*, trans. S. Heyvaert (Albany: State University of New York Press, 1984).

17. Antonio Negri and Michael Hardt, *Empire* (Cambridge, Mass.: Harvard University Press, 2000), 95.

18. The split cannot be limited to the cases of translation. For, as Briankle Chang suggests, the putative unities of the addresser and the addressee can hardly be sustained because the addresser himself is split and multiplies, as figuratively illustrated by the Plato-Socrates doublet in Derrida's "Envois" in *The Post Card*, trans. Alan Bass (Chicago: University of Chicago Press, 1987), 1–256. As to communication in general, Chang argues, "Because both delivery and signing are haunted by the same structural threat of the message's nonarrival or *a*destination, the paradox of the signature also invades communication. Communication occurs only insofar as the delivery of the message *may* fail; that is, communication takes place only to the extent that there is a separation between the sender and receiver, and this separation, this distance, this *spacing*, creates the possibility for the message *not* to arrive." *Deconstructing Communication* (Minneapolis: University of Minnesota Press, 1996), 216.

19. Sakai, *Translation and Subjectivity*.

5 • *BUTE DROMA* / MANY ROADS

Romani Resilience and Translation in Contact with the World

DEBORAH FOLARON

The practices of translation and interpreting are part of centuries-old traditions. Since its formal establishment in the 1980s as an interdisciplinary academic discipline, translation studies has followed a path of integrating diverse perspectives that further elucidate our understanding of the complex processes of this special type of communication. Translation programs throughout the world have incorporated a panoply of best practices both for professional translation procedures and for academic research. The translator's "toolkit" of theoretical concepts and practical skills is part and parcel of the foundation for translators in training around the globe. Today's practical palette of tools and resources includes such standard fare as monolingual and bilingual dictionaries and databases, terminology lists, bilingually aligned translation memories and bitexts, numerous glossaries, online and offline bilingual corpus and data sets, parallel corpora, grammar books, style guides, translator tips, reference materials—the list goes on. For many language pairs, a translator's initiation into the field of translation is fairly straightforward. Book stores, education and training programs, translator discussion forums, and access to the standard technologies suffice to get one under way. For many, language-relevant examples abound in the diverse texts and scholarly articles written on historical, linguistic, cultural, and sociological research approaches to the production and interpretation of translation in different contexts. Clearly, however, this type of experience is neither symmetric nor uniform for the world's nearly seven thousand languages, over half of which are still predominantly oral.

In this chapter, I consider the many roads of the centuries-old Romani linguistic condition from a translation studies perspective. "Romani" is here understood to refer not only to the diverse groups that identify by various Romani ethnonyms, but also in a collective sense to the broader category implemented for institutional and political purposes. Likewise, it refers to the language as an umbrella term for the range of Romani dialects, all of which share an original common core. To reflect on the Romani language and its history of migration, embedded within social, cultural, and political dynamics, invites a rethinking of some of the critical discourse used to conceptualize and frame translation. Carved out from a distinctive translational space, translation and interpretation practices in the ethnic, linguistic Romani context not only maintain a certain continuity with the Romani historical past, but also confront, as do other potentially endangered ethnolinguistic groups, new challenges in a fast-paced globalizing world configured by the dual hegemony of English, the internet, and other information and communication technologies.

TRANSLATION: IMPLICITLY ACKNOWLEDGING MULTIPLE SHADES OF "DIFFERENCE"

Translational space is here understood to refer to a conceptual and practical space generated by a broad spectrum of translation dynamics. A relational space of difference, it is motivated by a need and impulse to translate at the same time that it resonates from the effects of translation. An act of translation, as analyzed in the literature of the field, hinges on an assumption of "difference," however subtle it may be. It assumes at minimum the presence of two different languages, however defined, with their range of incommensurability bridgeable by virtue of translation. The act of "interpreting" a translation product or process directs the gaze through a "differential" lens. Reading and writing for translation, for instance, implies a cognitive shift in the mind of the translator, who reads with the intention of translating, or the translation-conscious writer, who writes with the intention of being translated. A translation-conscious reader of a translation, depending on his or her degree of familiarity with the source language from which the target text derives, reads in parallel, tracking the cues of the source language translation dispersed throughout the target language text. In all of these cases a translational lens of difference is foregrounded, through perimeters that are interlinguistic, intralinguistic, and intersemiotic, as broadly outlined by Roman Jakobson.[1] In this most conventional sense, a translational frame of mind implicitly acknowledges that linguistic, cultural, and, potentially, semiotic differences separate the existing source language text from the target language text that will be generated in translation activity. A translator acts in accordance with this knowledge. Metaphors abound to express and describe the crossing over from one linguistic-cultural domain to another that translation generally presumes.[2] Seeing the world through a translational lens, through the eyes of translation, may just be another useful metaphor. Like another language, but in distinct form, a translation functions as an/other lens through which to perceive, see, think, and understand the world.

Inevitably, the term itself encompasses not only its sensu stricto definition of linguistically transferring and transforming a text in written mode from one language to another. An act of translation defined broadly also shuttles between processes that are mental and physical. Defining when and how the mind "translates" is not an easy task; recent research in cognitive neuroscience shows that human beings are less compartmentalized linguistically than scientists had initially thought. The synaptic plasticity and capacity of the human brain and its mental conceptual structure can accommodate multiple languages in its repository of linguistic connections. Stanislas Dehaene has shown that literate humans appear to carry out their one- or multiple-language reading and writing activities across cultures in the same way, that is, in relation to a common "visual word form area" and within certain common constraints of brain circuits that organize and reorganize through "neuronal recycling."[3] Likewise, advances in research on multilingualism show that a multilingual frame of mind is not simply a mental agglutination of separate and discrete language systems. Speakers socialized into language bilingually or multilingually develop their linguistic resources (and diverse degrees of fluency) in a common repository and make use of their repertories to routinely negotiate subject positions in multiple language exchanges.[4] Bilingual and multilingual connections do not necessarily lead to equal measures of linguistic competence in all the languages of one's repertory—if indeed linguistic competence is commensurable with the criteria in place for standardized, normalized language use. The existence of a natural predisposition toward translating and interpreting is debated,[5] with some arguing in favor of a "natural translation" that occurs among bilinguals.[6]

RESISTING MONOLINGUALISM

The tangible act of translating or interpreting when one is continually immersed in internalized bilingual or multilingual realities and life experiences challenges some of our notions of translation. It problematizes the extent to which the definition and competence of translation can be analyzed, if only for the task of identifying the specific point at which translation proper cognitively occurs. Increasingly, the idea of multilingualism itself is being viewed as having been socially constructed as a response to a monolingual ideological mindset that assumes monolingualism as the norm; following this logic, hard and fast conventional linguistic categories such as codeswitching, mother tongue, and borrowing become problematic.[7] Along these lines, and drawing inspiration from George Abraham Grierson, Robert J. C. Young seizes on the notion of bounded language territories to rethink translation in a role of its "crystallization of languages as part of the institutional apparatus of the state": "[Translation enables] languages to become distinct and fixed enough for translation to take place. [It is] dependent on the spoken tongue's being 'reduced to writing': a stabilized, written form that allows the distinction between source and target. If we try to think of language and literature outside the triad of nation, state, and language, translation becomes problematic, because it requires the linguistic models that the triad invented."[8] While the notion of language may be unbound and language conceptually freed from constrictive borders, its actual practice is nonetheless configured and regulated by boundaries that are geographical, political, and social.[9] The attitudes toward, and perceptions of, difference are tangible realities. The lack of differentiating boundaries in the multilingual brain/mind confronts linguistic boundaries of multilingualism at the borders of geography and history. Given accelerating global communication and the impossibility of any one human learning all of the planet's seven thousand languages, the option of a translational interface acquires a heightened sense of urgency. The intensifying global interest in machine translation seems to bear this out. Translation, as Michael Cronin aptly underscores, expresses a fundamental human "right to difference."[10] Indeed, in the context of a rapidly globalizing world, to translate and be translated can be viewed as a human right, capable of supporting the inclusion of languages and cultures that have had little visibility, voice, and representation, and providing access to structures of power and global movements of information, goods, and services. In what ways does the Romani transnational context exemplify features of a translational interface of encounter designed by historical circumstances to engage "difference"? How can translation studies conceptualize its translational space?

A ROMANI TRANSLATOR TOOLKIT

The common translator toolkit profile mentioned earlier reflects certain underlying assumptions with regard to the translation environment in which translators are typically immersed. Those assumptions include literacy, language status, experiential knowledge, codification and standardization in language practice, and technical character encoding for computational environments, in addition to interlingual resources. A glance at the resources a translator would have available for purposes of translation in the Romani context already gives hints as to its unique character. For example, one finds no monolingual dictionary, encyclopedia, grammar, or other traditional work of reference published only in Romani. Nor is there any presence of a Romani state or geographical region where life, language, and cultural production have been exclusively and natively Romani. Nowhere has the Romani language served as the sole language of administration and institutional instruction, education, and learning. A more exhaustive search, however, reveals the existence of many bilingual "translation dictionaries" between Romani and national languages: Albanian, Bosnian, Bulgarian, Czech, English, Finnish, French, German, Hungarian, Italian, Latvian, Macedonian, Norwegian,

Romanian, Russian, Serbo-Croatian, Slovak, Spanish, and others.[11] A more comprehensive two-volume Kalderash Romani-English dictionary published in 2010 and 2011 by Ronald Lee is also available, the result of decades of Lee's practical interpreting and translation experience and acquired linguistic knowledge. Recent illustrated bilingual picture dictionaries, for example in Romani and Hungarian, are pedagogical and linguistically contextualized. Language learning materials and grammars, too, are bilingual. They are printed in "parallel" bilingual versions, for instance in Macedonian/Romani, or Serbian/Romani, or with prescriptive Romani grammar presented descriptively in another language, such as in English, French, Spanish, German, or Romanian. Transcriptions of Romani are presented multilingually as well, in a variety of scripts and alphabets. They include Latin/Roman characters with a varying range of diacritical marks, Cyrillic, and Greek. Interlingual and interdialectal linguistic databases such as RomLex have also been developed. At the outset, and from the perspective of translation, Romani appears to exist in direct relation to other languages, ones that complement and supplement its lexicon and linguistic functions. How does this affect the task of the translator in the Romani context?

TRANSLATIONAL BIAS OF LITERACY

Translation research in its descriptive form and translation pedagogy in its normative form have long conceptualized translation in terms of written source and target languages in general conformity with the conventional depictions of language groups. That is to say, language carries with it the associations of a "mother tongue" and a geographical territory assumed to be where the language is natively spoken. This assumption is a carryover from historical territorial borders, political nation-state concepts, and classification categories and descriptions from the humanities and social sciences. The contributions from cultural studies (including gender, postcolonial, poststructuralist approaches) to translation studies have incrementally problematized and nuanced this type of facile association, shifting translation's field of inquiry and analysis to one that embraces elements of heterogeneity over homogeneity or monolithicism. Translation studies, then, potentially offers a conceptual prism through which to examine the complexity of the Romani context and in so doing reveal its translingual, transcultural, transnational, and transterritorial dynamics. Some areas of particular relevance to Romani translational space are migration, minority language dynamics, hybridity, orality, bilingualism and multilingualism, language policy, and self-translation.

Orality, for example, is a distinguishing feature of the Romani language. The predominantly oral culture of Romani peoples has contributed historically to an asymmetrical relation between Romani and non-Romani languages. An overwhelming portion of Romani transcription and research has been conducted by non-Romani scholars. Despite some nineteenth-century letters found to have been written in Romani ("Germanized" Sinti and English Romani) and a recently discovered bilingual Romani (Lovari)-Hungarian dictionary written by Hungarian Roma Ferenc Sztojka in the late nineteenth century,[12] a written corpus of Romani texts penned by Romani peoples themselves was virtually nonexistent until the mid-twentieth century. Generally speaking, "interpreting" and contextualizing orality through conventional academic perspectives and disciplinary categories has been challenging and symptomatic of many fields, translation studies included, due in particular to the bias of literacy. From a translation perspective, furthermore, the process of translation is a double one, from oral to written representation followed by interlingual translation of the transcript, with the inscription of speech into writing and translation needing to depict the multiple oral narrative elements and aesthetic characteristics of oral tradition's iterations in more than one performance or storytelling session.[13] The characteristics of every oral culture are unique, and Romani culture is no exception. Citing the contents of Milena Hübschmannová's essay "My Encounters with Romano šukar laviben," Beate Eder-Jordan extrapolates some of the salient markers of Romani storytelling tradition as it transitioned from its traditional oral mode and materialized in the 1970s into some of the first examples of Czech-Slovak Romani literature "set in phonetic script."[14] They include the telling of stories and tales to fulfill the purpose of transmitting Romani ethics, values, and cultural norms, that is, "Romaniness" or *Rom(an)ipen*, in an oral tradition continued by some authors through the implementation of *divano*, or "talking narration," in written form. Equally prevalent and cited is the perceptible power attributed to the spoken word, emotion and feeling, the mix of reality and the supernatural, and an implied expectation to describe *romano čačipen* (Romani truth or reality) and to foster empathy.

Stories, performances, tales, and poetry are an integral part of oral culture, and they transition in written form as well into early Romani literature.[15] One of the first documented convergences of orality and translation, and perhaps the debut of a translation history of Romani literature, is the case of the early twentieth-century Polish Romani poet Bronislawa Wajs ("Papusza").[16] Having taught herself to read and write, she penned poems in Romani, which were subsequently translated and published in Polish by the poet Jerzy Ficowski. As Eder-Jordan notes, orality in the Romani context takes on other forms too. The historiography of Romani literature still has notable gaps due to the fact that many portions of it have not yet been written.[17] Exemplary is Eder-Jordan's account of her meeting with the Latvian Romani writer Leksa Manuš, who orally sketched out the history of twentieth-century Russian and Soviet Romani literature in an interview.[18] Knowledge about historical patrimony can be transmitted through oral interview, but translation also has a role to play.[19] From the perspective of translation studies, translational historiography has potentially considerable value. Translations can tell us about a given people's history, influencing as well the direction and depiction of cultural and political histories.[20] As Kathleen Davis argues, rendering visible a translation history that includes not only modern language translations but inter- and intralinguistic translations reflecting the historical trajectory of a language can "serve to connect the modern nation to its ancient heritage" and decenter the monolingualist focus that characterizes the writing of national narratives.[21] To what extent can a Romani literary historiography be written without the intervention of translation? As Michael Wogg observes, "time, geographic and social diversity, language and dialect diversity, notation and spelling diversity" are all factors that must be considered when laying out the vast landscape of Romani writers.[22] By any measure, it is clear that in order to successfully fulfill this task, translation must not be restrained by a bias toward literacy in the traditional sense.

TRANSLATIONAL BIAS OF THE MONOLINGUAL OPTIC

Classical approaches to and reflections on translation gravitate around evaluations of a translation and its source text through comparative linguistics and stylistics. By definition, language is the "systematic, conventional use of sounds, signs, or written symbols in a human society for communication and self-expression."[23] The criteria used to measure deviation or innovation with respect to the languages examined are grounded in prevailing norms and normative recommendations. As such, researchers rely on standard grammars, terminologies, and stylistic or rhetorical protocols to assist in analyzing the translation's reformulation and rewriting of grammatical structures, register, tone, language varieties, literary and poetic devices, and creative turns in language usage. Microlinguistic comparative analyses help pinpoint the ways different languages diversely express the same or similar thoughts and ideas, as well as their inherent structural differences. They unpack and divulge translator choices and decisions as options along a translational linguistic continuum that ranges from closely literal to loosely adaptive. A traditional Western analytical approach assumes linguistic boundaries for languages that in turn accommodate the notion of carrying meaning over or across in translation from one language to another. Every language has a history. By further studying its history, researchers decipher the provenance of its diverse features and etymology, and trace diachronically and synchronically the transformation of a given word or expression. Knowledge of a language's trajectory fills in the gaps and contributes to a more complete picture of its growth, expansion or retraction, and migration. It aids in understanding whether the usage of a term or phrase at any given point in time/space is indicative of a particular writer's or translator's repertory or the result of creative or strategic manipulation. The history of a language cannot be decontextualized, stripped of its social, cultural, political, and historical garb. A language's borders dynamically fluctuate and are reined in by a consensus, born of codified, standardized, and prescribed linguistic use, and implicit or explicit language policy. To what extent is this translation optic monolingually informed, presuming a linguistic transfer between two languages conceptualized monolingually as separate, discrete language systems? What if one of the languages in this equation were functioning by translational impulse, intrinsically multilingual by conception?

As suggested earlier in our brief assessment of the Romani translator toolkit, Romani appears to exist in relation to other languages and seems to be multilingually informed. That said, how do we define the Romani language for translation purposes without the historical support of territorial boundaries and traditional nation-state infrastructure? How would Romani translation be taught? How would a translation studies researcher understand the criteria that guide translators' decisions when they undertake translation of a text into Romani or a Romani text into another language? How would the translation be evaluated?[24] To answer these questions, it is necessary to turn to the critical role that historical linguistics has played and continues to play as linguists reverse engineer a more complete picture of the language from the data gathered in diverse linguistic communities.

THE ROMANI LANGUAGE

Despite its use for centuries in one form or another by Romani peoples around the world,[25] Romani was not clearly identified as a language in its own right until the late eighteenth and early nineteenth centuries, when researchers began to transcribe its oral utterances and linguists began to examine its structure more comprehensively. Points of consensus gradually emerged concerning its definition as a language. An Indo-Aryan core of lexical roots was confirmed as the original major source for all Romani dialects and its first point of origin established in India. A subsequent layer of pre-European Byzantine Greek roots was confirmed as a second major linguistic source, thus a second point of origin established in Byzantine Greek territory. Even though precise dates and details on early Romani migration routes are still debated, documentation from historical archives in various languages and countries confirms that Romani peoples were present throughout mainland Europe by the early sixteenth century, thereby explaining the presence of many other diverse lexical imports from other languages. Romani linguist Ian Hancock uses an apt metaphor in his Romani linguistics classes to describe the language by comparing it to an onion:

> An onion grows bigger layer by layer, with the deepest layers being the earliest. If we examine the vocabulary of the Romani language, the very first layer, at the heart of the onion, is Indian. The next layers include one after the other words from such languages as Phalura, Persian, Kurdish, Armenian, Greek, and so on, all acquired along the way, reflecting the geographical route taken by the Romanies' ancestors as they came westwards out of India.[26]

Broadly speaking, then, the structural layers of the Romani language—which manifests from sixty to eighty dialects—are basically three. Its core layer comprises approximately eight hundred pre-European, New Indo-Aryan (NIA) lexical roots interspersed with Persian, Kurdish, Armenian, and Greek, signaling its origins in the languages of India and those of early migration routes. The next layer overlays it with Byzantine Greek roots, most likely acquired between the twelfth and fourteenth centuries in Anatolia and the Balkans. Whether or not the language emerged as a kind of *koiné* in Anatolia among various migrants already speaking diverse Indian languages,[27] its linguistic development in the area of present-day Turkey, Greece, Bulgaria, Albania, Macedonia, and Kosovo is of historical significance.[28] The combination of these two layers constitutes a common core, which facilitates interdialectal comprehension among Romani speakers today.

The third and most expansive layer of the Romani language overlays the common core. It emerges from extensive contact with other languages in Europe and elsewhere, and transforms the lexical and syntactic structures in varying degrees, causing language variation and language loss. It is the layer that most significantly differentiates between all dialects. Hancock has proposed a historiographical periodization in Romani terms of the three main migration movements that correspond to these structural layers: *teljaripe* (out of India), *nakhipe* (crossover from Asia into Europe), and *buxljaripe* (migration out into the West).[29] Hancock observes, moreover, that both Asian and European grammar systems are reflected in the Romani language.

> One of the most interesting characteristics of Romani is that it has two sets of grammatical rules: one for its Asian component, called thematic, and one for its European component, called athematic. The thematic rules apply to all the words from languages up to and including Byzantine Greek; the athematic rules apply, broadly speaking, to everything acquired from Balkan Greek onward. The grammar for the thematic component is mainly Indian, and very regular, while the grammar for the athematic part of the language is more complex. For this reason, it isn't entirely accurate to call Romani a wholly Indian language; it seems to have finished taking shape only during the period of its contact with Greek, and so has a "Balkan" character as well. Thematic vocabulary is common to all Romani dialects, and it is the athematic loanwords from other languages that differentiate one dialect from another.[30]

By virtue of its historical roots and common core, therefore, Romani is linguistically defined as a language existing in the form of many dialects, each of which has been transformed to varying degrees by diverse historical circumstances and contact with many different languages. Some dialect groups have been more affected by isolation and earlier nomadism than others. Romani studies literature frequently remarks that all groups do not necessarily identify with one another and that a supra-group identity has not traditionally been a part of history collectively. Differences in what constitutes "Romani-ness" are historical, cultural, and linguistic, all of which resist the formulation of a single voice for any widespread collective movement.[31] Romani group identification with, and self-recognition in, an international nation-building discourse is not without challenges. Armillei and Mascitelli observe the "often conflicting discourses . . . running in parallel" in initiatives for recognition, representation, and minority and ethnic identity; they are not always uniform in objectives, with some advocating for Romani representation more globally while others act more regionally, nationally, and locally.[32] These conflicts reflect the tensions and challenges of a transnational or transterritorial group that is internally diverse and heterogeneous by its history, but which self-identifies as Romani by inherited oral traditions, family genealogy, and "Romani-ness."

Critical questions of language codification and standardization therefore go hand in hand with identity politics and modern nation-building strategies and visions that attempt to construct narratives on the basis of diverse concepts such as ethnicity, language, culture, nation, origins, historical discrimination and persecution, and so on. From one side, social stigmatization, segregation policies, and exclusionary politics, as well as former policies of assimilation by education into non-Romani culture, are well documented as having contributed to the dire socioeconomic situations of many Romani communities.[33] Although more recent Romani and EU political initiatives aspire to remedy the situation, the historical devaluing of Romani culture and language in many countries of Romani residence has had an impact on the sociolinguistic state of affairs. From another side, according to Hancock, the "non-core, or accreted, linguistic material" of the third structural layer that results from borrowing and loanwords from other languages in contact "constitutes the greatest barrier to inter-intelligibility."[34] The successive layers of second language (L2) influence are both old and recent, giving way to L2 stratification profiles that vary for individual dialects and communities of speakers.[35] Thus, for example, the diverse Romani dialects used in Italy may not be linguistically configured in the same way as dialects used in Poland, or Russia, or Argentina, due to the influence of other differing languages in contact over time. At the same time, acquisition of the Romani language natively is regarded as one of the key markers of Romani culture and identity and is attributed value in identity-shaping discourses for "nation building." Understanding the nature of the contact Romani has with other languages existing within nation-state territories is central to grasping the Romani translation context in practice and to conceptualizing the Romani translational space more abstractly.

MULTILINGUAL SOCIOLINGUISTIC UNDERPINNINGS OF ROMANI TRANSLATION PRACTICE

From early in its disciplinary history, translation studies availed itself of research areas from sociolinguistics. Eugene Nida's research on Bible translation and bilingual, multilingual, and oral cultural communities worldwide focused on translation and interpretation as a type of "interlingual communication . . . extend[ing] far beyond the mechanics of linguistic similarities and contrasts."[36] The translation of dialects has also been an important area of interest. Language varieties reflecting class, register, geographical variation, and historical time and space parameters are all considered in relation to a language standard and constitute a potential repertory for translation strategies.[37] As noted by Sara Ramos Pinto, interest in sociolinguistics dovetailed with translation studies' cultural (studies) turn in the 1990s, whereby language use was increasingly viewed as a complex, context-dependent social practice dynamically integrated within specific cultural practices.[38] From this vantage point, translation and interpreting are social-cultural practices connected with how language is used in practice, and directly relevant to translators. Upon request to translate a text from or into Romani, a translator may legitimately ask the question "which (dialect of) Romani?" The routine translation practice of assessing first the linguistic, cultural specificities of the target (translation) reader public, the genre and type of text, as well as the reasons and need for its translation entails knowing some characteristics of the Romani language context, and the extent of the language's use in Romani communities.

Despite the fact that linguist Marcel Courthiade's "international alphabet [of] meta-graphemes representing cross-dialectal phonological variation" was initially adopted by the International Romani Union in 1990, before the advent of widespread internet connectivity and communication, no officially codified, standardized version of Romani has been accepted by all for international use.[39] Regional codification efforts, however, have had some results. Among others, one noteworthy example is the initiative based on Rajko Đjurić's standardization and grammar in the Balkans: *Gramatika e Rromane Čhibaki. Nakhadipe pe rromani čhib* (2005) and *Standardizacija romskog jezika* (2012). An EU-focused policy of Romani "linguistic pluralism" as proposed by Yaron Matras has also gained traction.[40] Because the position of valuing any one particular Romani dialect over another is risky, a more generalized approach—allowing a dialect to develop naturally as a social practice and emerge into a standardized form by speaker choice and usage—has been adopted.

This process may already be under way. While a standard Romani dialect based on Vlax Polish Lovari had been proposed by Hancock due to its greater retention of historical core Romani features linguistically,[41] the Vlax Kalderaš dialect has been circulating more widely sociolinguistically. The Vlax group figures prominently in linguistic typologies devised according to classification schemes organizing dialectal similarities, structural developments, and their respective histories.[42] Frequently contrasted with non-Vlax, Vlax broadly denotes a historical distinction between dialects that emerged when Romani peoples classed as slaves for five hundred years in Moldovia and Wallachia were emancipated in the mid-nineteenth century. This more homogeneous, mutually intelligible cluster of dialects, including Kalderaš, was heavily influenced by Romanian, and spread through migration across Europe and to the same destination countries of other European migrants.[43] As noted by Ronald Lee, the differences within this Romani cluster are "slight," due mainly to "words borrowed from non-Romani languages which are common only to specific groups of speakers in a given country . . . roughly parallel to colloquial British English and American English or Mexican Spanish and Castilian Spanish."[44] The choice of which dialect to use for a Romani language translation implies, in a very real sense, a decision based on pragmatic communicative functions. Who will understand the translation, and which target audience is the translation destined for?

Romani peoples live in at least fifty-two nation-states; out of a population of around twelve million, approximately half speak Romani.[45] The fact that the Romani language manifests itself through dialects, with vocabulary and some grammar mirroring or shadowing the languages with which its speakers are in closest contact, yields a complex sociolinguistic reality that must be taken into account in determining translation practices. As Nazik Deniz, founder of the World Romani Dialects Interpretation Bureau in Canada, affirms, "We are all Roma, but our history and migrations have also made us linguistically and culturally diverse. It is in our organizing for . . . translation and interpreting diversity that we are able to encourage movement towards unity."[46] By creating a team of Romani dialect interpreters, she has sought to meet the specific needs of a unique population with unique historical circumstances. The Romani context, however, does not presuppose fluency in the Romani language, and linguistic competence in any given Romani dialect varies. Although more isolated communities may rely more heavily on communication in Romani, bilingualism and multilingualism constitute the norm once monolingual Romani children start school.[47] Language pairs, combinations, and directionality for translation therefore cannot be generalized. Situations are local, and personalized, with potential translation combinations endless and constrained only by the number of world languages. Briefly summarized, some use their dialect natively and daily within their neighborhood or community for communication purposes, but they interact with non-Romani peoples in the languages of the nation-state where they reside. Some use primarily the languages of the nation-state with both Romani and non-Romani peoples. Some do not speak any Romani at all and default to a shared common or international language. Finally, some use a Romani dialect in an international Romani context, but adjust for dialectal variation as they go along, defaulting to their other languages when and if the need arises. As Dafina Savić observes from her experience as a Romani interpreter in Canada, "At the level of general conversation, individual Roma from different countries who meet up together will be able to understand one another, but as soon as the discussion becomes more specific and in-depth, then individuals will borrow from the other languages they know or have been educated in."[48]

THE ASYMMETRIES OF THE ROMANI TRANSLATIONAL SPACE

The cultures of minority language groups, as Cronin explains, are "translation cultures par excellence," where the pressure to translate is a central rather than peripheral aspect of their experience.[49] However, not all minority cultures experience minority similarly. Romani language-culture is minority by default in every nation-state. Every literate Romani individual worldwide possesses a non-Romani "native" language as a result of his or her social exposure or education within non-Romani institutions of a non-Romani nation-state. This literacy increases the probability that individuals will choose to write and express themselves "natively" in one of the majority society languages of education. Thus, the Romani context is one that is always perceived relationally, with the language existing in relation to the other languages and dialects that constitute the linguistic repertory of the Romani individual. Linguistic competence in a Romani dialect may be constrained to aural comprehension and speech. Reading and writing literacies are very often more advanced in a non-Romani language. Some dialects are clearly endangered, while others are experiencing revitalization due to growing interest in Romani culture, language, and heritage.

LITERACY AND LITERARY TEXTUAL CONSIDERATIONS OF TRANSLATIONAL SPACE

Textual analysis and interpretation are a necessary preliminary step for professional, including literary, translators. In Romani writing, features inserted from oral Romani in contact with other languages may pattern the familiar oral code-switching and borrowings of bilingual and multilingual social contexts and diglossic societies. However, they may also be used strategically and artistically. With regard to literary expression in particular, Paola Toninato notes the importance of distinguishing the textual and intertextual evidence of oral and written hybridity, observing that literary criticism considers artistic, literary hybridity to be a "purposeful selection" of linguistic and cultural elements rather than "the passive reflection of an author's multicultural identity."[50] A text can exhibit hybridity at many levels.

> Within Romani literature, intertextual hybridity takes a variety of forms. First, intertextuality operates as a transposition of the oral tradition into written literature ("intersemiotic" hybridization). In this case, the hybridized materials are not just texts and motifs from the oral tradition but also oral modes of narration. Second, intertextuality concerns texts borrowed from both Romani and non-Romani literary traditions and subsequently hybridized ("intertextual" hybridization tout court).[51]

Interlingual textuality might also be viewed from another relevant angle, one that blurs any boundary between inter- and intralingual. By its history and ongoing language contact, the Romani language shadows non-Romani languages through its various dialectal forms. The notion of languages shadowing one another has been articulated by Harish Trivedi when considering Sanskrit and Prakrit, two slightly different but mutually comprehensible forms of the same language. The word for "translation" used in this particular context is *chhaya,* or shadow, "as if one of the languages were the shadow of the other."[52] Underscoring the Prakrit origin and mutual intelligibility of nearly all the major Indian languages, he problematizes the concept of translation as imported from Western discourse. From Trivedi's perspective, functional fluency in multiple Indian languages neither feels foreign nor poses a psychological obstacle, nor is in general conducive to translation as it is commonly understood in the West. Indeed, the concept is useful when reflecting on the Romani translational context. The internal shadowing among mutually intelligible Romani dialects or close intelligibility of core vocabulary among most Romani dialects, as well as the external shadowing of a Romani dialect with its closest language(s) in contact would appear to be operative.

This kind of internal and external "relationing" could mark a distinctive feature of the Romani translational space, indicative of a translational impulse that underpins transnational or transterritorial interlingual, intercultural communication. In practical oral conversation, speakers adjust for variation, commenting on the dialectal or linguistic differences they observe, sometimes stating their preferences. Their expectations of linguistic differences heighten their linguistic awareness and predisposition to listen. This disposition is both similar and different when it comes to writing. On one hand, the same linguistic engagement occurs when individuals of one dialect read texts written by individuals of another dialect. On the basis of many discussions and observations over the years, it is evident that they negotiate their reading through a prism of dialectal similarities and differences as well as ulterior language influences on the dialects. The act of writing can impose yet another "foreign" level of representation. Writers of a dialect adopt the alphabet and script most familiar to them from their non-Romani languages in contact. For example, Bulgarian Romani can be written in Cyrillic, Greek Romani with the Greek alphabet, and Eastern European Romani dialects in Latin/Roman script with various letter-diacritic combinations. This tendency continues in migration. Writers who write one way "natively" in their country of origin can end up transcribing their dialect differently in their host country. For instance, a Serbo-Croatian Romani dialect immigrant settling in an Anglophone country after the Yugoslav wars may later be influenced lexically and scripturally by English, and so on. Without a clear standard for orientation, a Romani writer's or translator's decision on which language, dialect, lexicon, and script to use can simply be a habitual, subjective one. However, it may also constitute a conscious or ethical position and political statement. For example, one's preference for a dialect or writing system can reflect a political statement in the face of language planning, codification, and standardization power struggles.

In sum, if we were to conceptually network the areas of Romani literate and literary expression in the Romani language dialects transterritorially, its first layer of translational quality would conceivably emerge as a sphere of writing that exists prior to any tangible act of translation. It is writing influenced by Romani-ness and the Romani experience in relation to a linguistic, cultural nation-state experience, and in relation to transnational interliterary and intertextual experiences. A similar sphere emerges for Romani writers writing in non-Romani languages (see Figure 5.1).

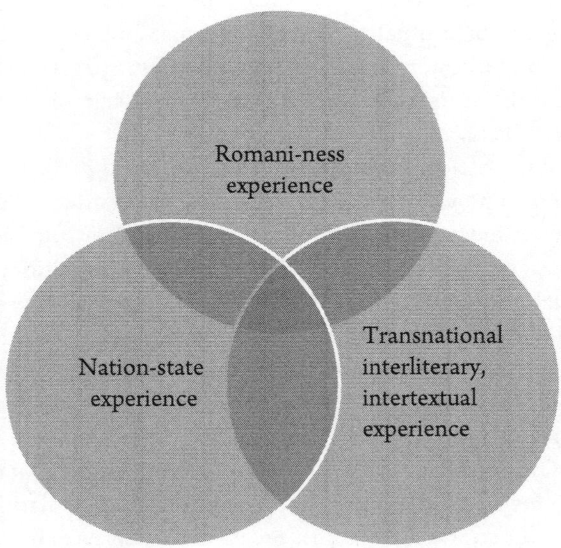

FIGURE 5.1 (Illustration by Deborah Folaron)

TRANSLATION TEXTUAL CONSIDERATIONS OF TRANSLATIONAL SPACE

Superimposing a concrete network of translation relations on the previously existing spheres of translational writing yields a strikingly diverse multilingual constellation of translation forms. Mapping directionality and language pairs transterritorially is challenging. In practice, translation processes must consider the relationing of Romani dialects to non-Romani linguistic and sociocultural environments, and in relation to each other. The predisposition to acquire lexicon from the majority and minority languages used in diverse nation-states and regions is translational. The translational impacts translation, in terms of the latter's production, reception, and criticism. The syntactic, lexical, semantic, and stylistic differences that emerge while shifting and adjusting between languages and/or dialects orient different translation strategies, procedures, interpretations, and explanations, for the translator as well as the reader of the translation. Because of this general situation, the actual practice of Romani translation problematizes such translation studies concepts as directionality, symmetrical correspondence, and source and target languages, which in turn complicates the criteria for establishing effective categories for analysis. Very broadly, the flows of multilingual translation directions fall into three basic spheres, with "non-Romani" signifying potentially all languages of the fifty-two nation-states in which Romani peoples live (see Figure 5.2).

Written translation involves literacy, education, and writing skills. Whether translation occurs in a Romani dialect or non-Romani language depends on the education, literacies, life experience, knowledge, and culture of each individual writer or translator. Translation into Romani of well-known literary works does occur; *Le Petit Prince* and the *Rāmāyana* into Romani are but two examples, as are several instances of theater translation and adaptation by the Pralipe and

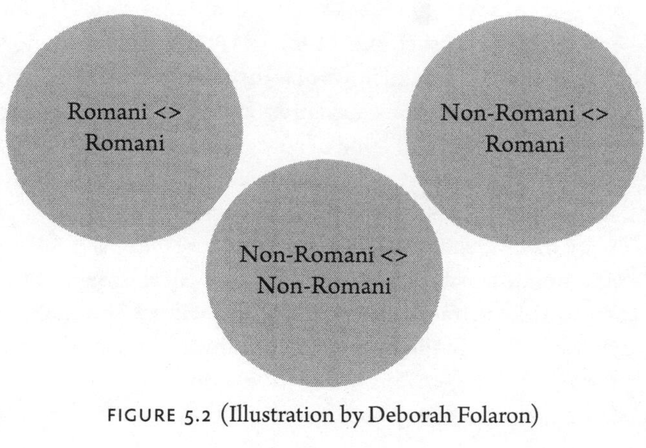

FIGURE 5.2 (Illustration by Deborah Folaron)

Romathan Romani theater troupes. Individual skills and circumstances shape Romani translation flows. As the volume of writing and translating activities rise, translation flows will acquire new contours and patterns in terms of specific language pairs and directions.[53] One illustrative case is that of the Romani author Mateo Maximoff, who translated the Bible into Kalderaš Romani, but also wrote at least ten novels in French.[54] For an English translation of his literary oeuvre, a translator would work from French into English, rather than from Romani. Romani authors elsewhere do similarly, tending to write literary works in the languages they were educated in. For example, the literary work *Füstos Képek* by the Hungarian Romani writer Menyhért Lakatos was translated from Hungarian, first into French (*Couleur de fumée, une épopée Tzigane*) and then recently into English (*The Color of Smoke: An Epic Novel of the Roma*). One exception is poetry, which seems to invite more frequent expression in Romani, with poems published unilingually, bilingually, and even multilingually in self-translation.[55]

MIGRATION AND MINORITY CONFIGURATIONS OF TRANSLATIONAL SPACE

Although many Romani communities have been settled for decades, even centuries, the force of migration weighs on the Romani condition, resulting in its minority status in all areas of the world. Both migration and minority dynamics shape the flows of translation and interpreting practices. At the outset, migration reconfigures a wide range of social relations, from the way migrants are initially categorized and administered to the way they are perceived and assisted once they have settled in their new host country. These factors inevitably condition the way migrants experience migration. Likewise, migration movements and resettlement shift the relational dynamics of certain ethnolinguistic groups and languages within geographical territories and areas, which contribute to shaping translation and interpreting as well, particularly in urban centers. Upon arrival on new territory, immigrants encounter a new set of cultural and linguistic relations in practice and/or defined by the host country. Official language policies and legislation structure the types, directions, and flows of translation activity, with officially recognized languages generating the translation and interpretation of administrative, legal, and government information in specific pairs and directions. Some, but not all, immigrant groups are beneficiaries of these legal mandates. As Reine Meylaerts notes, language policy always implies, implicitly or explicitly, some kind of translation policy that regulates translation in the public domain, be it for education, legal affairs, political institutions, administration, or the media. She puts forth the idea that an articulated translation policy could facilitate and enable immigrant and minority group rights in the framework of a more democratic "participatory citizenship" and in so doing ensure "translational justice."[56] The nonrecognition of certain immigrant language groups forces communities to organize translation and interpreting activities on their own. They do so to survive and participate in society, but also to retain their linguistic, cultural identity.

The range of official and unofficial translation and interpreting activities is as complex as it is diverse, shaping and configuring relations and interactions between the institutions of a nation and its migrants. Indeed, Loredana Polezzi calls attention to the fact that the extent to which migrants are implicated in translation activities suggests control over their degree of agency, that is, whether or not they perform as "objects" or "active subjects" of the translation processes.[57] Translator and interpreter visibility discloses the "struggle over the control of individual lives [and] social processes," thus potentially serving as a political act of witnessing.[58] All translation and interpreting activities are located within two general bidirectional flows; policies mandate and legislate hierarchically, or top-down, and actions organized in response to needs on the ground radiate, bottom-up. Within these flows, translators and interpreters play vital roles in encouraging and supporting migrant agency as interlinguistic, intercultural mediators. For many language groups with a long tradition of orality and with no support of an enforceable language policy, many of these activities revolve around oral interpreting practices. In the Romani context, these practices respond to different needs.[59] For example, Marushiakova and Popov mention that activists and linguists have acted as interpreters at International Romani Union events, working "between the different Gypsy communities [speaking] different languages or dialects of Romanes [Romani]."[60] Community interpreters are also frequently used to mediate in schools and hospitals and for legal, immigration, medical, and social services.[61] These interpreting situations vary considerably, from helping Romani parents and children understand educational policies and schoolwork to explaining diverse cultural practices. Romani interpreters frequently work between diverse Romani dialects and local contact languages and deal with the entire spectrum of literacy. They often describe in their discussions how an understanding of orality, oral expression, multiple dialects, and the way dialects function in general allows them to contextualize fluidly and rapidly while interpreting Romani dialectal speech, especially in urban contexts where Romani peoples of different origins settle after emigrating.

In the literature on translation and migration, Cronin presents "translational assimilation" and "translational accommodation" as "two possible translation strategies" of choice for minority migrants.[62] By assimilation he understands migrants choosing "to translate themselves into the dominant language of the community," mostly for its instrumentality, that is, the access it provides. By accommodation he refers to migrants choosing to acquire a host country's language, but also "to use translation as a means by which to maintain one's languages of origin."[63] Such nuancing of translational assimilative processes with the notion of accommodation acknowledges the distinctness of minority language migrant situations. In a postcolonial context, he notes, resistance to hegemonic language power through writing and translation strategies may take the form of linguistically rupturing and "foreignizing" the flow and logic of the master colonial language and discourse so as to allow the resistant "otherness" of the colonized to manifest itself. For a minority language to do likewise could be counterproductive, however, as "fluent strategies may well represent the progressive key to its very survival."[64] A certain pragmatism reigns, therefore, resulting in translation strategies that are more naturalizing and domesticating rather than foreignizing. Translators of nonstandardized or diglossic languages try to balance situations of natural interference and deal with the tension that exists between safeguarding the integrity of the language and flexibly allowing the language to usher in new concepts, terms, and expressions. It is, what Cronin aptly terms, the "classic double bind."[65] These tensions lead, in turn, to other types of resistance strategies. As Albert Branchadell stresses in the introduction to Branchadell and West, in this context the strategies focus on maintaining and cultivating one's language, language and translation policies, and nation-building initiatives and on positioning the language politically and ideologically "against dominant languages and dominant-language attitudes," including through symbolic, or emblematic, translation.[66]

TRANSLATION FUNCTIONS, TRENDS, AND STRATEGIES WITHIN ROMANI TRANSLATIONAL SPACE

In the Romani context, written translation activities reflect a broad spectrum of needs, goals, and motivations. A few functions are worth mentioning. For example, translation may be symbolic or emblematic. Supranational entities like the EU or regional and international NGOs request translations of documents into Romani even though Romani politicians, diplomats, activists, and intellectuals, as citizens of a (non-Romani) nation-state, are fully bilingual or multilingual. Translation may also be ethnic or "heritage." Local information and news are translated into Romani for newspapers, newsletters, pamphlets, posters, and other print formats for circulation within local communities. Another noteworthy activity is the translation of the Bible by religious organizations and individuals into one or more Romani dialects. This trend underscores the significance that Pentecostal evangelical churches and services currently have for Romani communities worldwide.[67] Translation may also be used for didactic purposes, that is, as a pedagogical strategy for teaching Romani through a second language in support of an identity-based bilingualism. In some cases, the focus is on creating interdialectal awareness. For example, Bakker and Kyuchukov describe children's booklets that portray the "same text in three different Romani dialects (one from Poland and two from former Yugoslavia)."[68] In another case, Gheorghe Sarău in Romania has used Courthiade's "unification model" of dialectal variation as a basis for writing a series of books that teach Romani language and literature (*I rromani ćhib thaj i literatùra*) to children. Included within are extracts of literary writing culled from texts written by Romani writers in Romania, France, Sweden, Ukraine, Colombia, the former Yugoslavia, and others, translated into Romani. (One assumes that the Romani authors first wrote in non-Romani languages and were subsequently translated into Romani, which may have functioned as a broader activist strategy.)

Translation activities are becoming more frequent in the digital sphere as well. Romani peoples all over the world have embraced technology: in the twenty-first century, the internet and social media have played a dramatic role in connecting Romani networks worldwide, both formally and informally. The current state of technical encoding of languages and scripts enables the exchange of information without need for special software. It facilitates multilingual communication and interaction across user communities, allowing for content to be written in diverse languages and scripts without users having to acquire additional technical expertise. Nonspecialized machine translation platforms like Google Translate are also popular, letting users get the gist of communication in real time. Many Romani websites today display content written and translated into Romani. One of the largest and most recent pan-Romani initiatives to date is the RomArchive "Digital Archive of the Roma." Spontaneous translation in online social media also occurs among Romani users from different countries managing multiple languages and dialects during their conversations. YouTube videos are subtitled by users, media work is posted online, and web content is translated and localized.

As identified by Cronin, the translational space of a minority, less-translated language and culture exists in strategic tension between translational assimilation and accommodation. In the Romani context, this tension seems to be mitigated through mutually reinforcing strategies of translational resistance and translational activism, both of which exhibit impulses of a decolonizing strategy to combat erasure from a history narrated by non-Romani hegemony. This implies, for instance, gaining Romani ownership over the historiography of their own cultural patrimony. International cultural patrimony is language-bound. Without translation, portions of this collective patrimony remain inaccessible to the Romani community at large; academic (and literary) works stocked in libraries and specialized documentation centers around the world are not all-language inclusive. As such, a Bulgarian Romani scholar may find a different selection of academic and literary works on and by Roma than his or her Russian, Romanian, English, Spanish, Hungarian, or Polish counterparts. Analogous to other language communities, academic scholarship also implies writing or translating one's work into English for international circulation and consumption. This step becomes vital for Romani peoples hoping to participate in discussions that could lead to policy making. Only recently have some begun to insist that codes of ethics be respected and that collaborative participation serve as a basis for research.

Translational resistance and activism are multifaceted, with resistance overlapping aspects of translational accommodation. In conventional translation terms, the Romani language viewed as either source language or target language already implies a certain dynamic of translational accommodation by default. The common core identifies each dialect as belonging to the broader Romani language, but each dialect is equally dependent on translational mechanisms through its contact with diverse other languages; linguistic and translational phenomena contribute to defining the dialect. At the same time, given the absence of adult Romani monolingualism and the Romani sociolinguistic situation, the Romani translation context implies translation into and out of non-Romani languages of diverse nation-states. Translation-related activities are likewise an intrinsic component. For example, codification, standardization, terminology, and lexicography are of very high value for revitalizing the language. Sustained efforts are under way to document words for inclusion in dictionaries and to coin neologisms for use in modern speech, writing, and translation. Linguists and lexicographers are guided politically and linguistically, making decisions based on their knowledge of early Romani, thematic and athematic elements, and languages in contact. As Hancock states, the strategies used to expand the Romani lexicon include linguistic incoining, phrasing, native retrieval, and foreign adoption.[69] Other activities support translational accommodation and resistance. For instance, translation is used as a tool to learn and advance one's knowledge of Romani language and history. It is used in self-translation to portray bilingual or multilingual relationing of the self in literary or artistic expression. It functions instrumentally in public spaces, when communities organically organize interpreting and translation activities to meet community communication needs. During one event I personally observed in Toronto, interpreters of three Romani dialects and national languages shared the stage and relayed from one language to another so that all members of the Romani immigrant community who had gathered could understand. It harnesses community knowledge of individuals who by virtue of their fluency in certain languages or dialects serve as interpreters and interlinguistic and intercultural mediators in a variety of educational, legal, medical, and other settings.

Translational activism is more concerted. It may be reactive (as when translation or interpreting situations need to be dealt with urgently or in timely fashion) or proactive (when more long-term translation projects, initiatives, and capacity-building activities can be worked on).[70] It attempts to transcend nation-state boundaries and national languages and cultures, with Romani peoples empowering themselves collectively and organizing in solidarity to challenge discrimination and racism in daily life. It aims to combat the ideologies and representations of them that have circulated within dominant discourse in many languages around the world for so long. It seeks to investigate and revisit the facts of Romani history as it has been written and uses translation as a means to access sources and share oral traditions (songs, tales, games), oral history testimonies (*Porrajmos* Holocaust survivors), sacred texts, pedagogical materials, information, and artistic, literary, and academic works, in both print and digital formats. The domain is inevitably multilingual and global. With the help of communication technologies and the web, informally and formally translated news and information circulate quickly through Romani and non-Romani networks—in Romani and non-Romani languages—and internationally in English.

CONCLUSION

Despite inhabiting a minoritized space asymmetrically configured by diverse power dynamics, Romani peoples do not compose a "translation culture" in any usual sense of the territorial, linguistic, and cultural terms of translation studies.[71] Their unique minority status evolves from a translational impulse that mutually shapes a translational response and is shaped by its effects. Moira Inghilleri insightfully observes in her studies on migration, translation, transnationalism, and multilingual signage that the juxtaposition of different languages and cultures in a given space can be articulated anew in a vocabulary of translation that has traditionally conceptualized translation in terms of separate language-culture entities. A more productive reading, according to Inghilleri, is one that interprets their aspects as "relational," in a condition of "intrinsic dialogism."[72] Applied to the transterritorial realm of Romani identity, these aspects of "relationality" and dialogism resonate with the adaptive (re)configuring dynamics of the Romani translational space. The Romani world has been a multilingual, heterogeneous one for almost a thousand years, since the time the first families left India. Multiple contacts with languages, cultures, religions, and different societies around the world make interpreting and translating between dialects and languages, sometimes in one and the same family, a natural response that emerges in the midst of so much diversity. Romani space would seem to be inherently translational, conjugating itself in relation to the non-Romani world, and in relation to the diversity it embodies within itself. The practice of translation, oral and written, meets a communication need. Alternating between interdialectal, interlinguistic, and adaptive translation procedures to borrow, calque, and create neologisms when interpreting meanings to reformulate Romani discourse,[73] modern interpreters and translators alike seem to be carrying on a tradition that has profound roots in the dynamics of the language itself, with many of its current roads leading back to reinvigorate and revitalize its source through translation.

NOTES

1. Roman Jakobson, "On Linguistic Aspects of Translation," in *The Translation Studies Reader*, ed. Lawrence Venuti (Milton Park: Routledge, 2012), 126–131.
2. Tan Zaixi, "Metaphors of Translation," *Perspectives: Studies in Translatology* 14, no. 1 (2006): 40–54.

3. Stanislas Dehaene, "*Reading in the Brain* Revised and Extended: Response to Comments," *Mind & Language* 29, no. 3 (June 2014): 320–335.
4. Claire Kramsch, *The Multilingual Subject* (Oxford: Oxford University Press, 2009).
5. Rachele Antonini, Letizia Cirillo, Linda Rossato, and Ira Torresi, eds., *Non-professional Interpreting and Translation. State of the Art and Future of an Emerging Field of Research* (Amsterdam: John Benjamins, 2017).
6. María Jesús Blasco Mayor and María Amparo Jimenez Ivars, eds., *Interpreting Naturally. A Tribute to Brian Harris* (Bern: Peter Lang, 2011).
7. Sinfree Makoni and Alastair Pennycook, "Disinventing Multilingualism: From Monological Multilingualism to Multilingual Francas," in *The Routledge Handbook of Multilingualism*, ed. Marilyn Martin-Jones, Adrian Blackledge, and Angela Creese (London: Routledge, 2012), 439–453.
8. Robert J. C. Young, "That Which Is Casually Called a Language," *PMLA* 131, no. 5 (October 2016): 1218.
9. See Naoki Sakai, "How Do We Count a Language? Translation and Discontinuity," *Translation Studies* 2, no. 1 (2009): 71–88.
10. Michael Cronin, *Translation and Globalization* (London: Routledge, 2003), 35.
11. Peter Bakker and Hristo Kyuchukov, eds., *What Is the Romani Language?* (Paris/Hatfield: Centre de recherches tsiganes and University of Hertfordshire Press, 2000), 128.
12. Anthony Grant, "When the Other Writes Back: Some Early Romani-Language Work by Roma and Others and the Cultural Context of Intellectual Capability," in Roma series 05, *Languages of Resistance: Ian Hancock's Contribution to Romani Studies*, ed. Hristo Kyuchukov and William New (Muenchen: LINCOM GmbH, 2017), 101–113; Marcel Courthiade and András Kányádi, eds., *Un dictionnaire Rromani oublié: le « Gyök-Szótár » de F. Sztojka* (Paris: INALCO and Rromani Baxt, 2007).
13. Paul Bandia, "Orality and Translation," *Handbook of Translation Studies* 2 (2011): doi:10.1075/hts.2.ora1.
14. Beate Eder-Jordan, "Oral and Written *Šukar Laviben* of the Roma. The Beginning of a Romani Literary *Historiography*," trans. Maria Willing, in *Or Words to That Effect: Orality and the Writing of Literary History*, ed. Daniel F. Chamberlain and J. Edward Chamberlain (Amsterdam: John Benjamins, 2016), 194–205; see Milena Hübschmannová, "Rencontres avec le Romano šukar laviben," trans. Ginette Ramognino, Janick Vrignaud, and Catherine Ingrand, *Études Tsiganes* 36 (2009): 98–135.
15. See, for example, Marcel Courthiade, ed., "La Littérature des Rroms, Sintés et Kalés," *Missives* 225 (March 2002); "Une ou des littérature-s Romani?," *Études Tsiganes*, no. 43 (2010); and "Littératures Romani: Construction ou Réalité?," *Études Tsiganes*, nos. 36–37 (2009).
16. See "Papusza. Poétesse Tsigane et Polonaise." *Études Tsiganes*, no. 48–49 (2011–2012).
17. Sofiya Zahova, "'The Romani People' Narratives in Books for Roma Children," in Kyuchukov and New, *Languages of Resistance*, 374–389; Hedina Tahirović-Sijerčić, "Romani Secret Road Symbols: The First Written Words in Romani or the First Translation of Romani," in *Translators Have Their Say? Translation and the Power of Agency*, ed. Abdel Wahab Khalifa (London: LIT-VERLAG, 2014), 65–82; and Paola Toninato, *Romani Writing: Literacy, Literature and Identity Politics* (London: Routledge, 2014).
18. Beate Eder-Jordan, "La littérature Romani: une aubaine pour la littérature comparée," trans. Danièle Tebaa, Cécile Kovacshazy, and Catherine Lederbauder, *Études Tsiganes* 36 (2009): 146–179.
19. See Julie McDonough Dolmaya, "A Place for Oral History within Translation Studies?," *Target* 27, no. 2 (2015): 192–214.
20. Outi Paloposki, "Translation History: Audiences, Collaboration and Interdisciplinarity," *MonTI. Monografías de Traducción e Interpretación* 5 (2013): 213–239.

21. Kathleen Davis, "Intralingual Translation and the Making of a Language," in *A Companion to Translation Studies*, ed. Sandra Bermann and Catherine Porter (Malden, Mass.: John Wiley, 2014), 586–598.
22. Michael Wogg, "Romani Literature" (Romani-Project Graz), http://romafacts.uni-graz.at/get_pdf.php?file=pdf_docs/ROMANI_LITERATURE/English/Li_2.0_literature.pdf; see also Rajko Đjurić, *Die Literatur der Roma und Sinti* (Berlin: Edition Parabolis, 2002).
23. David Crystal, *The Cambridge Encyclopedia of Language*, 3rd ed. (Cambridge: Cambridge University Press, 2010), 451.
24. Debbie Folaron, "Translation Romani" (2011), http://www.translationromani.net/en.
25. Peter Bakker, "A Text in Romani from 1622," in *Romani Studies: Contemporary Trends*, Roma Series 02, ed. Hristo Kyuchukov, Lukasz Kwadrans, and Ladislav Fizik (Meunchen: LINCOM GmbH, 2015), 10–26.
26. Ian Hancock, "Romani," in *Journeys of Besieged Languages*, ed. Delyn Day, Poia Rewi, and Rawinia Higgins (Newcastle upon Tyne: Cambridge Scholars, 2016), 161.
27. Ian Hancock, *Danger! Educated Gypsy: Selected Essays*, ed. Dileep Karanth (Hatfield: University of Hertfordshire Press, 2010).
28. Yaron Matras, *Romani: A Linguistic Introduction* (Cambridge: Cambridge University Press, 2002).
29. Hancock, *Danger!*, 119.
30. Ian Hancock, *We Are the Romani People: Ames am e Rromane džene* (Hatfield: University of Hertfordshire Press, 2002), 150.
31. See Ilona Klímová-Alexander, *The Romani Voice in World Politics—The UN and Non-state Actors* (Aldershot: Ashgate, 2005).
32. Riccardo Armillei and Bruno Mascitelli, "The Illusive Search for Identity and Citizenship in a Distant and Rhetorical European Union: The Case of the Romanies," in Kyuchukov and New, *Languages of Resistance*, 175.
33. See David M. Crowe, *A History of the Gypsies of Eastern Europe and Russia*, 2nd ed. (New York: St. Martin's, 2007), and Peter Vermeersch, ed., *The Romani Movement. Minority Politics & Ethnic Mobilization in Contemporary Central Europe* (New York: Berghahn Books, 2006).
34. Ian Hancock, *Handbook of Vlax Romani* (Columbus: Slavica, 1995).
35. Matras, *Romani*, 194–196.
36. Eugene A. Nida, "Sociolinguistics as a Crucial Factor in Translating and Interpreting," in *Encuentros Complutenses en torno a la traducción*, Actas V, ed. Rafael Martín-Gaitero (Madrid: Editorial Complutense, 1995), 43–50.
37. Jiří Levý, *The Art of Translation*, trans. Patrick Corness (1963; Amsterdam: John Benjamins, 2011), 98–99.
38. Sara Ramos Pinto, "Sociolinguistics and Translation," in *Handbook of Translation Studies*, vol. 3, ed. Yves Gambier and Luc van Doorslaer (Amsterdam: John Benjamins, 2012), 156–162.
39. Yaron Matras, "Language and the Rise of a Transnational Romani Identity," RomIdent Working Papers no. 24 (2013), 8.
40. Ibid., 17; and Yaron Matras, "The Future of Romani: Toward a Policy of Linguistic Pluralism," *Roma Rights Quarterly* 1 (2005): 31–44.
41. Dileep Karanth, ed., *Danger! Educated Gypsy. Ian Hancock. Selected Essays* (Hatfield: University of Hertfordshire Press, 2010), 115–116; see aslo Hancock, *Handbook of Vlax Romani*.
42. Edward Proctor, *Gypsy Dialects: A Selected Annotated Bibliography of Materials for the Practical Study of Romani* (Hatfield: University of Hertfordshire Press, 2008), 6.
43. Astrid Sabaini, Mozes F. Heinschink, and Dieter W. Halwachs, *Kalderaš Romani* (Munich: LINCOM GmbH, 2015), 3.
44. Ronald Lee, *Learn Romani: Das-dúma Rromanes* (Hatfield: University of Hertfordshire Press, 2005), 1.

45. Hancock, "Romani," 157.
46. Debbie Folaron, "Interpreting Romani—A Canadian Overview," *Circuit* 132 (2016), http://www.circuitmagazine.org/dossier-132/interpreting-romani-a-canadian-overview.
47. See Hristo Kyuchukov, Jill de Villiers, and Andrea Takahesu Tabori, "Why Roma Children Need Language Assessments in Romani," *Psychology of Language and Communication* 21, no. 1 (2017): 215–243.
48. Folaron, "Interpreting Romani."
49. Cronin, *Translation and Globalization*, 139, 146.
50. Toninato, *Romani Writing*, 129.
51. Ibid., 129.
52. Harish Trivedi, "In Our Own Time, on Our Own Terms. 'Translation' in India," in *Translating Others*, vol. 1, ed. Theo Hermans (Manchester: St. Jerome, 2006), 104.
53. See Milan Samko, "Linguistic Ideologies of Roma Mothers and Languages of Their Children," in Kyuchukov and New, *Languages of Resistance*, 354–362.
54. See Jaroslav Balvín, "The Life of Matéo Maximoff," in Kyuchukov, Kwadrans, and Fizik, *Romani Studies*, 246–265.
55. See Toninato, *Romani Writing*.
56. Reine Meylaerts, "Translational Justice in a Multilingual World: An Overview of Translational Regimes," *Meta* 56, no. 4 (2011): 743–757.
57. Loredana Polezzi, "Translation and Migration," *Translation Studies* 5, no. 3 (2010): 348.
58. Ibid., 353–354.
59. Debbie Folaron, "Challenging the Borders of Nation: Language and Translational Language Policy in the Plurilingual Romani Context," in *Minority Languages, National Languages, and Official Language Policies*, eds. Gillian Lane-Mercier, Denise Merkle, and Jane Koustas (Montreal/Kingston: McGill-Queens University Press, 2018), 281–314.
60. Elena Marushiakova and Vesselin Popov, "The Roma—Nation without a State? Historical Background and Contemporary Tendencies," in *Nationalisms across the Globe: An Overview of the Nationalism of State-Endowed and Stateless Nations*, ed. Wojciech Burszta, Tomasz Kamusella, and Sebastian Wojciechowski (Poznan: School of Humanities and Journalism, 2005), 433–455.
61. Folaron, "Interpreting Romani."
62. Michael Cronin, *Translation and Identity* (London: Routledge, 2006), 56.
63. Ibid., 52.
64. Cronin, *Translation and Globalization*, 140–141.
65. Ibid., 147.
66. Albert Branchadell and Lovell Margaret West, eds., *Less translated Languages* (Amsterdam: John Benjamins, 2005), 9–10.
67. David Thurfjell and Adrian Marsh, eds., *Romani Pentecostalism: Gypsies and Charismatic Christianity* (Bern: Peter Lang, 2014).
68. Bakker and Kyuchukov, *What Is the Romani Language?*, 114–115.
69. Hancock, *Danger*, 123–124.
70. Cf. Maria Tymoczko, *Enlarging Translation, Empowering Translators* (Manchester: St. Jerome, 2007).
71. Nadja Grbic, Gernot Hebenstreit, Gisella Vorderobermeier, Michaela Wolf, and Erich Prunč, eds., *Translationskultur Revisited: Festschrift für Erich Prunč* (Tübingen: Stauffenburg Verlag, 2010).
72. Moira Inghilleri, *Translation and Migration* (London: Routledge, 2017), 155.
73. Ronald Lee, "Writing and Translating Romani," in Kyuchukov and New, *Languages of Resistance*, 74–86.

6 • *EZHI-GIKENDAMANG AANIKANOOTAMANG ANISHINAABEMOWIN*

Anishinaabe Translation Studies

MARGARET A. NOODIN

Ojibwemowin odizhinikaadaanaawaa. Mii dash i'iw gichi-inendaagwak aapiji. Mii i'iw anishinaabemowin. Aanishinaa gigii-miinigowizimin. Mii i'iw ji-inwewang gii-nandodomaan. Mii dash i'iw imaa gakina gegoo ayaamagak imaa anishinaabemowining gakina gegoo izhi-gikendang anishinaabe inakeyaa ani-izhichiged. Mii go gaye i'iw naa gemaa anishinaabemowining maajiishkendang anishinaabe gaye ge-ani-izhichiged gwayak akawe ji-bimaadizid.
(They call it Ojibwe. And it is thought of very highly. That's the Indian language. We have been given that. It's intended for our speech. And everything is contained there in the language, everything the Indian knows and does. Contained in the language is the Indian knowledge of how to do things and how to live.)

—Mezinaankwad Robert Jourdain,
translated by Henry Flocken and Anton Treuer

Anishinaabemowin, also called Ojibwe, uses the word "aanikanootan" to convey the idea of translation. "Aanikanootan" is closely related to "aanikoobidoon," which is the verb for stringing things together or extending something by tying pieces together. There is an echo of both in "aanikoobijigan," which is an "an ancestor, great-grandparent, or great-grandchild," but nothing in the word signifies the nouns parent, person, or child. Perhaps the best way to understand both translation and ancestry is through the action of connection. As we translate, we connect languages and cultures. Our language also connects us to those who used it before us and those who will carry it into the future.

This essay examines the significance of twenty-first-century indigenous voices moving between languages to intentionally modernize oral and textual traditions while also reshaping cultural and geopolitical boundaries. The geopoetical diaspora and cultural network made visible by these translations offers yet another view of human evolution and the practice of translation. As Anishinaabe poetry moves between modern English and modern Anishinaabemowin, it is clear that translation is more than mediation or transfer between languages or cultures. It is a political act of connected empowerment. In *The Translation Zone,* Emily Apter explains that when it is "cast as an act of love, and as an act of disruption, translation becomes a means of repositioning the subject in the world and in history; a means of rendering self-knowledge foreign to itself; a way of denaturalizing citizens, taking them out of the comfort zone of national space, daily ritual and pre-given domestic arrangements."[1] When applied to indigenous literary and cultural studies, this quotation serves as a perfect description of decolonization, which is too often taken to mean a return to the past when it can more productively be aligned with the anarchic freedom of the individual to disrupt and rearrange linguistic, artistic, and political expectations. Writers recognized as Native American, American Indian, Indigenous, or Aboriginal in the United States and Canada maintain multiple identities; fully understanding their work requires the study of many languages. The fact that so many competing and different terms are used simultaneously for the field itself demonstrates its complexity and the continuing impact of linguistic resistance.

The history of translation in North America requires the recognition of complexity. Most indigenous cultures tell of at least two "times" in which stories are set, with one always being a time when translation and discourse was able to extend beyond humanity. In the times that followed, narration became limited to humans, but vast intertribal differences were acknowledged. Many stories and archaeological sites document extensive exploration and trade in North America, in some cases connecting sites to other continents. This interconnection would have necessarily involved a need for translation between languages. The diversity of indigenous languages and dialects that remain highlights the continual need for translation. It is along this continuum of change and linguistic evolution that the recent period of colonization led by English-, French-, and Spanish-speaking people must be viewed. Perhaps because there was less diversity among the languages and cultures of the colonizers, perhaps because so many encounters were focused on dominance, or perhaps because the "civilizing" settlers were unable to recognize oral systems of information, the recent colonial period resulted in incredible linguicide. The question is, when does this period end? Could it be now, with texts that move contemporary thought between global and local languages, using the English *lingua communis,* or gidinwewininaan, to support the creation of an Anishinaabemowin *lingua perpetuus,* or abiji-inwewin? Kathleen Shields has written that English is a pivot language, and asymmetric relations between languages and nations are increasingly evident.[2] This chapter argues that translation is a tool of decolonization, revitalization, and unsettlement; it is a means of connecting the past and future through language, through aanikanootan.

In translation, relation is everything. To proceed with a conversation about Anishinaabemowin and English, it is important to know the lineage of the languages. As identified by Paul Proulx, a Proto-Algic language was spoken in North America around seven thousand years ago.[3] According to Howard Berman, the Algic branches include Wiyot, Yurok, and Algonquian subdivisions.[4] Within the Algonquian group, Anishinaabemowin is one of thirty languages that became distinct twenty-five hundred to three thousand years ago.[5] J. P. Mallory explains that the Indo-European language family diverged from Proto-Indo-European around thirty-five hundred years ago, and most linguists agree English is approximately fifteen hundred years old.[6] These facts show that each is a highly evolved language predicated by many centuries of use. These facts also show Anishinaabemowin is likely twice as old as English. Both began as oral languages, both are now written, with Anishinaabemowin entering a period of alphabetic literacy only recently. Walter Ong notes that "the shift from orality to writing intimately interrelates with more psychic and social developments than we have yet noted."[7] It is pure speculation to wonder whether the Algonquian languages might have used, and subsequently evolved beyond, physical representation of language. We will likely never know the complete history of orality and why it was maintained for so long by cultures capable of many innovations. Could some ancient sessions of exchange have regularly involved marks in sand, clay, or bark? Could oral performance be the culmination of language evolution as the ability to consciously encode, store, and retrieve language increased in a society? As we witness the deconstruction and reconstruction of text through technology and the increasing variation of vocabulary and orthography, these are questions worth asking. English and Anishinaabemowin have different histories, which are a part of the translation equation if we wish to postulate theories regarding the way they are used in the present.

Formal descriptions note that English is a language with fixed syntactic rules and a focus on the noun or pronoun in each sentence with rich descriptive capabilities. Anishinaabemowin is a verb-based agglutinative language focused on action and direction. Students learning English are encouraged to use adverbs and adjectives to add detail to lyric, narrative, or informative phrases, which often begin with a subject followed by a verb. Students learning Anishinaabemowin are encouraged to begin with one or more root verbs and build phrases by adding prefixes and suffixes to the verbs in order to indicate what is happening and how it happened. Pronouns in English are separate words with a clear difference between male and female in the third person. Pronouns in Anishinaabemowin are variations of inflection appearing as prefixes and/or suffixes often depending on the pattern or intent of the narrative. Furthermore, the third person offers no way to indicate gender, and there are forms of "we" and "you" that either include or exclude the listener. Perhaps the most often cited and most misunderstood difference between the languages is the classification of nouns in Anishinaabemowin. Sometimes referred to as "animacy" or "gender," neither is an accurate translation, and most contemporary teachers find it most useful to simply use the demonstrative equivalent of "this one" or "that one" to communicate the class of a noun that is "wa'aw" or "i'iw" in the west and "maaba" or "maanda" in the east. This is of course a very basic summary of the contrasts between the languages, but it does reveal some of the challenges encountered by translation and alludes to the source of many cultural and political misunderstandings discussed at great length by ethnographers and historians.

This chapter is focused not on the linguistic aftershock of manifest destiny but rather on the practice of empowering and privileging an indigenous language. Four poets, who have published numerous volumes in English, recently chose to have their verse translated into Anishinaabemowin. All of the poets are considered minority authors in a national context. George Kenny and David Groulx identify as Aboriginal authors from Canada, Kim Blaeser and Heid Erdrich identify as American Indian or Native American authors from the United States. When we read these authors' work as Anishinaabe poetry moving from English into Anishinaabemowin, the dominant borders are erased and the formerly subaltern voice is at the center. What can be seen in both languages is undeniably part of Anishinaabe literary identity, and what is shifted from one language to another offers a view of translation and Anishinaabe epistemology in two contemporary cultural contexts.

A look at where these authors and translators come from, return to, and make their homes while teaching and translating illustrates the breadth of Anishinaabewakiing (Anishinaabeland). Their lives trace the north and western half of the Great Lakes to include forests and islands, dirt roads and highways, rural schools and universities, boarding schools and language camps. The eldest in the group began life in the first half of the 1900s when missions and welfare services forced assimilation and the use of English. The youngest of the group was born just before the civil rights movements of the 1970s led to political protest and cultural revitalization. Throughout the entire time the loss of elders and birth of children fueled a burning urgency for change and survival. In the late 1990s more nations earned federal recognition; legislation in both the United States and Canada supported cultural recovery and attempts at reconciliation. It is no coincidence that in the space of four years, between 2011 and 2014, four bilingual examples of English poetry translated into Anishinaabemowin appeared. The time for Anishinaabe-centered translation had arrived. When the language was no longer the first language of families, when the past century's attempts at translation for conversion were more distant memories, the focus finally shifted to preserving the creative power of Anishinaabemowin in the present.

Interestingly, the poets published translations of their work in reverse order, with the youngest poet, David Groulx, born in 1969, working with Shirley Williams to publish two editions of his book, *Bi-Gishkoziitwin Biidaanzhed* (*Rising with a Distant Dawn*) in 2011. In 2012, Heid Erdrich included a section of prose poems with my translations in her collection *Cell Traffic*. In 2013, Kim Blaeser, born in 1955, asked me to translate several of her poems, which later appeared in *Hayden's Ferry Review* in English and Anishinaabemowin. In 2014, George Kenny, born in 1952 and a speaker of Anishinaabemowin, published a bilingual edition of *Gaawiin Mawisiiwag Anishinaabeg* (*Indians Don't Cry*), translated by Patricia Ningewance. The fact that the younger poets pushed first for translation may indicate the experimental energy of poets born in the 1960s and the caution of the generation born in the 1950s, or it may be purely coincidence. All of the translators are also teachers of Anishinaabemowin and through their work contributed to the development of editorial and translation standards. Prior to these publications, occasional isolated examples occurred; for instance, in 2010 Rick Grescyk translated Jim Northrup's poems "Ishkonigani-odaabaan (Rez Car)" and "Nindooshtigwaanimashkikiwininiban (Shrinking Away)," but the translated versions remain unpublished. There are likely other samples as yet undiscovered of poets and teachers working together learning, unlearning, and relearning languages, but the important fact is that there is now momentum for translation from English to Anishinaabemowin, which should allow this synchronic analysis to become diachronic in the future.

The translators clearly state that the function of their translations is to focus on the future. Although they offer information about the way the language has been spoken in the past, their intent is to aid current and future students in understanding Anishinaabe lyric in the Anishinaabe language. The back cover of *Bi-Gishkoziitwin* states, "Mii dash ezhi-oditamang ji-gikendamang Anishinaabewaadiziwin" (So this is how we will obtain a knowledge of Anishinaabe ways of life). Echoing these sentiments, Patricia Ningewance's "Translator's Note" explains,

> It is my hope that the Anishinaabe language student or reader will enjoy reading this book of short stories and poems. There are not many books of length—fiction or nonfiction—that are written in Anishinaabemowin. It will help enhance a student's vocabulary and grasp of the Anishinaabemowin grammar. Stories and poetry in the Native language play a particularly important role in language revitalization, as they bring the language to life.[8]

Heid Erdrich describes the translations in her volume as "re-expressions" that "note interesting tensions between Ojibwe and English."[9] In the past, many translations of Native American, Aboriginal, and American Indian literatures have been the work of ethnographers and documentary linguists, and the function of these translations has been to reveal the maximum amount of information to the

English reader, or to recover and reactivate linguistic artifacts from dormancy. In this new generation of translation, the directional change from English to Anishinaabemowin is intended not to reveal one culture to another, but rather to connect one culture to itself, across multiple languages.

These translations are predicated on the presence of a population of editorial grammarians willing to engage in making art. All of the translators have careers that span decades of curriculum creation, instruction, and assessment. Their ears are tuned to the ways each language is most frequently misunderstood. Their translations begin with a fluent understanding of the meaning in English and move from a direct and literal first version to a more oblique and nuanced final version, which is a single strategy combining two methods in order to find the best match for meaning and the best aesthetic echo of sound, length, and pattern. Aids for translation are few for Anishinaabemowin. There are lexicons from the late 1700s and early 1800s, but orthography varies and few dictionaries were written by fluent speakers. There are also more recent resources across dialects including the *Freelang Online Ojibwe-English Dictionary* and the *Ojibwe People's Dictionary*. Richard Rhodes published the *Eastern Ojibwa-Chippewa-Ottawa Dictionary*, but it is viewed as a very regional document. It is likely that most translators turn data they have compiled on their own. Shirley Williams published *Gdi-nweninaa: A Collection of Ojibwe and Odawa Words*, and many of those words are found in her translation. Patricia Ningewance has published *Pocket Ojibwe: A Phrasebook for Nearly All Occasions*, which reflects her dialect and preferences. In each case, the translations are done by teachers who use the same dialect as the poet. Also in each case, the translation is a close conversation between members of the same culture. As the field of Anishinaabemowin translation grows, it will be interesting to see if translations produce a more standard orthography and usage. If so, will some works require deviation from that standard to reflect variations in vocabulary, grammar, syntax, and pronunciation, or will the standard be all-encompassing?

These translations are not to be read simply as decolonial poetic migrations backward in time from the present when Anishinaabemowin is not the dominant language to the time when it was. Rather, they are the spin of a wheel powered by language and culture, allowing one time to overlap another, one voice to be heard in two languages. Nor do they represent an attempt to render everything in two equal versions, which is neither linguistically nor culturally possible. If translation is the transfer of ideas from one language to another, these works require collation, the alignment of multiples to create a whole. These texts invite theories of translation and recombination that are both general and specific, and that add to the understanding of language, interpretation, translation, and comparison. Patterns appear and maxims become obvious. For instance, when trying to translate poems by Heid Erdrich, I found myself working with a few of Mona Baker's eight strategies for translation.[10] I could sometimes find a more general word or a more neutral word, or rely on a suitable paraphrase that either elaborated on the meaning or defined it by contrast. In a few instances I found a cultural equivalent, and in a very few cases it was best to keep a foreign word in the Anishinaabemowin text. However, working with an efficient agglutinative language that privileges repetition of meaning and construction of new words, I had a few other options. When faced with the lines:

> they offer tobacco at first thunder
> visit Ganesh and household gods, Buddhist shrines,
> and wonder if Jesus is some kind of benign zombie[11]

I created the following Anishinaabemowin version with a literal English line of decoding beneath it.

> sema bagosendaamowaad Nimkodaading
> (tobacco they offer when it thunders)
> mawadishawad Jejiibajikiimanido ednokiiwaad, izhaawaad Buddha anamegamig
> (they visit Ganesh and household gods, they go to Buddhas' places of prayer)
> mii enendamowaad Paguk gonemaa Zhesus aawed
> (then they think he's a Paguk maybe, that Jesus)[12]

Certainly the borrowing is easy to see, and the previously borrowed and adapted words are rendered in their Anishinaabe versions, but making up a new word is a definite option and will give no reader of Anishinaabemowin reason to pause. Making up new words or more complex versions of old words by using verbs is common, which is how the noun Ganesh becomes Jejiibajikiimanido (essence of the one with a wide swinging motion above the ground). Not indigenous to North America, elephants were described by their action when they arrived, so "jejiibaji" means to be swinging and the added "kii" indicates this happens close to the ground, which is a fairly accurate depiction of one of an elephant's most prominent features. The fact that the translation moves from a proper noun that is a borrowed word in the English poem to a multisyllabic name based on character actions in the Anishinaabemowin poem is a comment on the construction of both words and names in Anishinaabe culture. The direct use of such broader religious terms as "Buddhist" and "Jesus" could also be the effect of assimilation, while the use of Paguk for "zombies" reminds Anishinaabe readers of epic narratives where characters rise up and return to life. The choices for how to combine and recombine cultures through language are numerous.

In the same series, a repetition of words becomes a single word reduplicated, which showcases the morphological characteristics of the target language as another option for difficult words and phrases. Reduplication occurs when a phoneme is repeated for morphemic effect. In my translation, "money this and money that, not enough and we'll be OK" becomes "zhoniyaa, zhozhoozhooniya, zhibii'aaminid zhibiiga'aminid, gakina gegoo da onizhishin," which is literally "money, mon-mon-money, we write it we stretch it, everything will be fine."[13] The repetition of the first syllable turns creates a superlative relative to the original word. The same thing occurs in the translation of "Ishkwa Ikidowinan (After Words)" by Kim Blaeser, when "in these last years I've worn and worn and nearly worn out my black funeral shoes" becomes "odaanaang biboonong n'gii bababa-goneshkanan agaawaa ndo'bagidendamowin-makade-makazinan."[14] By adding the "baba" to "bagoneshkanan," the word takes on a delightfully complex translation literally meaning "in these past winters I have wor-wor-worn them out almost, my 'forgive and release' black moccasins." The translation also highlights the fact that the English word for moccasins is in fact the Anishinaabemowin word for shoes, and the only way to say funeral is to use the verb that means both forgive and release. In the minutiae we find new strategies for translation and refine the understanding of the Anishinaabe language. The fact that Anishinaabe writers appear to lean toward some of the patterns of Anishinaabemowin even when writing in English suggests that oral patterns have survived both the transition to written form and the transfer into another language.

The realm of poetic translation is especially difficult because, along with the science of matching the meaning, a translator makes choices that invariably influence the very nature and essence of the poem. The lingering sorrow or flight of hopelessness is not always translatable from one culture to another. In the case of these writers and their translators moving from a language that stands for settlement to a language that stands for survival, the goal is not to simply move the grief or ecstasy from one language to another, but to allow it to undergo subtle changes as it is enveloped by an alternate system. Consider the example of two poems and their translations. Written years apart by different poets, they offer a record of racism and its impact on youth.

For most of thirteen years
Awashme midaashi-niso-biboon

For most of thirteen years
dreams of screaming rides
on eagles
filled my night eyes
dreams that had their birth
in trying to escape
the sneers through public
then high school
"You dirty Indian"
and fighting for respect
an Ojibway youth

who lost as much as
he won
at night he cried into
his pillow
and through thirteen years
dreams of screaming rides
on eagles
filled his night eyes.
Awashme midaashi-niso-biboon
e-bawaadamaan ji-bimiwinishiwaad
gaa-biibaagiwaad migiziwag
gaa-inaabiyaan ako gii-dibikag
amii ko gaa-gii-onji-inaabandamaan
e-gagwe-giimiitooyaan
gii-igooyaambaan aki gikino'amaadiiwigamigong
biinish gii-ani-mindidiwaan
"Gaa-wwinziyan Anishinaabewish"
e-gii-onji-miigaazoyaan
anishinaabens
minik gaa-wanitood
gaa-gii-bakinaaged
gii-dibikag gii-mawid
odapikweshimoning
midaashi-niso-biboon minik
e-bawaanaad e-bimiwinigod
gaa-biibaaginid migiziwan
gaa-waabandang gii dibikaninig.[15]

Note the slurs captured in the words "dirty Indian" and "halfbreed," which are both rendered with explicit and direct simplicity—and nearly matching morphemes—into "wiiniziyin Anishinaabewish" and "abitooziinh." The "ish" at the end of Anishinaabewish" adds emphasis that is possible only through oral delivery in English and heightened by print in Anishinaabemowin. Also note the light salve of "bimi" that appears and reappears throughout both poems. "Bimaadizi" is the verb for being alive with "bimadiziwin" the noun for life. In addition, all words of personal motion begin with "bimi." As these poems of quiet desperation and a longing for escape move from one language into another, it could be argued that Shirley Williams and Pat Ningewance made choices that threaded life and motion through the poems serving as an unwritten major chord to the original minor, or perhaps as a star-spark of energy reflected off the chill of a mineral moon. Both poets are aware escape is futile and reckon the days and nights and years of their lives by surviving one more "biboon" ("one more winter"), which is the idiom used instead of "old" when one speaks of age. "How old are you?" becomes "Aan-iin endaaso biboonigiziyan?" literally, "How many winters have you seen?"

It is also interesting to compare the overall format choices of the translators. George Kenny wrote "dreams of screaming eagles," and translator Pat Ningewance held true to the patterns of sound, echoing the internal lines in each line, but shifting the repeat slightly from the center of the words to the front as she wrote "e-bawaadamaan ji-bimiwinishiwaad." Every choice has meaning. Her translation matches the original emotional intent with a surgical precision that confronts the English version head-on, allowing both to serve as pillars of poetry recording the pain of youth.

Transformations
    Ezhi-aanj-naagozing

I gave the first five years of my life
being human.
    Nmiigwen nbimaadiziwin naanan-biboon
    nbimaadiziwin
    aawiyaanh bemaadizid.
I spent the next fifteen years of my life
being ashamed and not knowing why (halfbreed).
    Miidash miinwaa gii-nokaaziiyanh
    eko-mdaaswi-shi-naanan nsabiboon nbimaadiziwin
    mi-gaajiiyaanh miinwaa kendiziiyaanh aanish iidik
    (aabitooziinh).
I lived the next ten years of my life
trying to end it.
    Ngii-ni-zhi-nbimaadiz dash pii (mii)nash mdaaswi-biboon
    bimaadiziwin
    gweji nzidiziiyaanh.
I'll live the rest of my life
trying to remember what it was to be human
    Nga-bimaadiz minik ge-ni-bimaadiziiyaanh
    gwejtoowaanh ji-mnjimendimaanh wenesh
    gaa-aawong bimaadiziiwin.[16]

David Groulx's poem is a variation on the same theme. As Kenny's poem asserts, it is painful to be "Indian," and it is just as painful to be only half "Indian." In Groulx's poem he writes of his transformation from desperation to resolution. The title in English describes a change that could take many forms, but the Anishinaabemowin describes a change in how one looks, which leaves open the possibility that a central identity may have remained unchanged. Unlike the translation of Kenny's poem, this translation of Groulx's poem adds line breaks and length. Words and lines are not simply longer, reflecting the difference between the languages, but there are breaks added where none were previously. Statements are stretched and separated in ways that add depth. In the English version we read "life" four times and "human" twice. In the Anishinaabemowin version "life" and "human" are both translated with variations of "bimaadizi," which then appears nine times. In a poem about living beyond a desire to die, Shirley Williams has woven a message about life into her use of the word that is "to live," "to be human," to journey forward.

Much is often made of the "oral origins" of indigenous writing, and there are some ways in which all of the English to Anishinaabemowin translations evoke the traces of performance that mark a more oral tradition. There are also ways in which some of these poets have pushed the boundaries of poetry and translation by using technology to combine sound, text, and image. Many languages in various phases of revitalization have used audio artifacts to teach, and the translations of early contributions in every language are treasured; they also stand, however, as isolates outside natural context prompted by objective observations or requests for elicitation, rather than inspired by artistic expression and cultural exploration. "Lexiconography 1: Aabjito'ikidowinan 1" by Heid Erdrich is one example of an Anishinaabe palimpsest created for more than one sense. The video poem is freely available on her website.[17] It lives in that space and is not mediated by publishing or any economy other than time. Those who give up some of their time to experience the poem are rewarded with a bilingual dance of wooden clothespins and clouds, ziinaakwa'iganan gaye aanakwadoon. An explorer of liminal spaces, Erdrich credits this poem to a page in *The Concise Dictionary of Minnesota Ojibwe*, which serves as a perfect metaphor for being positioned between languages. She began with a word and created a chain of memories in English, then invited a response in Anishinaabemowin. The video poem traces memories moving from one language to another by mixing the sound of wood and wind with a reading in both languages. Images distract the eye as two languages wash over one another, not leaving space between lines but also not allowing one language to ever drown out the other. Both the English and Anishinaabemowin versions emphasize the action and play with the bright purposeful sound of pinning clothes on a line or the profound silence of clouds. In this case, there was no emphasis on exact equivalents in translation, only a desire to evoke a matching mood. Alliteration moved across languages even though the meaning shifted slightly. For instance, "collapsed clouds of clothing" became "bisikiigamaang biizikiigan-aanakwadoon" which is literally "folded clouds of clothing." At other times, each language references culture differently through clothing. On the one hand, "lines of a man's clothes, heavy denim" is simply "miikanot miinawaa bitomiikanotan" ("pants and underpants"), leaving the American legacy of "denim" for English readers. On the other hand, "woman's clothes" become "gaawiin ziibaaskasiigoodenan," literally "dresses without jingles," representing all of the everyday clothes that might be hung on the line and the handmade dresses for healing, which would not be washed and placed on display unattended. Erdrich's game-like format for hypertext verse carries orality into modernity.

The liberties taken by translators can connect poems and poets to create a third dimension, a collated space that is neither solely English nor solely Anishinaabemowin. The result is a resonance between languages, which is a product of assimilation, acculturation, and translation. These are not poets and translators who live in two worlds. They are artists living in one world with two languages. They are sorting out the power and patterns of each language to create a single more resilient identity. In *Born in the Blood: On Native American Translation,* Brian Swann describes the traditional task of translating Native American literature and lyric, which has been to "make something available without making it assimilable; to make it similar and different at the same time while taking it seriously all the time; to keep it simultaneously intriguing and challenging; to create beauty, respect and admiration with the desire to share and participate without the need to appropriate."[18] A close reading of the method and message produced by these Anishinaabe poets and translators moving between English and Anishinaabemowin demonstrates how fine art can be inimitable, how the translation of Native American narrative and verse is entering a new era. Readers are not likely to imagine they could or should claim any of the feelings or experiences expressed by the poets; they are instead invited to consider oral and literary lyrics in a global context. Translation creates a space for understanding that did not exist prior to the contact between languages. Mii dash I'iw imaa gakina gegoo ayaamagak imaa eneweyang.

NOTES

1. Emily Apter, *The Translation Zone: A New Comparative Literature* (Princeton: Princeton University Press, 2006), 6.
2. Kathleen Shields, "Challenges and Possibilities for World Literature, Global Literature, and Translation," *CLCWeb: Comparative Literature and Culture* 15, no. 7 (2013): doi.org/10.7771/1481-4374.2381.
3. Paul Proulx, "Proto-Algic I: Phonological Sketch," *International Journal of American Linguistics* 50, no. 2 (April 1984), 165–207.
4. Howard Berman, "Proto-Algonquian-Ritwan Verbal Roots," *International Journal of American Linguistics* 50, no. 3 (July 1984), 335–342.
5. See Ives Goddard, "Central Algonquian Languages," in *Northeast*, ed. Bruce G. Trigger, vol. 15 of *Handbook of North American Indians* (Washington, D.C.: Smithsonian Institution, 1978), 583–587, and Marianne Mithun, *The Languages of Native North America* (Cambridge: Cambridge University Press, 1999).
6. J. P. Mallory, *In Search of the Indo-Europeans: Language, Archaeology, and Myth* (London: Thames and Hudson, 1991).

7. Walter J. Ong, *Orality and Literacy: The Technologizing of the Word* (New York: Methuen, 1982), 175.
8. See David Groulx, *Bi-Gishkoziitwin Biidaanzhed Biidaabang* and *Rising with a Distant Dawn*, trans. Shirley Ida Williams (Toronto: Bookland Press, 2015), xii.
9. See Heid E. Erdrich, *Cell Traffic: New and Selected Poems* (Tucson: University of Arizona Press, 2012), 3.
10. Mona Baker, *In Other Words: A Course Book on Translation* (London: Routledge, 1992).
11. Ibid., 74.
12. Ibid., 74.
13. Ibid., 69.
14. Kimberly M. Blaeser, "After Words," trans. Margaret Noodin, *Hayden's Ferry Review* 54 (Spring/Summer 2014): 57.
15. George Kenney, *Gaawiin Mawisiiwag Anishinaabeg: Indians Don't Cry*, trans. Patricia M. Ningewance (Winnipeg: University of Manitoba Press, 2014), 174–175.
16. Groulx, *Bi-Gishkoziitwin Biidaanzhed Biidaabang*, 48.
17. See Heid Erdrich, "Lexiconography 1," http://heiderdrich.com/video/lexi1/.
18. Brian Swann, *Born in the Blood: On Native American Translation* (Lincoln: University of Nebraska Press, 2011), 6.

7 • "IF YOU COULD ONLY UNDERSTAND MY LANGUAGE"

Counterfeit Script, Make-Believe Translation, and Actor-Spectator Complicity in *The Toll of the Sea* (1922), *Mr. Wu* (1927), and *Hollywood Party* (1937)

YIMAN WANG

In 1764, a book titled *Memoirs of ****, Commonly Known by the Name of George Psalmanazar; a Reputed Native of Formosa*, was published posthumously, as intended by its author. In this memoir, Psalmanazar repented his vile act of passing for a Formosa native and a Christian convert who, furthermore, concocted a reputed Formosan script and ethnography in his best-selling book *An Historical and Geographical Description of Formosa* (1704, 1705), which he described as "hatched in my own brain, without regard to truth and honesty."[1] Ironically, despite his repentance of this act of forgery, his memoir still carries his imposter name, while his real name, rendered as ****, remains a glaring absence, mocking his posthumous attempt at self-exposé.

The curious case of Psalmanazar, who successfully passed for a Formosa native despite his "authentic Caucasian looks, blond hair and blue eyes," has sparked much scholarly interest.[2] For Jack Lynch, Psalmanazar foregrounded the performative nature of Orientalism.[3] For Lydia Liu, Psalmanazar figured as a "supreme parodist" and "a caricature of the Enlightenment dream and a parody of ethnographic imagination."[4] Liu further uses this case to interrogate the production of meaning-value in the process of colonial encounter and its attending power inequity. Liu argues that Psalmanazar's book, *An Historical and Geographical*

Description of Formosa, fabricated a society with no referent, just as his imposter name did not refer to a real name. His rebuttal of a missionary's report based on real-life experience in Taiwan, calling the latter a forger, raises questions of "meaning as face value and writing as parody of other writing."[5] Psalmanazar the parodist undermines the very legitimacy of any claim to authenticity and the original, for they are revealed as being already steeped in the overarching colonialist, ethnographic fantasy of the racial and cultural Other. In this fantasy, the originator of the text about the Other and the translator of the text blend into one, for they both feed upon and reinforce the same enclosed signifying system of Orientalism that is predicated upon Western obliteration of the historical Other. In other words, the fundamental problem in this signifying system is its a priori exclusion of the Other, which inevitably leads to undervaluation, even devaluation of the Other, even in its attempt to translate the Other.

If Formosa (and the rest of the "Orient") in the eighteenth century could be conveniently packaged as a thoroughly contrived fiction, hatched in the Western brain, the situation had changed drastically by the 1930s. With China's modernization drive and the Nationalist government's assertion of its soft power on the international stage and, most importantly, with Hollywood's voracious appetite for the international market, China, emerging as an important interlocutor, posed a problem that Hollywood had to reckon with. This in turn led to a different approach to the foreign (in this case the Chinese) language and culture, resulting in varied translational politics and strategies.

The American comedian Harold Lloyd's 1934 comedy *The Cat's Paw* (dir. Sam Taylor) is symptomatic of precisely this shift. This film narrates the story of an American boy traveling to China with his missionary father, and then returning to his American hometown as a young man, only to get entangled in the local political chaos. Raised and educated in China for twenty years, he has studied Ling Po, a reputed Chinese poet and philosopher. Yet upon returning to his native Stockport, California, he finds himself confused by American mannerisms, while his English, transliterated from the American Orientalist imaginary of Chinese diction, similarly baffles the Californians. Lloyd's stranger-in-hometown character identifies with Chinese culture and language despite his Caucasian looks. In this sense, he echoes Psalmanazar's imposter identity, with one significant difference: Lloyd's character claims a Chinese identity through acculturation (rather than genetic heritage as Psalmanazar did), which was supported by Lloyd's extradiegetic efforts. According to the film's publicity, Lloyd studied two Chinese dialects for the role, although the few lines he delivers phonetically are barely intelligible.[6] The publicity further claimed that the "Oriental sequences" at the beginning of the film were made with the assistance of the Chinese Nationalist government, implying that their visual, cultural, and linguistic accuracy was endorsed by the Chinese government.[7]

While the film seemed to go out of its way to appease the Chinese government, its deployment of Chinese written and spoken language remained problematic. Shortly after the opening of the film, a missionary family is shown arriving in a Chinese village. The American boy (played by a child actor before Lloyd essays his adult version) is given a Chinese book, the cover of which reads 靈普哲學心理論述. This title is left untranslated, and is merely introduced as "funny writing" (according to the boy). In the following sequence, he is shown holding the book and reading, which then cuts to a close-up of a page inside the book, revealing more untranslated "funny writing." Another cut shows two Chinese boys sitting down next to him, speaking in Chinese (Cantonese, to be exact), to which the American boy responds, "You'll have to talk slower," and finally, "I guess I just don't understand." On that note, one of the Chinese boys proceeds to turn the book around, suggesting that he has been trying to tell the American boy that he is reading the book upside down, which adds a comic spin to his imitation reading gesture. Subsequently, a wipe and a dissolve take us to 1934—twenty years later; a camera close-up reveals the same book on a small desk, right next to another book with a cover reading 明心宝鉴, again untranslated.

In this section, Chinese writing and speech are deployed visually and acoustically, but not semantically, since the film offers no translation of the book titles or the Chinese boy's lines. The mainstream, non-Chinese-speaking, mostly white audience was thus encouraged to treat the Chinese language as arcane and inscrutable "funny writing," even if the use of the valid Chinese script ostensibly paid due respect to Chinese censorship. Furthermore, the focus on the inert and impenetrable physiognomy of the Chinese language masks significant misplacements of the Chinese text. While indicative of Hollywood's fundamental trivialization of the Other, these misplacements offer Chinese-speaking viewers comic moments unintended by the filmmaker (judging from the film's publicity that stressed the producer's effort to "get it right"). For instance, Chinese-speaking viewers recognize that the Chinese titles are composed of valid characters. However, the first title, 靈普哲學心理論述, loosely meaning "Ling Po's Treatise on Philosophy and Psychology," is not a real book, but Hollywood's concoction for the sheer purpose of introducing the fictional Chinese poet-philosopher Ling Po. Since the book does not exist, the page within the book, shown in close-up and upside down, is grafted from Confucius's *Analects*. The second title, 明心宝鉴, shown on the small desk twenty years later, is an actual book, but is geared toward juvenile education, which mismatches with the male protagonist's current adulthood in 1934. It is, however, the very first Chinese classic translated into a Western language (Spanish in this case) by Juan Cobo, a Dominican missionary who presented the translated version to the Spanish prince in 1595. It is unclear who (or whether the Chinese government that purportedly helped with the "Oriental sequences") suggested the inclusion of this book in the film, and whether the production team attached any special significance to this book (other than its iconic Chinese looks). The Chinese bricolage, stranded in the nonsignifying realm, thus constitutes a glaring present absence that produces variant viewing responses depending on the spectator's knowledge of Chinese history, culture, and languages.

The two instances I outline above share the fundamental structure that the originator and the translator of the Other's language and culture are one and the same; and that is the party occupying the empowered position and commanding the authority to present, explicate, and construct the disempowered Other. Given the colonial-era power inequity and the correlated Orientalism, it is not surprising that translation (or lack thereof) serves as a crucial venue of massaging and managing the Other's difference as exotic, innocuous, and disposable. On the other hand, these two instances also invite us to refocus on the obverse; namely, in what ways the colonized subject or the marginalized performer and spectator negotiate their compromised position, what energy they generate in embodying the foreign Other in the film's production and reception, and what kind of translational politics they instigate through their active, belabored, and nonnormative performance and spectatorship. My goal here is not to simply rediscover the subaltern agency in terms of individualist will and capacity to accomplish self-empowerment. Instead, I am interested in recognizing the possibility of what I call the *paradoxical agency* that is immanent and situated in the processes of negotiating and troubling of the colonialist binary politics. Such paradoxical agency does not necessarily rewrite the rules of the game once and for all, but rather keeps problematizing and rerouting the hegemonic meaning-value so as to make room for other modes of meaning-making and self-positioning through working with the mainstream mass media such as Hollywood cinema. In this article, I specifically examine translation, or the marginalized performer and spectator's encounter with Hollywood's scriptural Orientalism, as the multivalent site for developing such disruptive, paradoxical agency.

I further implicate and reflect upon my own position as a bilingual viewer and film critic who engages with the early twentieth-century Hollywood films nearly a century after their original release. What new relevant perspectives (in addition to identifying and critiquing mistranslations and misinformation in these films, which many may perceive as historical relics that we have already transcended and left behind) do I offer with my lingua-cultural knowledge and academic expertise? What is the significance of foregrounding my own role in producing and vectoring translational politics and its import? And how does this self-reflexive methodology contribute to translation studies in general?

To address these questions, which all center on strategies of mobilizing various hermeneutic positions, I evoke Ella Shohat and Robert Stam's "question of address," which considers "Who is speaking through a film? Who is imagined as listening? Who is actually listening? Who is looking? And what social desires are mobilized by the film?"[8] In a similar vein, Christopher Faulkner urges us to attend to "listening formations" and "the social dimension of speech and audition."[9] Faulkner defines listening formations as "the whole context of audition for historically specific audiences, taking account of expectations formed for them by the whole culture and technology of speech and hearing of which they are a part."[10] He urges us to "understand the formation . . . of a normative and hegemonic 'speaking degree zero,' along with *departures from it*," which means to comprehend "how people understood their material, lived existences in historically specific instances."[11] He further stresses "*the relation of spectator to film*," the expectations that an audience brings to a text and, the "kinds of *social and cultural knowledge*" that a text is able to engender.[12]

Building upon Shohat and Stam's "question of address" and Faulkner's notions of "listening formations" and the spectator's agency to depart from normative formations, I ask in what ways untargeted or peripheral spectators (especially those whose bilingual and bicultural ability allow them to see and hear beyond the "degree zero") strategically allow themselves to be addressed by the manifest film, or interrupt such an address through alternative methods of transcoding the film. Relatedly, I consider this question with regard to similarly positioned film performers who can see and hear beyond the "degree zero." In their strategic engagement with the mainstream film as spectators and performers, they undertake the task of translation (be it implicit or explicit), and reveal it as a cognitive and affective sieve functioning as a barrier for some spectators and performers who can stay on only one side of the film. Translation can, however, also become a porous channel for others who are apparently sifted out and eliminated from the film, but paradoxically gain the privilege of seeing the sieve as a sieve, that is, a mechanism and an apparatus shot through with flaws *and* unforeseeable possibilities. It is in engaging with the question of address and problematizing the listening (as well as viewing) formation that one can start to understand how translation works semiotically, affectively, and politically for the unintended and peripheral as well as intended addressees. This study sets into relief the translational interaction and friction between the enunciative act of the mainstream film and the nonnormative performative-spectatorial positions in the border-crossing power dynamic.

In this study, I first examine the power operation of translation (or the absence of translation) as a *visual episteme* (rather than simply a narrative device or a communicative practice) in two silent films: *The Toll of the Sea* (1922) and *Mr. Wu* (1927). In both silent films, the linguistic dimension is necessarily visualized as intertitles on title cards. Such visualized translation, or lack thereof, calls for a careful dissection of the cinematic techniques deployed to encourage preferred or dominant meaning production. After dissecting the ideological work of translation as a visual episteme, I then focus on the Chinese American performer Anna May Wong's performative mobilization of translation in *Mr. Wu* and later work. Contrary to the ways in which the films' preferred meaning-making system affects, addresses, and sutures the audience, I argue that Wong's double-register address to her audiences speaks to them differently, as if from both sides of the sieve, which in turn enables audiences to relate to her through different political dynamics. Such an address does not necessarily undermine Hollywood's hegemonic power. In fact, it might even play into Hollywood's desire to expand its international market. However, my study demonstrates that such complicity is hardly a done deal, and that its doubleness inevitably introduces unexpected discordance into the field of semiotic translation and affective transmission.

PHYSIOGNOMY OF THE COUNTERFEIT SCRIPT

In view of the shared "Oriental" narrative of a doomed interracial relationship in *The Toll of the Sea* and *Mr. Wu*, linguistic translation necessarily plays an important role in positing the racialized Other, and in managing the Self-Other relationship. My central concern, however, is not how translation tends to mistranslate or misrepresent the Other; that argument has been well-rehearsed since Said's original theorization of Orientalism. Rather, through the lens of visualized translation or non-translation, I argue that the Other is phantasmatic to begin with, and that visualized translation helps to create an illusion of the existence of the Other and the Other's "original" language, only then to repress them once again. To put it differently, the "original" Other language in visualized translation does not necessarily exist, or is used in a nonsensical manner (as demonstrated in the cases of Psalmanazar and *The Cat's Paw*).

The counterfeit script, as presented in *The Toll of the Sea* and *Mr. Wu*, can be understood as the linguistic counterpart to yellowface casting. It constitutes a form of scriptural yellowface. Béla Balázs implies the continuity between the script and the actor's visage in silent cinema in his theorization of "physiognomy." He takes note of "the emotional effect" of the spoken word as "indicated in the written word by the shape and weight of the lettering." Thus, according to Balázs, "Those who remember the titling of silent films may also remember that excitement, tension, weariness, despair or passion were *made visible in the forms of lettering*, in the expressive black-and-white of the titles."[13] The visualization of emotions through lettering in the intertitles forms the physiognomy of the script, as if the characters' psychosomatic states inevitably seep into the lettering. As he describes, "The physiognomy of the pictures had to be continued in the *physiognomy of the lettering*, in order to preserve the *visual continuity of atmosphere*."[14] Balázs associates such emotional lettering that deemphasizes objective images with abstract film.

In my analysis of visualized translation in *The Toll of the Sea* and *Mr. Wu*, I emphasize the political ramifications of scriptural physiognomy as a visual episteme. I use the notion of physiognomy to highlight the shared make-believe visuality between the counterfeit script and yellowface makeup, both of which stem from the entrenched colonial power disparity. Yet, they also open up an opportunity for the unintended or peripheral audience with a bilingual and bicultural background to challenge the hegemonic white authorship and translation of the Other.

In his essay "Global English Ideography and the Dissolve Translation in Hollywood Film," R. John Williams argues that dissolve translation facilitated the universalization of English as "global English"; the way it called attention to itself as an act of translation taking place outside the diegesis led to a disruptive experience, rupturing the diegetic illusion for the audience, which in turn led to the demise of this practice after the 1940s. This argument persuasively unpacks the meta-cinematic quality and alienation effect of dissolve translation. However, Williams ignores an important element; that is, for the audience who understand both the source language and the translation, the feeling of alienation already sets in with the first title card that precedes the translation montages, and is supposedly the source language. This alienation effect is not necessarily associated with the meta-cinematic insertion of the title card, or the extradiegetic translation of the aural into the visual. Rather, it is oftentimes triggered by the simple fact that the purported source script is no more than a counterfeit script; or there is absolutely no connection between the source script and the supposed translation in the following title. In recognizing the misplaced translation and disfigured scriptural physiognomy, the bilingual, bicultural audience encounters a make-believe game that can simultaneously repulse, alienate, and amuse them, while leaving the unsuspecting monolingual audience duped, yet safely protected behind the English intertitles that mesh perfectly with the colonialist narrative.[15]

Anna May Wong, the most recognized early twentieth-century Chinese American actress, played the female protagonist (a Madame Butterfly character) in *The Toll of the Sea* and a supporting maid in *Mr. Wu*. Her physical looks were harnessed to authenticate the Chinese themes, especially in *Mr. Wu* where the lead roles were played in yellowface by Lon Chaney and the French émigré actress Renée Adorée, in a make-believe Chinese garden designed by the MGM art director Cedric Gibbons (with the advice of a Chinese director, Moon Kwan, who happened to be touring a film in the United States and was recommended by Wong to MGM as a consultant). Like Wong's Chinese looks and the Chinese garden look-alike, the "Chinese" script was deployed to round out a conventional Orientalist fantasy for the white audience.

In *The Toll of the Sea*, the counterfeit script mimics the supposed picturesque look of Chinese ideograms. It is also presented vertically in two equal-length lines, suggesting the genre of Chinese couplet that is frequently inserted into classic poetry, or pasted on the two leaves of the front gate at the beginning of the Lunar New Year. Despite these "Chinese" visual cues, the script per se is sheer make believe, with no actual Chinese referent or any meaning. In other words, the counterfeit script serves simply to pictorialize phantasmatic Chineseness to the non-Chinese-speaking audience. As Balázs might argue, the "foreign" language exists as "non-verbal speech landscapes," encouraging the spectator to perceive the for-

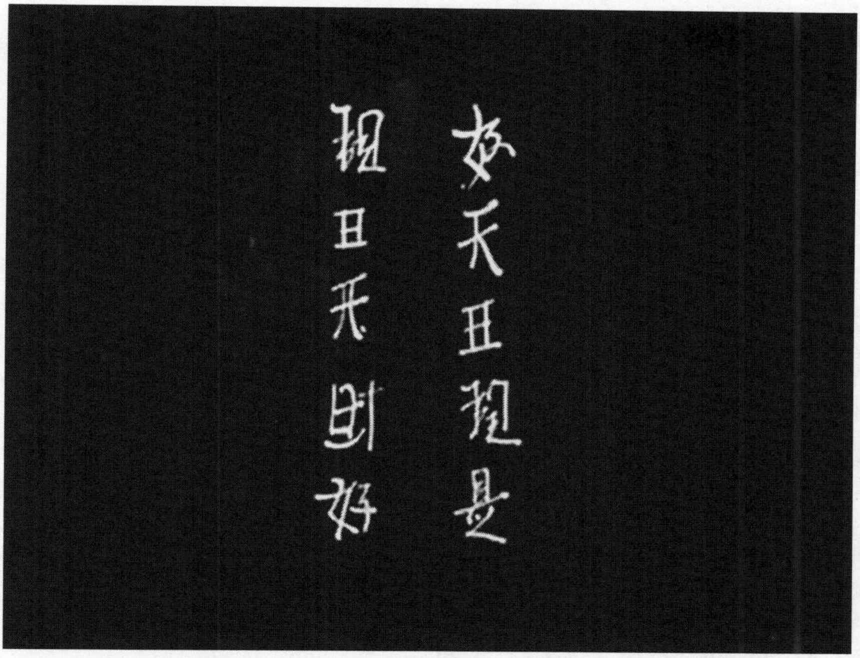

FIGURE 7.1 (Image from *The Toll of the Sea*. Directed by Chester M. Franklin. Los Angeles: Metro Pictures, 1922)

eign language as unintelligible, yet innocuous exotic foreignness.[16] To the extent that the script is associated with Chinese writing only through presumption, rather than actual connection, the script exists as an icon in the Peircian sense, its phantasmatic physiognomy resembling visual yellowface that presents an iconic "Oriental" image in place of an actual Asian actor or character (see Figure 7.1).

Given the counterfeit nature of the "original" script and its utter lack of a referent and meaning, the following English intertitle ("We're happy to observe the day is pleasant"), which poses as a translation, is actually non sequitur. Yet, it is also not just an empty gesture. As R. *John W*illiams argues, this "dissolve translation" manifested "Hollywood's mission to bring 'other' voices to its American monolingual audiences."[17] Robert Stam calls this practice a discourse of "pseudo-polyphony," which "marginalizes and disempowers certain voices, and then pretends to undertake a dialogue with a puppet-like entity that has already been forced to make crucial compromises."[18] Thus, dissolve translation is complicit with Hollywood's hegemony in rendering differences digestible, assimilable, yet also irrelevant.

In Mr. Wu, we find similar counterfeit "Chinese" script, with the significant difference that no translation is provided. This counterfeit script is used to indicate the dialogue between Renée Adorée as a Chinese Mandarin's daughter,

Nang Ping, and Anna May Wong as the maid, Loo Song. During their gestural and "linguistic" interaction, Gregory, the white Englishman who is courting Nang Ping, expresses confusion and frustration with being left out of the conversation. In response, Nang Ping makes a teasing comment, shown in an English title card, "If only you could understand my language," then turns to Loo Song in another English title card, "We understand him very well, don't we?" Aside from the two English lines, all communication between Nang Ping and Loo Song is written in the counterfeit script that is a purely picturesque nonverbal speech landscape (à la Balázs). To the extent that the foreign/Western spectator (Gregory) is literally excluded from the conversation, the omission of translation of the counterfeit script simulates his frustration with the impenetrable and untranslatable Other. To use Balázs's terminology again, the counterfeit script affects the viewer with its physiognomy suggestive of mood and emotions, but not semiotics. In a more critical vein, yet sharing Balázs's emphasis on the script's intransitive and abstract nature, Williams calls the counterfeit script "Chinese chatter" with no reference to Chinese characters: "it is the representation of the characters as exploding that carries meaning, that is, as a reflection of Wong's exasperation with her mistress."[19] The linguistic Otherness is thus reified through its reduction to an ornamental form, depleted of content.

Within the broader context of the film, however, the ornamental Chinese chatter takes an unexpected twist that reveals its inadequacy and irony all at once. These are the moments when the ethnic Chinese actress, Anna May Wong, makes a surprising eruption into the foreground, transcending her supporting role as the maid. This eruption points out the limitations of simple criticism of Orientalist stereotypes, while highlighting the complexity of the extradiegetic as well as diegetic language manipulation. In the above-described sequence, the linguistic difference takes place purely on the textual level in the physiognomy of the intertitles. The illusion of a Chinese dialogue, created through the counterfeit script, presents visual illegibility matched with its supposed aural unintelligibility. It is in sharing the impenetrable foreign physiognomy of the counterfeit script that Nang Ping and Loo Song—the inscrutable Orientals in the diegesis—form an exclusive bond.

However, this exclusive bond is make believe, just like the counterfeit script. In the extradiegetic realm, due to Wong's inadequate Chinese ability and Adorée's complete lack of it, they most certainly would have spoken English to each other (just like Ralph Forbes who played Gregory), despite Lotta Wood's dialogue script that specified that the maid and the mistress should speak Chinese. To the extent that they all spoke English extradiegetically, there was no language barrier among the three performers, or special lingua-cultural bonding between Adorée and Wong. In this light, Adorée's lines—"If only you could understand my language" and "We understand him very well, don't we?"—become necessarily ironic. On the one hand, it can be understood as an insider's joke on the make-believe Chinese script/dialogue (i.e., the one-sided, incommutable understanding never really happened on the set thanks to the absence of a non-English-speaking Other). On the broader systemic level, however, these lines hint at a foreignness right on the edge of Hollywood's "global English." Its existence is intractable and irreducible, even when it takes the trivialized form of exotic counterfeit script, or "pseudo-polyphony."

Given the racial and colonial politics subtending Hollywood productions, this foreignness was ultimately perceived as being embodied by Wong in the context of this film. Unlike Adorée who expediently yellowfaced a Mandarin's daughter without compromising her white French heritage, Wong was perceived as a permanent foreigner by dint of her Chinese heritage (even though popular media readily hyped her modern girl/flapper image in life). As argued previously, her casting as the maid was intended to authenticate the Chinese theme and mise-en-scène of this film. This is demonstrated in the film's publicity that showed Wong teaching Adorée how to use chopsticks the Chinese way.[20]

Given's Wong's perceived foreign status, the teasing comments by Adorée's Chinese mistress—"If only you could understand my language" and "We understand him very well, don't we?"—would have been more appropriately articulated by Wong, a minority actress always typecast as an exotic, enigmatic Other in Hollywood films. On a deeper level, what frustrated the dominant white industry and market's ability to understand her was her *composite* identity, which derived from Orientalist reification of her Chinese heritage, combined with her active flaunting of modern American femininity (as suggested by her flapper image). The meeting of the twain (the East and the West), judged to be impossible (according to Rudyard Kipling) or mind-boggling, caused an epistemological crisis, which pushed and exceeded the limit of Orientalist, essentialist cognition.[21] Wong's composite identity rendered her untranslatable to the dominant white industry and audience because Euro-American centrism forestalled any genuine engagement with her complex Self-Other symbiosis. Consequently, Wong's Chinese linguistic and cultural heritage was simultaneously capitalized on and quarantined in the margins and the background. Her career was ironically premised upon the industry's failure to understand her, therefore creating emblematic Orientalist situations (both diegetic and extradiegetic) where she could only wish "you could understand my language" (the "language" here going beyond just linguistic communication), while she could "understand [her white colleagues and audience] very well."

Signaling the asymmetrical and incommutable premise in the intercultural and interracial relationship, these lines virtually flipped into a self-irony performed by the mainstream film industry (unintentional as it may be). It satirized the industry's inherent logic of marginalization and exclusion, coupled with consumption of the perceived Other. However, when voiced by Adorée—the white performer—these lines simply constituted a tongue-in-cheek joke. It takes an ethnic Chinese actress like Wong, who was coded and excluded as a permanent foreigner, to actually bring out the irony of these lines (even if unintended by the original film). The thorny issue of translation is thus shown to be a conundrum in at least three ways. First, it is unnecessary to the extent that the entire cast actually spoke English in making the film, and the film participated in promoting what Williams calls the "global English." Yet, it is also obviated and impossible since any foreignness or differences are already reduced to mere unintelligible, tokenized, picturesque icons. Ultimately, however, translation is intractable given Wong's conspicuous, composite visibility that is read differently by different audiences. In other words, the conundrum of translation becomes coterminous with the conundrum of Wong's composite identity, both of which were produced by the epistemological framework premised upon the entrenched colonialist, racial, and gender power inequity.

Perceived as a conundrum, Wong mobilized this status as an opportunity to erupt into the foreground despite her supporting maid role, thereby to defy the stereotypical tokenizing casting. She accomplished this by edging out intertitles with pantomime, thereby replacing the impenetrable linguistic Otherness (i.e., the counterfeit script literally put into her mouth through the silent cinema technique of intertitle insertion) with the more legible bodily performance. This is demonstrated in a later scene that completely disposes of language (including the pulsating counterfeit script). In this sequence, Loo Song desperately warns Nang Ping of her xenophobic father Mr. Wu's arrival during her last tryst with Gregory. Here the communication between the two women is rendered completely visually through close-ups of their intense facial expressions and body gestures, without recourse to the counterfeit script. The rapid cross-cutting between Loo Song, Nang Ping, and the approaching Mr. Wu leaves no space for inserting intertitles, leading the audience to exclusively focus on the characters and actors' bodily performance. It is in highlighting the intense visual, embodied performance that Nang Ping (Renée Adorée) and Loo Song (Anna May Wong) receive equitable camera attention, enabling us to recognize and examine Wong's laborious efforts to portray the maid with a vivacious presence that challenges simple criticism of her stereotypical casting. In this sequence, Wong's facial and bodily performance registers a gamut of emotions that far exceed her role as a maid. Her intense acting (perhaps overacting, given her supporting role) makes her an active interlocutor intervening in the white actors' make-believe, yellowface interracial romance. Wong's emotional acting coupled with her nonwhite identity enable her to usurp the emotions of Adorée's role that more properly befit her, for the doomed interracial romantic scenario was a situation Wong (not Adorée) had to constantly battle extradiegetically as well as diegetically. Wong thus *vicariously* plays the doomed female protagonist caught in the anti-miscegenation quandary. Despite her marginalized role, Wong foregrounds the problematic politics of intercultural and interlingual translation and communication by strategically performing her "foreign" power in a legible physical idiom.

My emphasis on Wong's performative disruption of *Mr. Wu*'s manifest Orientalist fantasy and yellowface casting by no means presumes Wong's individualist free will and agency. It goes without saying that Wong, as a marginalized minority actress, had to largely operate within Hollywood's confines (which was to fill a supporting role scripted without her consent or input). Her lines and screen time also hardly ever reflected her intervention in the creative process. Nonetheless, to the extent that she was arguably the most prominent Chinese American actress, and had received much media attention and curiosity since the early 1920s, it is not surprising that her "Oriental" presence was much fetishized on the screen and the correlated star(let) discourse. A case in point is Todd Browning's silent film *Outside the Law* (1921), in which Wong plays an uncredited Chinese girl. A mere extra, she nonetheless received a major frontal close-up in which she visibly delivers a line even though it does not get translated into an intertitle. The paradox of being uncredited on the one hand and being spotlighted on the other emblematizes Wong's curious position in Hollywood entertainment. Arguably, her simultaneous invisibility and hypervisibility affords a liminal space analogous with the sieve of translation, discussed above, in that it represents the power structure without taking it as the final word, and it makes possible negotiation and agency without guaranteeing their realization. It is precisely in this liminal space, working with the sieve of translation, that Wong could stake her disruptive presence through versatile performance, in spite of the film's structural erasure of her. This is what I call her paradoxical agency.

I have argued that Wong's performance presents a self-conscious "foreign" text that orchestrates its linguistic and visual physiognomy so as to compel, channel, and defy translation all at once. She repurposes translation as a versatile sieve that on the one side dupes the non-Chinese-speaking white audience and, on the other side, affords bilingual and bicultural film workers (like herself) and viewers the ability to see not only the manifest filmic representation, but also its obverse seams. To understand exactly how Wong's ironic performance in the liminal screen space generates new channels, strategies, and political efficacy of translation, we must examine her multifaceted relationship with her transnational audiences. Recalling Shohat and Stam's "question of audience address," and Christopher Faulkner's provocative emphasis on the departures from the normative "listening formations," I examine the possible ways in which the audiences respond to Wong's "audience address" when she ostensibly fills in the prescribed "Oriental" roles.

WONG'S DOUBLE-REGISTER AUDIENCE ADDRESS

In the light of Wong's composite identity and interstitial position outlined previously, I argue that when Wong adopted a Chinese stance in addressing her audience, she did not unproblematically identify with Chineseness (however defined), but rather deployed the stance as a strategic position of enunciation, and a performative identity that provisionally laid claim to what Spivak calls "strategic essentialism." This performative identity was especially pronounced when she seemingly spoke as a "native informant" and a translator of her "native" culture.

Like the white colonialist who pretended to play both the author and the translator of another language and culture (as illustrated in the cases of Psalmanazar and white characters in Hollywood productions), Wong performed an authority claim in her act of authorship and translation. The purpose, however, was very different. For Wong, authority claims based on her performative embodiment of the "native informant" fulfilled two functions. For the naïve audience, her authority claims were understood to derive from and reaffirm her authentic "Chineseness," which also constituted the raison d'être of her paradoxical tokenizing inclusion in and ultimate exclusion from the film industry. For the audience who shared or came to share her bicultural knowledge and experience of the lopsided race and gender politics, however, her translation and authority claims suggested an audacity to perform, even to forge (in the sense of producing *and* faking) a version of "Chineseness." The purpose of this performance was not to mimetically represent Chinese identity, nor to simply create another "China" myth (as the white colonialists had been doing), but rather to question the divide between authenticity and forgery. Thus, she contributed to producing a polemic and a counterhegemonic meaning-value (à la Lydia Liu) for "Chineseness" as it continued to be entangled in the global circulation of cultural-political icons.

One example illustrating Wong's double-register audience address is her 1930 essay, titled "The Chinese Are Misunderstood," in which she assumed the role of a Chinese cultural diplomat and a translator. Here she negated all Western understandings of the Chinese, and instead described the Chinese as pleasure-seeking, relaxed, intensely emotional, trustworthy, and respectful.[22] This essay may easily lead us to take for granted Wong's Chinese identity. It almost reads like her following up the line "If only you could understand my language" with an offer: "Let me translate my language into yours." Nevertheless, it is important to note that the role she performed in this essay was not simply a native Chinese informant imparting an accurate image of the Chinese people. Rather, her portrayal or translation of the Chinese character was counterposed to the Western image of the Chinese. One may even argue that she constructed the Chinese image in reaction to the Western hegemonic imaginary. Assuming the role of author-producer of the counterhegemonic meaning-value and cultural translator of Chineseness, she derived her authority claim from her interstitial position, her composite identity and the correlated dual perspective, rather than her Chinese heritage. Armed with the dual perspective, and negotiating the treachery and possibility of translation and mediation, she produced and translated a meaning-value of "Chineseness" that contested the Euro-American Orientalist imaginary while inviting Euro-American readers or audiences to a fresh engagement with the Chinese character.

Wong's act of translation also occurred frequently in her stage performance and short films where she performed in multiple languages (including German, French, Swedish, Italian, Yiddish, and her ancestral Taishan dialect, as well as English with a British accent), showcasing her linguistic cosmopolitanism. Yet, she did not simply enact a linguistic bricolage, but also skillfully played the languages with and against each other so as to maximize her appeal to the transnational and cross-racial/ethnic audiences and, more importantly, to address them in different registers with divergent messages. This was illustrated in a short film, *Hollywood Party in Technicolor* (dir. Roy Rowland, 1937), produced by Louis Lewyn Productions and distributed by MGM. Like *Mr. Wu*, this short film is an unapologetic extravaganza of yellowface performance, with the entire Caucasian cast enacting a mishmash Orientalia amid a plethora of Oriental motifs, this time supposedly representing an East Asian tea party. Wong, again, is the most prominent nonwhite performer in the show, participating in and ostensibly authenticating and endorsing the Orientalist fanfare. Upon being introduced in the middle of the film as "China lady of fashion" by a Fu Manchu look-alike (played by Charley Chase), Wong is revealed behind bamboo blinds, modeling new fashions she recently acquired during her 1936 China trip. With each dress change, the blinds are opened by a purple-clad Chinese woman at the gong signal sent by a green-dressed Chinese woman. Then Wong speaks to the camera/audience, across the blinds, highlighting the texture and (most likely fictionalized) imperial history of each dress.

In the film, Wong assumes the task of introducing and promoting modern Chinese female fashions to the West, in a manner similar to the role she adopted in "The Chinese Are Misunderstood." Directly addressing the camera, and by extension the presumably white audience, she shares with them her firsthand experience in modern China, making them privy to what she has learned (such as the symbolic meanings of the colors and fabric of the dresses). Contrary to the flapper image of her earlier career, she now performs and embodies her newfound Chinese identity. Her performative translation/mediation of Chineseness is further foregrounded in her speech. Freed from the counterfeit script put into her mouth (as in *Mr. Wu*), she addresses her American audience in British English, using the broad "a" and dropped "r" in words like "smart" to assert her cosmopolitan sophistication. Her accurate rendition of the upper-class sociolect sets her co-player Charley Chase's Fu Manchu-esque fake Chinese accent (or what I call the yellowface accent) into comic relief. Yet, in the midflow of the King's English, Wong abruptly turns to the green-clad Chinese woman and asks a question in Chinese. The woman answers in idiomatic American English, "I'm sorry, but I only understand Cantonese." Wong turns to the audience with a wink, a smile, and a quip, "Oh, I thought I could brush up my Mandarin." Then, without missing a beat, she resumes her description of the dragon dress in the King's English.

To the white audience that does not speak Chinese, Wong's brief untranslated Chinese "aside" dishes up another unintelligible, exotic, nonverbal speech landscape. In that sense, it is no different from the impenetrable counterfeit script to the Western eye. The irony, however, is that her "Chinese" remains equally unintelligible even to her "fellow Chinese." This failed connection deconstructs the make-believe bond based on a shared foreign language that is taken for granted in *Mr. Wu* between Adorée's mistress and Wong's maid. Indeed, the very expectation of such an easy bond is mocked as a myth, a wishful reduction and homogenization of Chinese consanguinity. With this missed connection, Wong introduces to her American audience the heterogeneity of Chineseness, composed of multiple lingua-regional cultures and geopolitics, including the tension between Cantonese and Mandarin Chinese. Such heterogeneity and tension undermine the Orientalist myth of a reified uniform China. Thus, skipping translating her purported Mandarin line for her countrywoman, and instead switching between accented Chinese and the King's English, Wong highlights differences within Chinese and within English. She plays these two languages and their internal differences against each other, *and* against the addressees' different listening formations. As a result, she teases out the complexity (including the ever-present breakdown) of interlingual and intralingual translation.

Furthermore, the intralingual communicative breakdown (as suggested by the green-clad woman's failure to understand Wong's Mandarin) is *staged* so that Wong could orchestrate a game of identity and power play in response to the political circumstances in 1937 and to Hollywood's changing approach to China-themed films starting around the mid-1930s. When the green-clad woman self-identifies her "Cantonese" background, and indicates her inability to understand Wong's Chinese aside, this staged miscommunication allows Wong to highlight her Mandarin skills, recently acquired during her trip to China (along with the Chinese dresses). Her emphasis on the new linguistic skill responds to two specific sets of circumstances. The first concerned the emerging U.S.-China alliance following the eruption of the Second Sino-Japanese War in July 1937. In building the alliance, the governing Chinese Nationalist Party's generalissimo Chiang Kai-shek and Madame Chiang made frequent trips to the United States to promote the image of modern China and to step up the war-relief fund-raising campaigns. One consequence of this national-image promotion was the denigration of Chinese immigrants from southern China and their descendants in the United States (like Wong) as less educated, retrogressive, and incapable of representing modern China. In place of their ancestral southern dialects, including Cantonese, Mandarin Chinese was promoted as the language of modern China.

The second set of circumstances pertained to Hollywood's changing attitude toward China and ethnic Chinese performers. As the Chinese government became increasingly vocal in resisting Western—especially Hollywood—"China-humiliating" films, as illustrated in the 1930 protest against Lloyd's *Welcome Dan-*

ger referenced earlier, it also more actively contributed to shaping Hollywood's production of China-themed films. The most salient example was MGM's mega-production *The Good Earth* (dir. Sidney Franklin, 1937), adapted from Pearl S. Buck's award-winning novel, which narrates a Chinese farmer family's saga through severe drought and political turmoil. The Chinese government's intervention in shaping the film was laboriously documented and has been studied in detail. The only requirement that the government initially stipulated in the agreement with MGM, but ultimately relented on, was the demand for a Chinese cast; Paul Muni and Luise Rainer played the leading Chinese farmer couple in yellowface. The film scored a huge success, winning Rainer a second best actress Academy Award.

The underside of the Sino-Hollywood collaboration in making *The Good Earth* was the elimination of Anna May Wong, whose vigorous lobby for the female protagonist role (Muni's wife) failed. She did audition for the role of Muni's concubine, but the MGM records of her audition indicated that she was considered not attractive enough to be convincingly seductive; the role went to the Austria-Hungary-born Tilly Losch. The reasons for Wong's exclusion from this high-profile film were complex. Historian Karen Leung refers to Madame Chiang's directive for MGM to not use Wong due to her scandalous reputation in China for portraying hypersexualized, low-class Chinese female characters.[23] In other words, Wong's self-Orientalism, tailored for the Hollywood appetite, was deemed "out of style"[24] by the mid-1930s as Hollywood sought to appease the Chinese government with more politically correct Chinese depictions.

In light of the shifting configuration of Sino-U.S. political and filmic interactions, Wong's self-claimed adoption of Mandarin Chinese registered her bid for modern Chineseness in defiance of both Hollywood and the Chinese government's denigration of her based on her racial/ethnic identity, linguistic heritage, and educational background. That the short film *Hollywood Party* was distributed by MGM in April, merely three months after the studio's release of *The Good Earth*, was suggestive of Wong's desire to harness the film as her own stage to perform her newfound alignment with modern China. As inconsequential as *Hollywood Party* was relative to *The Good Earth*, Wong managed to use it to speak back to MGM's exclusion of her from *The Good Earth* by revalorizing and upgrading her "Chinese" identity. She attempted this through linguistic makeover—from her ancestral Taishan dialect to Mandarin Chinese, from the regional to the national, and furthermore, from the old to the new.

And yet, despite her desire to realign herself with Chiang Kai-shek's China, Wong's display of the new identity promoted by the Chinese government must be understood as a tongue-in-cheek strategy couched in the form of an inside joke. The green-clad woman was complicit in co-staging this identity display, for they both must recognize that Wong's proclaimed Mandarin line was not really Mandarin, but something closer to her Taishan dialect—a distinction easily lost on her white audience. To the Chinese ear, Wong's failed attempt at Mandarin could be simply due to her lack of proficiency. However, the fact that she and the green-clad woman co-staged a seamless drama of Mandarin versus Cantonese, while maintaining them both as an unintelligible "speech landscape" to the foreign ear, points to the two sides of the lingual sieve. The code-switching game was less a demonstration of Wong's true multilingual proficiency than a staging of her versatile identity performance in response to the shifting configurations of the Sino-U.S. national-regional power struggle. Instead of subscribing to the Chinese government's self-righteous image of modernity, Wong's professed desire to acquire Mandarin Chinese was meant to pay a kind of lip service to this "new" Chinese image. Given her dual-register address to her audience of different backgrounds, Wong's Chinese aside constituted a make-believe performance, one that took advantage of the ambivalent meaning-value of the quasi-Mandarin speech, taken at face value by some, yet recognized as a charade by others, so as to open up axes of multiple potentially contradictory interpretations, interactions, and alliances.

ACTOR-SPECTATOR COMPLICITY

In the above analysis of counterfeit script, quasi-Mandarin speech, make-believe translation, and orchestrated code-switching without translation, I focus on the physiognomy of language (both the script and the speech), and examine the ways in which it is deployed and performed to generate different meaning-values, both by a mainstream industry like Hollywood and by marginalized film performers such as Wong. My concern is not to judge which meaning-value is authentic and good, and which is fake and bad, but rather to delineate what kind of performative processes and audience addresses are involved in generating such meaning-values and with what political ramifications, and how they impinge upon each other. A crucial set of questions in generating meaning-values and political ramifications focus on audience address and engagement: which audience is addressed; how the audience is addressed (when audiences of different backgrounds are involved, how they are addressed differently); and what processes of translation and mediation are involved in addressing the audience. My analysis demonstrates that the physiognomy of language functions as a sieve; its visual (il)legibility and vocal (un)intelligibility are orchestrated by processes of translation and mediation to suggest different meanings for audiences with different backgrounds and knowledge. This sifting mechanism in turn instigates different configurations of actor-viewer relationships.[25]

In the cases I am discussing here, audiences assume different degrees of agency in relation to the diegesis and the performance. Some remain on the manifest side of the sieve, blocked and duped by the impenetrable physiognomy of language. They comply with what Christopher Faulkner calls the normative listening formations and viewing formations, deriving pleasure from the film's face-value Orientalia. Others find the physiognomy of language shot through with holes (both meaningless and meaning laden), propelling them to shuttle back and forth between the manifest side and the underside, simultaneously engaging and disengaging with multiple, even contradictory modes of address. For these viewers who are likely bilingual and bicultural, the liminality between legibility and its failure takes on special significance not simply because it pushes the envelope of semantic communication, making their bilingual ability a vantage point but, more importantly, the liminality exposes the film as emphatically a film, that is, a performative and make-believe construct of the Other, the Self, and their shifting relationality, rather than a straightforward representation of authenticity. Thus, this liminality instigates audience address and performer-viewer interactions unintended by the manifest film, which imbue the counterfeit script, the quasi-speech, and the make-believe translation (or non-translation) with new meaning-values and alternative interactive and affective meaning-making processes.

Importantly, such performer-viewer interactions hinge upon translation, transcoding, and orchestration of the liminal space between legibility/intelligibility and its failure. In this light, the drive toward a "universal language" attributed to silent cinema is always haunted by the failure to be universal and the resurfacing of the thorny issue of translation and its breakdown. As it traveled and seeped into all corners of the world, ostensibly demonstrating the irresistible legibility of the modern idiom of moving image, silent cinema also simultaneously intertwined with questions of audience address, situated engagement, detoured intentions, and generation of new meaning-values and relations. By studying the implicit and explicit translation work performed by Wong in the mainstream American film industry, I move beyond the well-rehearsed ideological criticism that demystifies the counterfeit script and make-believe translation as nothing but Orientalist monopoly over the interpretation of the Other. I emphasize the ways in which Wong countered or mobilized the counterfeit script, quasi-Mandarin speech, and make-believe translation (or non-translation) to fashion a double-registered address to speak differentially to audiences with different preknowledge.

This is a labor-intensive undertaking for both Wong and her complicit spectators, and it has no guaranteed of success, in terms of becoming visible or recognized by the dominant system. As Danae Clark argues, performers and viewers "are 'film workers' who perform specific labors in relation to the cinema."[26] They come to "occupy similar positions and to experience similar struggles in terms of labor power and subject identity" due to their navigation of "politicized space of cultural practices," including cinema. In this process, they "form alliances that are vastly different from the narrow star (as object)-viewer (as subject) relation posited by mainstream film studies. Here the star/actor signifies a positionality and rallying point for matters of cultural resistance that are inflected by, but go beyond, the industrial context of Hollywood entertainment."[27] Clark's emphasis on the process of building a shared positionality and political alliance between the actor and the viewer is especially instructive for our understanding of the significance of Wong's laborious, double-registered audience address. It suggests the possibility of evoking and cultivating collaborative audiences across space and historical periods (even if such audiences did not exist in her time).

One reason mainstream Hollywood productions remain valuable is precisely that their ostensible "errors" are ripe not only for deconstruction but, more importantly, for retranslation from previously marginalized perspectives. By recognizing these perspectives and their facilitation of the diachronic actor-viewer alliance, we come to see how Hollywood films' counterfeit script and mistranslation (or missed translation) meet resistance or become detoured through minority performers and viewers' negotiative and translational practices as analyzed above.

In delineating the labor-intensive and situated agency that the bilingual, bicultural performer and viewer exercise in cocreating, encoding and decoding the physiognomy of language and translation, I also reflect upon my own position and agency as a bilingual, bicultural film viewer-critic with a specific gendered, raced, and class identity. I challenge the oversimplified "native informant" paradigm that ultimately supports the binary of misrepresentation versus authentic representation by simply separating the true from the false. I strive to deploy my bilingual and bicultural ability beyond mere positivist, empirical knowledge to actually underscore the importance of active mediation and translation in producing new meaning-values, feelings, positions, and politics. Ultimately, I mobilize my situated encounter with the above-analyzed films and with Anna May Wong to position film as fundamentally a translation device that works like a sieve to afford different entry points and meaning-makings for different viewers. This understanding veers away from a judgmental evaluation of Hollywood cinema, and instead refocuses upon this popular medium's intertwinement with linguistic and cultural translation in the process of constructing the Self and the Other. Both the film medium and lingua-cultural translation turn upon the underlying power dynamic between different parties involved, which leads to a process of constant shifting and negotiation.

In my analysis, the viewer's lingua-cultural knowledge and positioning function as a platform that interfaces with the film dispositif on the one hand, and with a performer's audience address on the other. The triangulated interaction then channels the viewer's mediation of the film, whether complying with the listening and viewing formations encouraged by the film dispositif, or departing from and derailing them. As a viewer-critic with my own specific platform, I have chosen to depart from the films' preferred listening and viewing formations, and to privilege ways of allying with the marginalized Anna May Wong, interacting with her double-registered modes of addressing her transnational audiences. Echoing her "Chinese aside," I trace sites of translation where the tongue forks into a different language, geared to a different listener, and implying a different set of listening/spectatorial relationship, where the script and speech jostle against the diegesis to become meta-cinematic, and where the very processes of meaning-making come under scrutiny and are thereupon reconfigured. These sites of translation oftentimes marshal an impenetrable physiognomy of language, not to reenact the Orientalist monolingualism (as Williams might argue), but to instigate a desire to understand the Other by departing from the significatory freeway and taking a detour through the "aside" and through subterranean pathways. It is in this process that the ostensible "non-verbal speech [and scriptural] landscapes" exceed words to stimulate situated relations, meaning-values, sentiments, and political articulations. This is also the starting point to reconfigure the power dynamic underlying the film medium and lingua-cultural translation.

NOTES

I would like to thank the editors for their thought-provoking suggestions and meticulous editing. All errors that might still remain are my sole responsibility.

1. George Psalmanazar, *Memoirs of ****, Commonly Known by the Name of George Psalmanazar; a Reputed Native of Formosa,* (London: Davis, 1764), 5.
2. Lydia H. Liu, ed., "The Question of Meaning-Value in the Political Economy of the Sign," in *Tokens of Exchange: The Problem of Translation in Global Circulations* (Durham, N.C.: Duke University Press, 2000), 13–44, see 15.
3. Jack Lynch, "Forgery as Performance Art: The Strange Case of George Psalmanazar," in *1650–1850: Ideas, Aesthetics, and Inquiries in the Early Modern Era* 10 (2005): 21–35.
4. Liu, "Question of Meaning-Value," 18.
5. Ibid., 18.
6. *Photoplay Magazine* 46–47 (1934): 36–37, http://archive.org/stream/photo47chic#page/n303/mode/2up.
7. Ibid. Lloyd's courtship of the Chinese government was arguably prompted by the government's vehement campaign against his *Welcome Danger* in 1930, criticizing it for denigrating Chinese American characters in San Francisco's Chinatown and furthermore issuing an order to suspend not only this film but also all Paramount productions in China until Lloyd's formal apology. Importantly, this campaign coincided with the issuance of the Hays Code, which contained a section on National Feelings that specifically requested "fair" representation of the "history, institutions, prominent people and citizenry of other nations" (http://www.artsreformation.com/a001/hays-code.html). For a detailed analysis of and the cross-purposes manifested in the Sino-American filmic, economic, and political encounter, see Yiman Wang, "The Crisscrossed Stare: Protest and Propaganda in China's Not-So-silent Era," in *Silent Cinema and the Politics of Space,* eds. Jennifer Bean et al. (Bloomington: Indiana University Press, 2014), 186–209.
8. Ella Shohat and Robert Stam, *Unthinking Eurocentrism: Multiculturalism and the Media,* 2nd ed. (London: Routledge, 2014), 205.
9. Christopher Faulkner, "Rene Clair, Marcel Pagnol and the Social Dimension of Speech," *Screen* 35, no. 2 (1994): 157–170, see 165–166.
10. Ibid., 165–166.
11. Ibid., 165–166, emphases added.
12. Ibid., 166, emphases added.

13. Béla Balázs, *Theory of the Film (Character and Growth of a New Art)*, trans. Edith Bone (London: Dennis Dobson, 1952), 183, emphases added.
14. Ibid., 183, emphases added.
15. Here lies a key difference between yellowface casting and scriptural yellowface. Contrary to yellowface casting that is recognized by all viewers as the pure effect (or feat) of makeup and make believe, the counterfeit script most likely goes unnoticed by viewers who do not know the language. They are therefore duped into taking the dissolve translation at face value.
16. Béla Balázs, *Schriften zum Film. Band 2: "Der Geist des Films," Artikel und Aufsätze 1926–1931* (Munich: Carl Hanser Verlag, 1984), 165, quoted in Anna Sofia Rossholm, *Reproducing Languages, Translating Bodies. Approaches to Speech, Translation and Cultural Identity in Early European Sound Film* (Stockholm: Stockholm University, 2006), 65.
17. R. John Williams, "Global English Ideography and the Dissolve Translation in Hollywood Film," *Cultural Critiques* 71 (Spring 2009): 119.
18. Robert Stam, "Bakhtin, Polyphony, and Ethnic/Racial Representation," quoted in Williams, "Global English Ideography," 125.
19. Williams, "Global English Ideography," 106.
20. *Photoplay Magazine* 31, no. 2 (January 1927): 48.
21. In his "The Ballad of East and West," Rudyard Kipling opens with the famous statement, "Oh, East is East and West is West, and never the twain shall meet." In the following lines, he reveals that the only time when "neither East nor West, Border, nor Breed, nor Birth" matters is when "Earth and Sky stand presently at God's great Judgment Seat"—an image pointing to the end of history and time, i.e., beyond the limit of current epistemology.
22. Anna May Wong, "The Chinese Are Misunderstood, Says Anna May Wong," *Rexall Magazine* 7, no. 77 (May 1930): 3–4.
23. Karen J. Leung, *The China Mystique: Pearl S. Buck, Anna May Wong, Mayling Soong, and the Transformation of American Orientalism* (Oakland: University of California Press, 2005).
24. Ibid., 75.
25. While I focus on Wong's differentiated audience address geared toward audiences of different backgrounds, I do not mean that she was the one and only player in orchestrating the multiple channels of address, translation, and mediation. As one of the volume editors, Patrice Petro, points out, in the light of the Hollywood mission of expanding its international market, Hollywood producers undoubtedly seized the opportunity to plant non-English script and dialogue to not only cater to the mainstream audience's Orientalist fantasy but also appeal to foreign audiences who might identify with the included foreign languages. The key difference between Wong and Hollywood's deployment of differentiated audience address, however, is that Hollywood had full conviction that the included foreign language could appeal to the corresponding foreign audience with commercial gains (or it simply did not matter if the film was not to be marketed in that country). Wong, on the other hand, demonstrated that the face value of the foreign language was invariably skewed when encountered by the foreign, bi-/multilingual and oftentimes peripheral audience (whether intended or not). As a result, translation and communication were foregrounded as problematic (instead of being taken for granted). Such encounter and disfigured face value of the supposed foreign language were instrumental in generating unexpected feelings and modes of engagement, ranging from alienation, repulsion, and frustration to playful performance and resignification.
26. Danae Clark, *Negotiating Hollywood: The Cultural Politics of Actors' Labor* (Minneapolis: University of Minnesota Press, 1995), 122.
27. Ibid., 124.

PART 3 TRANSLATION'S PRACTICES AND POLITICS

8 • PERSPECTIVES ON TRANSLATION STUDIES IN LATIN AMERICA

MARTHA PULIDO
TRANSLATED BY LORENA TERANDO

If we ground ourselves in the Translation Studies Map designed in 1972 and published in 1975 by James Holmes, noting that 1975 marks the official birth of translation studies, then we can use that date as a point of departure for a reflection on translation studies in Latin America. At that point, scholars in the discipline took ownership of it and began to feel a sense of autonomy. This date also marks the point when the reflection on and practice of translation began to distance itself from the structural linguistics blueprints inherited from Saussure and developed, in the late 1950s and through the 1960s, in books that focused on equivalence (Vinay and Darbelnet 1958) or that demonstrated a preliminary, albeit timid, concern with the translator rather than just the text alone (Mounin 1963).

While Holmes's map is generally viewed as marking the birth of translation studies, the 1975 publication of George Steiner's *After Babel* was key to translation studies in Latin America. The book arrived in the Spanish- and Portuguese-speaking Americas even before its translation into Spanish or Portuguese.[1] In its second chapter, "Understanding as Translation," Steiner included an important intervention based on the hermeneutic movement: his book made the figure of the translator clearly visible.

In 1990, Susan Bassnett and André Lefevere published *Translation, History and Culture,* demonstrating that the singular concern for the text was not sufficient for the study of the phenomenon that is translation. Their book brought into relief how the historical and cultural contexts of source and target languages affect the translator's position with respect to his or her practice of translation and, by extension, the final product. This book was followed by the 1991 English translation of the book *Text Analysis in Translation* by Christiane Nord (heir to Katharina Reiss and Hans Vermeer). Extremely valuable pedagogically, this functionalist book presents the German translation studies concept of *Übersetzungswissenschaft*, which focuses on the process of translation from many pragmatic perspectives. It makes, however, no comment on history.

In 1994 Cátedra Editoriales in Madrid published one of the first anthologies of texts on translation, *Textos clásicos de teoría de la traducción*, by Miguel Ángel Vega. While it is written in Spanish and is clearly ethnocentric, it offers a panorama of translation studies in the French, German, Spanish, and Russian contexts, and it opened the way for other anthologies. The anthology required significant research, and is tremendously useful for translator training. It stands out for its lengthy introduction, in which Vega demonstrates how the discussion of translation was less productive in Europe in the nineteenth century, especially in its second half.[2] This was, according to Vega, because the focus of translation shifted from literary to pragmatic texts; translation ceased to be considered an art because scholars sought to consider it as science. The question of whether this epistemological shift resulted in loss or gain for translation as a practice and object of study has yet to be answered. In any case, as we read this book, the need for an anthology of translation studies in the Americas becomes obvious.[3] Other continents have shown us the way. We have China's *An Anthology of Chinese Discourse on Translation. Volume I: From Earliest Times to the Buddhist Project*, begun by Martha Cheung, whose untimely death left the project incomplete. Hopefully another scholar will take up her pen.

After two decades of searching for its own school of thought, translation studies had a very productive year in 1995. Jean Delisle and Judith Woodsworth published the monumental *Translators through History*, with its international and interlinguistic dynamism that began to respond to concerns about translation's relationship to history. The text is a continuous succession of translational acts, from the very writing of each one of its chapters to the fact that it appeared simultaneously in English and in French. In that same year, Lawrence Venuti published *The Translator's Invisibility* and thereby placed the translator squarely at the forefront of analysis. Antoine Berman's *Pour une critique des traductions* was published in France and marked both the historical/cultural turn in translation studies and the birth of translation criticism, with respect to which the field must still position itself. In these texts, the translator was placed front and center and acquired more significance than the text. This was also the year of Gideon Toury's *Descriptive Translation Studies and Beyond*. Toury used Even Zohar's polysystem theory as a springboard to make it clear that translation was active in constructing culture in the target polysystem. Since the appearance of Holmes's map, Toury had been questioning the concept of equivalence in a number of his articles; his work on descriptive translation studies distanced the broader field of translation studies from structural linguistics as a means to think about translation, much as Steiner's work did. Also in 1995, Mary Snell-Hornby's *Translation*

Studies: An Integrated Approach was published in its second edition (the first appeared in 1988). It introduced a translation studies perspective that is somewhere between *Übersetzungswissenschaft* and translation studies: *Translationswissenschaft*. For Snell-Hornby, Translationswissenschaft is a discipline that encompasses translation and interpreting in theory, practice, training, and research. It includes all aspects of language for specific purposes and some aspects of terminology, literary and audiovisual translation, conference interpreting, media interpreting, court interpreting, dialogue interpreting, and the interaction of all of these with other disciplines.[4]

There are many more authors and turns to discuss, but this chapter does not aim to give a historical account of translation theory. Rather, its goal is to situate Latin America in relation to the global context of the field of translation studies.

In recent years, translation studies has begun to look toward Latin America. To be specific, research published in Spain integrates the work of scholars from several regions in Latin America. Francisco Lafarga and Luis Pegenaute propose research projects, organize conferences, and publish the results and proceedings of these events in volumes like *Aspectos de la historia de la traducción en Hispanoamérica* and *Lengua, cultura y política en la historia de la traducción en Hispanoamérica*, both of which were published in 2012. Lafarga and Pegenaute also undertook the arduous task of coordinating the writing of the *Diccionario histórico de la traducción en Hispanoamérica* (2013) and launched the "Biblioteca de traducciones hispanoamericanas" (Cervantes Virtual).[5] Mexican scholar Nayelli Castro collected essays on translation studies in Latin America and published them in her *Traducción, identidad y nacionalismo en Latinoamérica*, also in 2013. Jana Kralova at Carolina University in Prague published a compilation of texts on translation theory, including Latin American texts, in 2015.[6] Finally, since its creation by Miguel Ángel Vega, the working group HISTRAD, subsequently known as MIHSTRAD, has focused a significant part of its research on the Americas, in particular on missionary translation.

This recent panorama, which is by no means exhaustive, demonstrates that translation studies focused on Latin America has been for the most part concerned with the history of translation, and is largely critical in nature.

While this section of the chapter also cannot cite every important work, those that are included illustrate the tendency toward working on translation studies history and criticism. This is clear in books like Patricia Wilson's *La constelación del sur, traductores y traducciones en la literatura argentina del siglo XX* (2004), which gathered reflections on translated and national literature, and allows us to consider translation from the very moment of the creation of the work that is to be translated. In Peru, Ricardo Silva Santiestebán has also demonstrated this tendency to build a history of translation; he compiled texts on translation theory in Peruvian translation in his "Breve historia de la traducción en el Perú" (2013). He has also undertaken the tremendous task of compiling texts for an *Antología general de la traducción en el Perú*, the publication of which is forthcoming from Universidad Ricardo Palma. Gertrudis Payas led an earlier project to compile and systematize information in the critical edition *Biblioteca chilena de traductores ordenada por J.T. Medina* (2007), which presents a valuable testimonial of the intellectual contacts that Chile established abroad from the time of the printing press, recording the foreign works—and their translators—that helped build its national culture.

Hungarian-born Brazilian Paolo Ronai published his translation experiences in Europe and in Brazil in his 1981 book *A tradução vivida*. Haroldo de Campos presented his position as translator in articles like "Transluciferação Mefistofaústica" (1981) and "Tradición, traducción, transculturación, historiografía y excentricidad" (2010).[7] Then, in 2008, four translations of Walter Benjamin's "Die Aufgabe des Übersetzers" (The Task of the Translator) into Portuguese were released, three of which were written in Brazil. The first was Fernando Camacho's version from 1962. To put this into perspective, Harry Zohn's English translation was not published until 1968.[8] That the first translation of Benjamin's work was done into Portuguese and in Brazil constitutes a significant event in Brazil's early translation studies scene. Germana Henriques Pereira de Sousa has contributed to scholarship on the relationship between translation and history with her recently edited book on *Historia de la traducción y traducción literaria* at Universidad de Brasilia (2015). Pereira de Sousa and Thiago André Veríssimo also edited *História e historiografía da tradução: Desafios para o século XXI* in 2016. The recent publication of "Múltiplos horizontes da tradução na América Latina" in the March 2018 issue of *Trabalhos de linguística aplicada* (UNICAMP) offers many perspectives on translation in Latin America.

The Graduate Program in Translation Studies at Universidad Federal de Santa Catarina supports this area of study up to the doctoral level, and publishes a great deal of scholarship, including annual translations authored by its faculty. A digital collection of those works is publicly available.[9] Recent highlights of publications include the book *Estudos da Língua Brasileira de Sinais III*, by Ronice Muller de Quadros and Markus Weininger (2014). The University of São Paulo now includes translation studies in "Research in the Humanities" and various projects are under way.[10]

At the very moment in the nineteenth century when critical thought on translation began to lose dynamism in Europe, it gained momentum in Colombia. This is true for all Latin American countries, as writers, politicians, and translators were leading intellectual thought and taking the reins of the countries that had recently won their independence. While they were not writing treatises on translation proper, their essays, introductions, prefaces, and other work demonstrate critical thought about translation that aligns with the ideologies that each of them professed. Translation studies scholars Juan Guillermo Ramírez and Paula Montoya at Universidad de Antioquia focus their research on the nineteenth century. Ramirez and Montoya have published a number of articles on the relationship between translation studies and history, and their work has begun staking out the position of translation studies to which I refer in this chapter.[11] I offer Colombia as an example because I know more about what is going on there, but this is happening in other Latin American countries, too. My hope is that this chapter serves as an invitation to further research and writing on the subject.

The discussion shifts from translation "is" to translation "as": translation *as* reflection that offers bits of information about the journeys of some of the languages we speak.[12] Ricardo del Molino García's 2007 book *Griegos y Romanos en la primera república colombiana: La antigüedad clásica en el pensamiento emancipador neogranadino (1810–1816)* is an example of a work that discusses the act of translation—visible or invisible—as an element that allows us to analyze aspects of a country's history. Jason McGraw's *The Work of Recognition: Caribbean Colombia and the Postemancipation Struggle for Citizenship* (2014) takes up the liberation of slaves between 1850 and 1910. McGraw's book recounts the history of Afro-Colombians seeking citizenship rights, and was inspired by the Black poet Candelario Obeso (b. Mompox, 1849). Obeso happens to be a translator of Shakespeare (*Othello*) and Victor Hugo,[13] and his poems are translated by McGraw as an epigraph. Both Del Molino García's and McGraw's histories, while they do not mention translation explicitly, can be understood only through the intellectual history of a Colombian elite that nourished its thought on works in translation, an elite that was itself a dedicated practitioner of translation. Translation as a conceptual tool to reflect on the construction of Colombia in the nineteenth century is explicit in Rodríguez García's 2010 book *The City of Translation: Poetry and Ideology in Nineteenth-Century Colombia*. Paula Montoya's doctoral thesis defended at Montreal University in 2014 is even more specific in its use of translation as a conceptual tool to consider the construction of the education system and its policies from the nineteenth century to now.[14] Montoya and Elisa Galeano also have published on translation as cultural transfer in the Colombian pedagogical context.[15]

Historians do not study translation. The task is ours. It belongs to translation scholars who dedicate themselves to the history of translation. The history of translation mobilizes the thought behind translation studies and historical thought. Through translation we can establish relationships between history and the search for what could be called a recognition of oneself, what has been called—perhaps mistakenly—"identity." Latin America's malaise is contained in this way of defining ourselves and accepting for ourselves our "Latin American identity" without fully understanding what that implies, acknowledging that what signals "identity" cannot actually "identify" us. We do not feel completely at home within this identification. Looking at translation studies from the perspective of Latin America could help us establish these relationships among our fragmented histories, which in turn could lead to a better understanding of what we have been and what we strive to be.

For my discussion of translation as *translatio studiorum*, the phenomenon of *translatio* of cultural patrimonies, in this case from Latin America, I examine the pre-Hispanic literary work *Popol Vuh* and its translations to Spanish, French, and English. It has also been translated into German, but I do not include that here.

Those of us in the Americas are responsible for the translatio studiorum that is projected from our geographic space. To mention just one of the many elements that make up our cultural patrimony, we could for instance study the transmission of Christian values through the transference of Amerindian aspects that ended up integrated into the Christian tradition. The Brazilian example has a great deal to contribute to this topic with respect to the ways in which European languages are transformed when they come in contact with the American world; how words are divested of their ancestral meanings to acquire new meanings (just consider what has happened with the word *santidade*). If from the European perspective translatio studiorum is essentially the task of bringing books back to life, then the task in the Americas is first and foremost that of rebirthing: to rebirth, in this geographic space, that which has always been here, to bring knowledges, narrations, perceptions, thoughts, rituals, and emotions that were already here, back to life so we can then project ourselves as beings with a history.

Raphaël Girard lived for over thirty years in Guatemala. He wrote an exegetic, historical/critical translation of *Popol Vuh* (1954) that considers the work a cultural text, its content as historiography, and its authors as historians. Girard consulted the text in Spanish (the Ximenez translation, 1700–1704) and in French (Brasseur's, 1861); he also studied K'iche' Mayan and consulted with speakers of K'iche' Mayan. Mircea Elíade reviewed Girard's translation and in the review highlighted the clarity with which Girard unveiled the four eras of the world, the four cultural cycles: the primitive, horizon and the age of the formation of the K'iche' Mayan culture, the age of matriarchal-horticulture, and the patriarchal-agrarian cycle.[16] In the introduction to her doctoral thesis on *Popol Vuh*, Ana Maria Sackl describes the text as

> a cosmogony of the K'iche' Mayan culture that originated in MesoAmerica between the III and VIII centuries AD. Sometime between 1554 and 1557, a K'iche' scribe transliterated the texts that were possibly painted and logosyllabic of *Popol Vuh* to K'iche', but in the Latin alphabet. . . . It is believed that this manuscript was written in *Santa Cruz del Quiché*, near *Q'umarkaaj*, the capital of the kingdom that the Spaniards occupied and destroyed in 1524. . . . The text was taken later to Chichicastenango, where the Dominican friar Francisco Ximénez found it, transcribed the K'iche' Mayan, and translated it into Spanish. The friar finished his work . . . between 1700 and 1704.[17]

Now the text has gone from the oral in the K'iche' Mayan context in Mesoamerica to the written in K'iche' Mayan in the Americas of the Conquest to the written in the Colonial American Spanish of Ximénez to the French geographic space where Brasseur's translation became the point of reference for others.

In 2003, Allen J. Christenson published the results of twenty-five years of his work in Guatemala: *Popol Vuh: Sacred Book of the Ancient Maya*. After this exceptional translation experience, Christenson says of translation, "Translation is an art whose cloth is woven from a variety of threads. Any defects are solely the fault of the weaver. Its beauty is solely dependent on the threads themselves."[18] This beautiful and colorful Guatemalan concept of translation is already integrated into Christenson's way of thinking. An ethnologist, a linguist, and a professor of comparative literature at Brigham Young University, he lived for twenty-five years in Guatemala, where he dedicated most of his time to studying *Popul Vuh*. He read the Ximénez translation, then he compiled a K'iche' Mayan/English dictionary. His translation includes a fifty-page translator's preface and a forty-nine-page introduction. His functional translation includes 892 footnotes and is followed by a literal, interlinear K'iche' Mayan/English translation with 121 explanatory notes. In his preface, Christenson notes that the Maya themselves did not have access to the text in their own language for many centuries. His intention was to salvage the literary cultural power the Maya were robbed of centuries ago, bringing to the present the ancient Maya voice. Christenson's work is monumental; it presents the "original" K'iche' Mayan transcription of *Popul Vuh*, a pronunciation and spelling guide, and the K'iche' Mayan transcription in modern spelling on one side with its literal English translation on the other. It offers a functional English translation with linguistic and ethnological explanations on the poetic nature of *Popul Vuh*, and historical explanations of the manuscript and the translations consulted.

Translations of *Popul Vuh* have been the motivation for literary creations in many languages and contexts. That is how translatio studiorum is felt from the geographic space of Mesoamerica to the space of the Americas of the Conquest, to Colonial America, to the European space, to the U.S. space, only to return again to the geographic space of today's Guatemala, where it was born.

The Latin American translation studies school of thought today has the task of making visible the translatio studiorum occurring since the seventeenth century, both for this very geographic space itself in its many historical contexts and for other spaces as well. This becomes possible by recording the history of translation. We have several tasks before us: we must look into our American histories to see how processes of translation were experienced here, how we were translated, from what languages, into which languages, and in what time periods. We must draft critical editions of those translations that have been published, as well as comparative analyses of the different languages in which they were written.[19] It is also crucial to translate into Spanish the works that were written about us in other languages. It is essential to become historians as we translate and, as a result, to motivate translators in training to become historians of translation themselves. Using translation as a methodological tool to study our American histories will certainly throw light upon obscure passages of our past, and perhaps also draw unexpected horizons for our future.

NOTES

1. Adolfo Castañón's translation into Spanish was published in 1995, while Alberto Franco's translation into Portuguese was published in 2005. Cf. Andréia Guerini, "George Steiner, Depois de Babel: questões de linguagem e tradução," *Cadernos de Tradução* 1, no. 19 (2007): 264–267.
2. By contrast, in Latin America the nineteenth century was a very productive time in translation studies.
3. Colombian Sergio Bolaños Cuellar published his *Introducción a la traductología. Autores, textos y comentarios* in 2016 (Universidad Nacional de Colombia/Universidad del Rosario, Bogotá). See the book review by Laura Esperanza Venegas Piracón, "Introducción a la traductología: Autores, textos y comentarios, Sergio Bolaños Cuellar," *Mutatis Mutandis* 10, no. 2 (2017).
4. Gustave Althoff and Alice Leal, "Interview with Mary Snell-Hornby," *Scientia Traductionis* no. 9 (2011): 365–388.
5. Francisco Lafarga and Luis Pegenaute, eds., "Biblioteca de traducciones hispanoamericanas" (Cervantes Virtual), http://www.cervantesvirtual.com/obra/biblioteca-de-traducciones-hispanoamericanas/.
6. *Mutatis Mutandis* dedicated an issue to Jiří Levý, "The Art of Translation: Jiří Levý (1926–1967) y la otra historia de la traductología," *Mutatis Mutandis* 9, no. 2 (2016). See also Jana Králová, "La recepción de la traductología latinoamericana en Chequia: inspiraciones temáticas, metodológicas y didácticas," *Ars & Humanitas/Studije/Studies* 11, no. 2 (2017): 44–55.
7. Rosario Lázaro Igoa, "Haroldo de Campos: recorrido por sus textos teóricos sobre traducción y estado de traducción al castellano" *Mutatis Mutandis* 5, no. 2 (2012).
8. I am grateful to Vassia Silveira, a master's student at UFSC, for sharing this reference with me in 2015.
9. See their website: http://www.pget.ufsc.br/BibliotecaDigital.
10. See their website: http://research.fflch.usp.br/node/83.
11. Paula Andrea Montoya Arango and Juan Guillermo Ramirez Giraldo, "Rafael Pombo y Candelario Obeso: Traducción e intercambios culturales en la Colombia del siglo XIX," in *Traductores y Traducciones en la Historia Cultural de América Latina* (México: Universidad Nacional Autónoma de México, 2011), 159–174.
12. See *Filosofía e historia en la práctica de traducción* (2003, 2014), which focuses on the act of translation. http://aprendeenlinea.udea.edu.co/revistas/index.php/mutatismutandis/article/view/23689/19453.
13. Juan Guillermo Ramírez, "Candelario Obeso," in *Diccionario Histórico de la traducción en Hispanoamérica*, ed. Francisco Lafarga and Luis Pegenaute (Madrid: Iberoamericana, 2013), 303–304.
14. Paula Montoya, "Traducción y transferencia cultural en la reforma educativa radical en Colombia: Descripción y análisis de *La Escuela Normal* (1871–1879)" (PhD diss., Universidad de Montreal, 2014).
15. Paula Montoya Arango and Elisa Galenao, "Benedikta Zur Nieden de Echavarría, traductora: transferencia cultural en el contexto pedagógico colombiano a mediados del siglo XX," *Mutatis Mutandis* 8, no. 2 (2015): 485–516.

16. Mircea Elíade, "Raphaël Girard. Le Popol Vuh. Histoire culturelle des Maya-Quichés," *Revue de l'histoire des religions* 147 (1955): 262–263.

17. The doctoral thesis by Ana Maria B. C. Sackl, "Paratradução do Popol Wuj: paratextos e excertos de Gênesis," is available at http://www.pget.ufsc.br/curso/teses/Ana_Maria_B._C._Sackl_-_Tese.pdf.

18. Allen J. Christenson, trans., *Popol Vuh: Sacred Book of the Quiché Maya People*, 16, http://www.mesoweb.com/publications/Christenson/PopolVuh.pdf.

19. Anthony Knivet, *As incríveis aventuras e estranhos infortúnios de Anthony Knivet: memórias de um aventureiro inglês que em 1591 saiu de seu país com o pirata Thomas Cavendish e foi abandonado no Brasil, entre índios canibais e colonos selvagens*, ed. Sheila Moura Hue, trans. Vivien Kogut Lessa de Sá (Rio de Janeiro: Jorge Zahar Editor, 2008). Kogut Lessa de Sá translated this work from the English: Anthony Knivet, "The Admirable Adventures and Strange Fortunes of Master Antonie Knivet, Which Went with Master Thomas Cavendish in His Second Voyage to the South Sea, 1591," in *Hakluytus Posthumus; or, Purchas His Pilgrimes. Contayning a History of the World, in Sea Voyages and Lande Travels*, ed. Samuel Purchas (London, 1625). Kogut Lessa de Sá also offers an edited version of the text in English: Anthony Knivet, *The Admirable Adventures and Strange Fortunes of Master Anthony Knivet: An English Pirate in Sixteenth-Century Brazil*, ed. Vivien Kogut Lessa de Sá (Cambridge: Cambridge University Press, 2015).

BIBLIOGRAPHY

Althoff, Gustave, and Alice Leal. "Entrevista con Mary Snell-Hornby." *Scientia Traductionis*, no. 9 (2011): 365–388.

Bassnett, Susan, and André Lefevere, eds. *Translation, History and Culture*. London: Pinter, 1990.

Berman, Antoine. *Pour une critique des traductions: John Donne*. Paris: Gallimard, 1995.

Castro, Nayelli, ed. *Traducción, identidad y nacionalismo en Latinoamérica*. México: Bonilla Artiga Editores, 2013.

Cheung, Martha, ed. *An Anthology of Chinese Discourse on Translation. Volume I: From Earliest Times to the Buddhist Project*. Amsterdam: John Benjamins, 2006.

Christenson, Allen J., trans. *Popol Vuh: Sacred Book of the Quiché Maya People*. www.mesoweb.com/publications/Christenson/PopolVuh.pdf.

de Campos, Haroldo. "Transluciferação Mefistofaústica." In *Deus e o Diabo no Fausto de Goethe*. São Paulo: Perspectiva, 1981.

Delisle, Jean, and Judith Woodsworth. *Translators through History*. Ottawa: Presses de l'Université d'Ottawa, 1995.

Eliade, Mircea. "Raphaël Girard. Le Popol Vuh. Histoire culturelle des Maya-Quichés." *Revue de l'histoire des religions* 147 (1955): 262–263.

Lafarga, Francisco, and Luis Pegenaute. "Biblioteca de traducciones hispanoamericanas." www.cervantesvirtual.com/obra/biblioteca-de-traducciones-hispanoamericanas/.

———, eds. *Diccionario histórico de la traducción en Hispanoamérica*. Madrid: Iberoamericana, 2013.

Montoya, Paula "Traducción y transferencia cultural en la reforma educativa radical en Colombia: Descripción y análisis de La Escuela Normal (1871–1879)." PhD diss., Universidad de Montreal, 2014.

Montoya Arango, Paula, and Elisa Galeano. "Benedikta Zur Nieden de Echavarría, traductora: transferencia cultural en el contexto pedagógico colombiano a mediados del siglo XX." *Mutatis Mutandis* 8, no. 2 (2015): 485–516.

Mounin, Georges. *Les problèmes théoriques de la traduction*. Paris: Gallimard, 1963.

Nord, Christiane. *Text Analysis in Translation: Theory, Methodology and Didactic Application of a Model for Translation-Oriented Text Analysis*. Amsterdam: Rodopi, 1991.

Payàs, Gertrudis, and Claudia Tirado, eds. *Biblioteca chilena de traductores (1820–1924) ordenada por J.T. Medina*. Santiago de Chile: Centro de Investigaciones Diego Barros Arana, 2007.

Ramírez, Juan Guillermo. "Candelario Obeso." In *Diccionario Histórico de la traducción en Hispanoamérica*, edited by Francisco and Lafarga and Luis Pegenaute, 303–304. Madrid: Iberoamericana, 2013.

Ronai, Paolo. *A tradução vivida*. Rio de Janeiro: Nova Frontera, 1981.

Sackl, Ana Maria. "Paratradução do Popol Wuj: paratextos e excertos de Gênesis." PhD diss., Universidade Federal de Santa Catarina, 2015.

Silva Santiestebán, Ricardo. "Breve historia de la traducción en el Perú." In *Al humanista, traductor y maestro Miguel Ángel Vega Cernuda*, edited by Pilar Martino Alba, Juan A. Albaladejo Martínez, and Martha Pulido. Madrid: Dykinson, 2013.

Snell-Hornby, Mary. *Translation Studies: An Integrated Approach*. Amsterdam: John Benjamins, 1995.

Steiner, George. *After Babel. Aspects of Language and Translation*. Oxford: Oxford University Press, 1975.

Toury, Gideon. *Descriptive Translation Studies and Beyond*. Amsterdam: John Benjamins, 1995.

Vega, Miguel Ángel, ed. *Textos clásicos de teoría de la traducción*. Madrid: Cátedra Editoriales, 1994.

Venuti, Lawrence. *The Translator's Invisibility: A History of Translation*. London: Routledge, 1995.

Vinay, Jean-Paul, and Jean Darbelnet. *Stylistique comparée du français et de l'anglais. Méthode de traduction*. Paris: Didier, 1958.

Wilson, Patricia. *La constelación del sur, traductores y traducciones en la literatura argentina del siglo XX*. Buenos Aires: Siglo XXI Editores, 2004.

9 • FROM INTERPRETING TO COLLOQUIAL TRANSLATION

Tools Indispensable to Literary Creation

OLGA BEHAR
TRANSLATED BY LORENA TERANDO

What in the world can an interpreter be doing, galloping on horseback over the dirt roads of the Cordillera de los Andes in Chile toward the tomb of her favorite woman poet? What is the point of setting out in a small boat on an endless journey down the Magdalena River, or sleeping in a hammock in La Guajira Desert "to understand the importance of dreams" in the author's world, if the end goal is to translate a Nobel Prize winner's work into Japanese?

Satoko Kamura, the adventurer in question, has interpreted a number of Latin American authors into Japanese, and understands that the flavor of the writer's day in, day out is key for readers in other languages not only to read, but also to assimilate and understand the meaning of the literary creation. Kamura is quite an inspiration for those of us who are writing and hope to be read by a more global public that can't access our languages.[1] I, in particular, am captivated by the ability of interpreters like Kamura to put themselves in another's shoes, and tease out the author's emotions and feelings that are beyond words. "Even though some of Gabo's works had been translated into Japanese, they were not very well done. That's why I needed to come and hear the pitch of the voices and take in the scenes of the characters," said Kamura, explaining why she decided to set out on this adventure to the Caribbean of Gabriel García Márquez, which twenty years later still hasn't come to an end.

In general, when I use the term "translation," I refer to a more literal exercise that includes what I call "simultaneous translation," and it can include an oral or written transfer of information. When using the mode of simultaneous translation, linguists maintain a nearly exact fidelity in terminology used in the source language event. When I use the term "interpreting," I refer to an exercise that is much broader. In my vision as a writer, interpreting can be written (i.e., letters, diaries, etc.) or oral, and it is intended to encompass the historical, social, and geographical context as well as the life and the thought processes of the character in a story, in order to transfer his or her discourse to another language.

Bearing this in mind, I admire simultaneous translators. I don't understand how they can hear what a person says, and interpret it while that person is still talking. It's magical, something more akin to a machine than to a human being. Sharpening their senses so as not to miss a single word, and perfectly translating the content—it's a mystery to me. However, I rarely use the services of this kind of linguist. Other linguists concentrate on the translation of written texts. Real time is not their dictator, even though they have a specific timeline. I admire their ability to understand the meaning of that which is expressed, beyond even the value of the word found in the dictionary. Still another variety of linguist is the kind I try to work with when the need arises, the kind who understands idiosyncrasies, slang, and gestures an interviewee might use, even if this linguist hasn't studied translation and doesn't have academic knowledge of languages. Let me explain why I seek them out.

Ana Ramos Calvo, professor at the Universidad Autónoma de Madrid who translates important texts from Arabic to Spanish (prose in particular), notes,

> In addition to facing the difficulties that any translation presents, literary translators must also attend to the beauty of the text, to its styles and its lexical, grammatical, and phonological devices, all the while bearing in mind that the stylistic devices in one language may be different in another. For example, Arabic does not have a formal "you" form like the Spanish "Usted," which could be crucial in translation. Finding the right solution for certain markers of respect or affection, like the Arabic "ya aini," is also crucial.[2] Translators must achieve a translation that is equivalent in quality to the original text, without neglecting the integrity of its content.[3]

Her task of translation is theoretically grounded in J. C. Catford's statement in *A Linguistic Theory of Translation* that "translation may be defined as follows: the replacement of textual material in one language [source language] by equivalent textual material in another language [target language]."[4] Ramos Calvo goes on,

> This definition necessarily leads us to reflect on a key term: equivalence. The fundamental challenge for translators is to find equivalents that produce in readers of the translation the same effect that the author wanted to produce in the readers of the source text. This forces translators of literary texts to think of the text as the

> basis for continuous "negotiation" with the author, so the language of the new text may present terms that are equivalent in value to those in the original language, without neglecting their force, their dynamic elements or their aesthetic quality. It is generally accepted that we don't translate meaning, but messages, so the text should be considered in its totality.[5]

We can see one potential point of rapprochement between the writer and the translator in this reflection: when this rapprochement is imperative not only in the task of translating a work that has already been completed—and usually published—but also in the process of constructing of the work.

Tradition has it that to interpret texts in which the characters are everyday people, one must know the "language of the people," which may be considered vulgar by some. "Refined language" is considered to be closer to official language. This language is grammatically polished and boasts an extensive vocabulary, but is not necessarily technical even if it is used in official documents, statements, speeches, and so on. It is the language spoken by the upper classes, while the "language of the people" is used by the lower classes, or those with little cultural or academic education.

By contrast, instead of "language of the people," I prefer to use the term "colloquial language," which is different from refined language in its use of local or regional terminology, turns of phrase, and expressions, and resists distinguishing between social classes or academic backgrounds.

This is not just about geography; within colloquial language one can also distinguish social groups, urban tribes, and narrative and/or historical epochs. According to the theories of Peter Newmark, cited by González de Sande, a translation is successful when it restores the meaning of the original text and gives readers of the target text the same cognitive and emotional effect that the original text gave its readers. This is what Newmark calls "communicative translation," in contrast to "semantic translation," for which the translator would attempt to reproduce the contextual meaning of the author, bearing in mind the syntactic and semantic restrictions of the original text, regardless of whether readers can understand it.[6]

It is even more complicated when, as in my case, the writer is not translating a previously written work, but is carrying out interviews that are necessary for researching a topic. In this case, unlike other authors who prefer idiomatic textual translation, I prefer to work with the colloquial interpreter, though sometimes that person may not even speak Spanish well. This is particularly true when we are talking about the challenge of facing a reality that is at first distant, but that comes closes to the writer as she develops her characters, until it is absorbed into her bones and in her heart more than it is in her mind and her intellectual capacity. This is even more necessary when the writer—as in my case—works with texts that combine nonfiction with fiction.

How does this process take place? Using the tools of journalism (in particular the genres of the chronicle and the interview) to appropriate characters that existed in real life, as did the history in which they were immersed, and their geographic, social, and political locations.

That is, when the legal, narrative and journalistic supports, and many times the information required to construct the narrative scaffolding that contributes to contextualization are found. Newspapers, legal reports, letters, photographs all contribute to feed the plot that is, up until this point, basically made up of nonfiction elements.

So the narration begins to be constructed from creation and setting, dialogues, monologues, and other resources used from the fictional literary toolbox to assemble a clear, credible text that captures the attention of its readers.

Three years ago I was beginning to work on *The Klein Case: The Origin of Paramilitarism in Colombia.*[7] I cowrote this book with political scientist and diplomat Carolina Ardila. We carried out preliminary research and wrote in Spanish. The nonfictional person on whom we based our main character is a colonel in the Israeli Army who trained paramilitary groups in Colombia; he does not speak Spanish, speaks broken English, and the only language in which he can communicate with ease is Hebrew. Carolina had arrived in Israel a year before we began our work, but she had not yet mastered Hebrew. On top of everything else, Yair Klein, the nonfictional colonel, is gruff and distant and hates journalists.

After two visits by Carolina, in the company of a colleague with perfect command of Hebrew and whose Spanish was passable, Mr. Klein agreed to give us an interview. The questions Carolina and I had were: How can we make a connection with this person? How can we open him up, make him talk about what he's hidden for twenty-four years, what he hasn't wanted to confess to anyone?

In addition to the journalistic techniques used in interviews and obtaining testimony, we needed a crucial element: the consecutive interpretation of what was said. There were several options, but the most logical one was to contract an interpreter with complete mastery of Spanish and Hebrew. Other media interviews with Klein that had required interpretation had proven unfruitful; the cocksure, reticent man who appeared at the start of the interview hadn't changed a bit by the end. So bringing in a translator who would exacerbate this situation was not a solution.

After a great deal of searching, we concluded that Carolina's colleague, David (not his real name), was the perfect person to take on this task. We decided to ask him to be our ally in the task of understanding how and why Yair Klein had trained those Colombians in military tactics. Although David was trained in the sciences, he had grown up in a home where Spanish is spoken (his mother is Colombian) and had trained himself to speak it well by reading, conducting internet searches, and watching a lot of Latin American film. He had a thick Israeli accent, but he was proficient enough to be able to interpret what Klein would tell us. I also thought it was important for David to be interested in the political issues relevant in Colombia and for him to know Colombian idiosyncrasies well.

David told us that he had been to Colombia when he was a teenager, and he had noticed that his Spanish was rather limited. He spoke it only with his closest family members in Israel. He bought a dictionary and, when he got home, took on the challenge of learning fifteen words per day. At the end of a year, he had acquired about two hundred new words for his vocabulary, and some of them included their derivations and conjugations. This independent learner was up to the task we had in mind for him, but when we told him of our plan, he was shocked and stated flatly that he was incapable of such a feat. He is a heritage speaker of Spanish, using it on vacation trips to Spanish-speaking countries and for light reading. We convinced him with our argument: we needed someone who could build trust, not someone who would build a wall between our interviewee and us.

When we got to Yair Klein's house for the first interview session, he was surprised too. Even more so when he offered us a coffee and our magnificent interpreter went into the kitchen with him, to chat while the coffee brewed. When we sat down at the table and turned the recorder on, Mr. Klein felt so comfortable he had no trouble at all opening up straightaway about one of the trickiest issues we would discuss. Our interpreter made him feel like he was chatting with a friend.

Now, the obvious question is: how faithful can an interpretation be if the interpreter is not trained? Indeed, this is really a challenge. We had to stop the interview on several occasions to ask Mr. Klein to explain with different words, or in greater depth, those things our interpreter didn't understand. I remember one of the concepts we didn't understand had to do with military ranks, like "brigade-chief," or the specific types of command or weapons. The fact that our interviewee wanted the interpreter to understand so that he could interpret correctly turned into a didactic exercise that made him feel more important. And it had quite a positive effect.

Once the six interview sessions were complete, we confirmed to Mr. Klein that everything recorded was going to be reviewed by a professional. I am pleased to say the linguist we hired felt the work was well done. She noted that the way some words were rendered was incorrect, but that what Mr. Klein had expressed in general had remained intact. In the second stage of the project, the transcribed text was translated professionally and more questions cropped up. They were resolved with no problem by Mr. Klein; trust had been built between our interpreter and Carolina (who stayed in Israel, while I returned to Colombia) and Mr. Klein. That allowed us to add more depth to the information.

Once published, the book was very controversial because of Klein's revelations. He agreed to give some interviews, always with assistance from Carolina. By that time she had mastered Hebrew; she knew idiomatic expressions and colloquial language. He felt that if she was the interpreter, the interpretation would be correct. On one of these occasions, the TV channel Caracol hired a professional translator for Klein's interview. Carolina was present, but as a contact to help with the interview. The translator, who was Argentine, made a mess of one of Klein's early answers, and Carolina had to step in for him. Mr. Klein was talking about places in Colombia and specific, everyday Colombian habits, which were out of the reach of the professional.

The situation was even more challenging when Mr. Klein agreed to a teleconference interview with the Tribunal for Justice and Peace to clarify for investigators of paramilitarism in Colombia the aspects of training that he had led. The tribunal is part of a structure that was created through the Santa Fe de Ralito Agreement signed on July 15, 2003, by the paramilitary organizations and the administration of Colombian President Alvaro Uribe Vélez, which made possible the demobilization of thirty-four blocs of the paramilitary group Autodefensas Unidas de Colombia (United Self-Defenders of Colombia).[8] The agreement resulted in Law 975 of 2005, known as the Law of Justice and Peace. It was through this law that Transitional Justice was created, with the goal of prosecuting the perpetrators of thousands of crimes committed by this illegal military organization. Transitional Justice is administered through special tribunals. The Tribunal for Justice and Peace hired a simultaneous translator whom Carolina had to correct constantly to ensure that Mr. Klein's sworn testimony would be accurate.

Interpreters working on testimony with a high degree of colloquial language content must have extensive knowledge of the circumstances, the context, the interviewees' personalities, and possibly the content of what will be said. When working with complex personalities, it is also important for interpreters not to play a professional, distant role that may make it difficult to build the trust needed for the person to decide to divulge sensitive information. It is also imperative to have interpretation/translation experts involved in the content to guarantee the truth and accuracy of everything that will be published, but those experts should come after the work of the colloquial interpreter is done.

At this time I am taking on new challenges in my historical novel set in a region of Poland that is now part of Ukraine. It was invaded by Nazis and was later invaded, lost, and subsequently recovered by the Russians. I am working with a colloquial interpreter to interpret fifty-four pages of a diary written in prison in extremely tiny script by the woman on whom the main character is based. We also used some letters and official documents. While I can distinguish between German and Russian, my interpreter noted that the calligraphy complicated the task, to the point that I had in some instances confused Polish with Ukrainian. She was very generous, and was able to interpret both languages. Thus in this case of interpretation of extremely colloquial texts, I needed the help of a very specialized interpreter who also understood the historical, political, and social context in which the documents and letters were written.

It was not possible to use books to research some of the terminology native to this area of Poland or used colloquially in the 1930s and 1940s; it wasn't easy to find. But as we worked together, paragraph by paragraph, we consulted one another as well as dictionaries, friends, maps, Google Poland images to contextualize objects, customs, and even flowers, and sometimes Google Earth to fully comprehend the land that was so crucial to the story. By combining the various modes of translation and interpretation, through three very dynamic months of hard work, we managed to find the meanings we were after.

It is this close relationship between the colloquial interpreter and the writer that makes it possible to take on such a challenging literary text. The diary was written in such detail that at times we had to dedicate hours to searching one word or colloquial situation before we could finally create the atmosphere we needed. When the book—now written in Spanish—is translated into English or another language, only a true expert will be able to reconcile the multiplicity of languages in it so that, as is our goal, the real winner will be the reader.

NOTES

1. The adventures of Satoko Tamura, the translator of Gabriel García Márquez's *One Hundred Years of Solitude*, are recounted in Colombia's *El Tiempo* newspaper, May 10, 2012, http://www.eltiempo.com/archivo/documento/CMS-11760524.
2. Translator's Note: "Ya aini" literally means "my eyes." It is used to describe or address someone who is very important to the speaker or writer, and whom he or she loves dearly. In some areas of the Spanish-speaking world, "mis ojos" would be a familiar rendering ("niña de mis ojos," for example). An English translation that renders the literal and figurative meanings at the same time would be more challenging.
3. See Ana Ramos Calvo, "Teoría y práctica de la traducción literaria" (June 27, 2016), http://hottopos.com/mirand8/anaramo.htm.
4. J. C. Catford, *A Linguistic Theory of Translation* (Oxford: Oxford University Press, 1965).
5. Ibid.
6. See Gaite Mercedes González de Sande, "Reflexiones sobre la traducción del lenguaje coloquial en Nuvolosita Variabile de Carmen Martín," http://193.147.33.53/selicup/images/stories/actassevilla/conferencias/GONZALEZ_SANDE.pdf.
7. Olga Behar and Carolina Ardila Behar, *El Caso Klein. El origen del paramilitarismo en Colombia* (Bogotá: Editorial Ícono, 2012).
8. The United Self-Defense Forces of Colombia was a paramilitary coalition of right-wing death squads contributing to Colombia's long history of political unrest, displacement, drug trafficking, kidnapping, and extortion. It targeted peasants and labor union leaders and is considered a terrorist organization in many countries. It was disbanded in 2006.

10 • LANGUAGE, POLICY, AND DIS/ABILITY IN SENEGAL, WEST AFRICA

ELIZABETH R. DRAME

Current data by UNESCO and the African Child Policy Forum show that one in every ten children on the continent of Africa has some type of disability. National and international policy mandates regarding the rights of children with disabilities intersect in ways that influence the practice of inclusion in West African countries such as Senegal. The Special and Inclusive Education arm of the Quality Education for All Program (EQPT) of the World Bank conducted a study examining existing and needed resources for effective implementation of an inclusive education model in Senegal.[1] Its initial findings, as presented by Carleton Aslett-Rydbjerg, indicated that one major challenge is that of establishing an actual need for inclusive education given a lack of credible and reliable data on the number of affected children, owing to the stigma associated with disability in this culture. The negative perceptions contributing to this stigma include viewing children with a disability as a burden or a curse, and as less capable or incapable. These general perceptions, given voice by those without disabilities and expressed in language and attitudes, lead to greater social exclusion, lower self-esteem, and lack of future aspirations in this at-risk Senegalese population. Family members, motivated by fear of exclusion or abandonment and by a desire to protect their children, are pushed to confine their children to their homes rather than enroll them in school.[2]

Even if parents wanted to enroll their children in school, there are limited public education options for children with disabilities in Senegal; private education options are accessible to only a few with the financial means. Aslett-Rydbjerg highlights the need for ongoing awareness campaigns to destigmatize disability and to help educators, children in "regular" schools, and the Senegalese population in general to understand the benefits of inclusive education. Additionally, in order to support the physical and meaningful inclusion of children with disabilities in schools, it is critical to address chronic physical inaccessibility of buildings, classrooms, and materials. Aslett-Rydbjerg proposes a model of capacity building that relies on developing a system of pilot schools that would implement an inclusive education model with specific supports—teacher training, building modifications, materials and resources, and awareness campaigns. These pilot schools could become models and resources for the surrounding schools.

Principles of inclusion should undergird learning pedagogy in all schools for all children, rather than being a separate add-on. This will require a sea change in thinking and teacher preparation, a national Senegalese curriculum that starts with the reconceptualization of disability as socially constructed, and a reframing of the associated colloquial discourse and policy language.

My chapter examines the cultural conceptions of ability and disability embedded within La Loi d'orientation sociale, the Senegalese government's disability rights and inclusion mandate that was signed into law in 2012. Fundamental to my analysis of Senegalese policy are notions of ableness in Senegalese society, as well as myths and misconceptions of disability. I assess specific psychological, cultural, physical, and economic obstacles preventing the full integration and inclusion of individuals with disabilities, and I contrast the policy language with the language of the "street." I proceed with consideration given in particular to potential implementation challenges and opportunities inherent in the law, and its potential to change daily life for individuals with disabilities by emphasizing education. Selected personal narratives help ground my policy critique in lived experience, and I conclude with ideas for policy implementation, specifically addressing the role of discourse in opening or closing doors for individuals with disabilities. To accomplish this, I take up several theoretical perspectives including ableism, critical disability theory, and postcolonial translation theory to inform a critical discourse analysis of colloquial and policy language related to disability in Senegal.

The United Nations Secretariat for the Convention on the Rights of Persons with Disabilities (2007) provided a summary of international policies related to disability rights. Its summary highlighted the need to ensure equality and access for people with disabilities in the exercise of the same rights—political, cultural, economic, health, social, and other forms of rights—as nondisabled people. A shift to equal access necessitates a shift in focus from caretaking and social services (which amount to rehabilitation toward a "norm") toward a focus on equal access to rights, opportunities, and societal participation available to persons without disabilities. Corrective measures are required to address existing discrimination and to promote opportunities for persons with disabilities to participate on the basis of equality in both social life and development. United Nations human rights conventions such as the Convention on the Rights of the Child protect the rights of individuals with disabilities by virtue of the universality of their application. In addition, other international and regional human rights conventions, such as the African Charter of Human and People's Rights, make specific mention or provision for protecting the rights of persons with disabilities.

La Loi d'orientation sociale is situated within, and heavily influenced by, these international education and disability rights conventions, as well as by nonbinding international instruments including standards, resolutions, and declarations, such as the Declaration of the Rights of Disabled Persons and the Salamanca Statement and Framework for Action on Special Needs Education. Legislation at the nation-state level is critical for the promotion of human rights for people with disabilities. Corresponding legislation at the level of a single country is most impactful when the goal is to effect social change for a marginalized group. Typically, international mandates, resolutions, and norms provide a useful starting point for how domestic legislation must reflect domestic conditions. These mandates may, for example, acknowledge needed social change in order to eventually produce durable, long-term improvement in the lives of marginalized groups.

Susan Peters, a special education researcher with experience working in sub-Saharan African contexts, uses a conceptual framework that views international disability policy as discourse rather than as a neutral representation of official decisions (a representation that nonetheless necessarily communicates power relationships).[3] Her perspective of policy as discourse provides an appropriate context for framing and situating my critical discourse analysis of the law, illuminating the problematic colloquial language by which disability is labeled in Senegalese society. Discourses codified in policy language are value-laden and need to be deconstructed to understand what subtext is being promoted related to disability rights. Peters's analysis traces the change in discourse around disability embedded in the context of historically important international policy documents produced between 1960 and 2007, documenting shifts from a welfare and caretaking perspective to a rights-based approach. A brief summary of Peters's policy discourse analysis (provided below) is instructive.

According to Peters, international conventions and mandates initially focused on preventing and eliminating discrimination and exclusion in education by providing access to educational environments, even if these environments were in separate settings. This initial emphasis on separate access shifted to a focus on an individual's need for specific services to reach his or her potential, as a means of ensuring integration to all aspects of life: familial, economic, professional, recreational. At this time, there was greater emphasis on education within the ordinary school system (World Programme of Action Concerning Disabled Persons, 1982), though only when such pedagogies were readily in place or otherwise conveniently feasible. The World Programme of Action still supported the use of separate facilities for an "appropriate period of time" as long as the quality was equal to general education settings. At this time, disability was viewed as an experience that all could share, with disablement appropriately viewed as part of normal life experience.

Peters argues that the focus then began to move away from solely the individual to systemic contextual factors such as resources, partnerships, and environments. In 1989, the Tallinn Guidelines began the discourse on continuum of placements (general education, resources, separate classes), recognized diversity within the population of persons with disability (deafness, gender, culture, language), and the need for training of general education teachers regarding disability. The Convention on the Rights of the Child in 1990 moved the discourse back to a medical model focused on individual deficits, but by contrast, in the same year, the World Declaration on Education for All stressed a social model of disability that stated that equal access should be integral to general education (rather than being an add-on, integrated into an already established system). Importantly, organizations were deemed accountable for providing resources and funding based on access and equity rather than availability and cost.

The 1994 Salamanca Statement discussed human differences as a normal part of life, focusing on abilities rather than disabilities, and promoted a broader conception of disability across the life span, including also attention to gifted and talented learners. At this time, the policy discourse moved beyond access and equal opportunity to stress quality and accountability. The 2000 Education for All Framework for Action in Dakar and the 2004 Education for All flagship initiative—the Right to Education for Persons with Disabilities—were developed to address unique and persistent challenges with achieving Education for All goals for people with disabilities. As a result of pressure from disability organizations for a disability-specific convention, the Convention on the Rights of Persons with Disabilities was signed by eighty countries in 2007.

Addressing inequity in quality of life and social inclusion among the differently abled is a significant aspect of reducing and eliminating poverty. Lack of opportunities to contribute as full, productive human beings and citizens and continued exclusion and discrimination have a significant and negative economic impact on all societies, but particularly those with high rates of poverty like Senegal. Peters's policy discourse analysis revealed contradictory language in international conventions, reflecting a lack of consensus on differential conceptions of disability as either an inherently medical and individual condition or a socially constructed label. This vacillation is then perceptibly reflected in national policies when nations attempt to align their laws with international ideals.

Cultural lenses color every aspect of education and day-to-day life for individuals with disabilities. The influence of Western-centric cultural notions of disability is thus clearly evident in the framing language used to describe disability, whether in the individual, the environment, or both. Conflicts surrounding equity and justice in service delivery and social integration arise when Western ideas about disability are imposed on non-Western cultures, particularly when these ideas are packaged in the language embedded in international policies adopted as national and state-level dictates. An analysis of culturally contextual language and labeling that surrounds disability is therefore critical to developing an understanding of how government-driven, proposed, or sanctioned access and services are received, perceived, and broadly implemented.[4] Rather than rejecting non-Western beliefs about disability and its origins—such as supernatural, spiritual, or situational causes—as backward, efforts must be made to understand the roots of these beliefs so that they are specifically addressed when they interfere with the acceptance and inclusion of individuals with disabilities. Non-Western beliefs have the potential to lead toward positive supports, expectations, acceptance, and resilience as well. An interrogation of beliefs rooted in colloquial and policy language and discourse, for instance, can result in a movement from a binary dichotomy of Western views situated within objective, scientifically validated evidence, to a dual system of beliefs where cultural perspectives of parents are no longer devalued, but are instead integrated into systems of support and inclusion.

Ableism and *disablism* are useful terms to consider in this context.[5] Ableism involves the active, but often unconscious, production and reproduction of the "perfect" body; anything less is viewed as different, undesirable, negative, and fundamentally deficient. Ableism is deeply embedded in the fabric of all aspects of many societies, such that language, practices, and values reflect a specific physical standard for what is considered minimally normal, beautiful, and perfect and ultimately acts as arbiter for what is worthy of full humanity. Notions of disability or disablism result in preferential, paternalistic, and discriminatory treatment stemming from discourses and behaviors related to inferiority and superiority. These play out in diverse ways for people deemed disabled. Disablist attitudes can also be seen in the provision of rehabilitative or compensatory solutions and well-meaning services for the disabled, in order to tacitly encourage assimilation to a normative standard of ability.

Critical disability theory critiques the deficit lens that colors language, discourse, images, and actions toward those who do not fit societal norms about ableness.[6] It also serves as a tool for examining well-intentioned international policies that aim to support the human rights of individuals with disabilities, but which could paradoxically have an opposite effect: an emphasis on caretaking and charity serves to disenfranchise people with disabilities from full participation in social and institutional systems and structures, as well as in cultural practices and traditions. Marginalization and exclusion exist, however, even when stigmatization is not a significant factor, because the design of all social organizations is based on core assumptions of normality and able-bodiedness, which in turn influence ideas about how we "should" engage in daily life activities.

Critical disability theory views disability as a social construct rather than an innate, predetermined reality resulting from impairment. Among other factors, it seeks to dissect the language, attitudes, and values of societies that give rise to systemic inequities. Words and images used to describe or label disability have a strong and enduring influence on conceptions and perceptions of disability and the status people with disabilities occupy in society. Even when attempts are made to use alternate, nonstigmatizing labels, there is still the risk that the discourse around disability results in daily actions that disempower, devalue, and dehumanize those with disabilities. To preserve the social rights and equality of people with disabilities, the reinforcement of the social construction of disability on a foundation of deficit-oriented labeling, attitudes, values, and discourse needs to be challenged in countries around the globe, particularly in the realm of national and international policy.

Finally, postcolonial translation theory acknowledges that the very act of translating non-Western cultural beliefs and understanding into Western categories or labels can be viewed as an act of recolonization, influencing ideas and behaviors in ways that conflict with, or do not acknowledge, cultural norms, particularly when the Western language of translation is the colonizer's language. Postcolonial translation theory intervenes by raising questions about what is communicated about power when cultural concepts are translated or codified into the language of the colonizer; in the case of this chapter specifically, concepts of disability are translated into French within an extremely diverse Senegalese society made up of numerous ethnic groups with their own languages and beliefs. Postcolonial translation theory thus challenges translation within colonial contexts as a "collusive activity that participates in the fixing of colonized cultures into a mould fashioned by the superior power."[7] It is important to point out some limits to this perspective, however, as it assumes that translation from a less-dominant language into the language of the colonizer is always illegitimate, and an act of cultural appropriation. This position calls into question, in somewhat extreme fashion, the validity of any translation other than translation into non-dominant languages.

With these theoretical frameworks as a guide, I proceed now to the second half of this chapter: my methodology, findings, and analysis of conceptions of disability evident in policy language in French, alongside colloquial language in Wolof—one of the indigenous languages of Senegal—to see how this tension plays out in the context of a developing West African country.

I conducted a participatory evaluation at a specialized education center for children with disabilities during an eight-month period in 2011–2012 in Dakar, Senegal. This work explored conceptions of disability held by different stakeholders, ascertained through observations, large group meetings, and individual interviews. I gathered qualitative data from disability advocates, parents, educators, and administrators, with a focus on values, beliefs, behavior, and language related to individuals with disabilities in Dakar. These views were captured through extensive field notes, observation notes, and collaborative projects such as co-developed and co-delivered intervention sessions and document reviews. The results paint a picture of differentials and variations in lived experiences of children and their families with various disabilities. Informant interviews were conducted with different stakeholders involved in disability advocacy work (including Save the Children Sweden, Special Olympics Senegal, USAID, and UNESCO staff).

All interviews were conducted primarily in French, audiotaped, and transcribed. Though French is the professional lingua franca of Senegal, interviewees interspersed Wolof terms, particularly when asked to explain conceptions of disabilities from all language perspectives as part of the interview. I transcribed all interviews directly from their primary language (French or Wolof). Most interviewees self-translated Wolof terms and phrases into French, which facilitated my translation process of Wolof terms. I also cross-checked Wolof to French translations with at least two native Wolof speakers. Data sources included transcriptions from a total of thirty-four individuals who participated in interviews, focus groups, professional development sessions, and classroom observations. These individuals included educators from two specialized centers for children with intellectual and physical disabilities, a number of teachers from the building housing students with significant intellectual disabilities, administrators, service providers (one or more doctors, social workers, or occupational therapists), parents, and participants from local and international disability advocacy organizations. The text of La Loi d'orientation sociale was an important data source as well.

Discourse analysis acknowledges that meaning embedded in language is deeper than the superficial information communicated.[8] It raises questions about how meaning and power are constructed and reinforced through language.[9] Critical discourse analysis examines the role of discourse in production and reproduction of dominating power relationships resulting in the creation of social inequity. Additionally, it is concerned with how language structures produced by dominant and subjugated groups reinforce dominance relations in a society. I have attempted to capture integral understandings and potentially conflicting conceptions of disability through an analysis of discourse in French, English, and Wolof, to better understand culturally embedded notions that may be unduly determined by postcolonial influences.

The inductive coding of the qualitative data involved an initial review of raw data (e.g., legislative documents, interview transcripts) and a cross-data source initial summarization of broad themes related either to an individual medical model of disability or to a socially constructed model of disability. This analytical process occurred over at least two cycles of review.[10] The initial organization of themes into these two broad categories was modeled on Peters's analysis from 2007, discussed at length above, in which she reported on shifts between two Western models of disability embedded in policy discourse over time. As these models have proven influential in Western constructions of disability, this chapter is concerned with examining Western impacts on Senegalese disability conceptions.

In what follows, I organize my analysis in the following manner: First, I provide a more detailed description of the two Western models of disability—the medical model and the social model—in order to frame my initial findings.[11] Subsequently, I analyze evidence of medically or socially driven conceptions evident in the text of La Loi d'orientation sociale, after providing contextual background on the law's genesis. Alongside this, I examine labels related to specific disability areas, excerpted from transcribed interviews and observations, for evidence of the two models of disability.

The medical model of disability views a person's disability as intrinsic to the individual, necessitating the need for a cure or a fix. As a result of physical or functional "abnormality," a person with a disability requires intervention (typically in the form of services and treatment) to remediate the presumed impairment, and better approximate normative concepts of ability. The practice of placing people with specialists—either temporarily or permanently away from families, friends, and communities—results in segregation. To compensate for what they are lacking, people with disabilities are given special services and benefits, but this marginalization impacts the value placed on individuals with disabilities, as they are indicated to be inferior and disadvantaged, rather than productive, citizens. The medical model is grounded in the belief that an individual's impairment is what prevents his or her full inclusion in society, rather than attributing the individual's disenfranchisement to problematic, self-reinforcing systems of society.

In the social model, most challenges experienced by individuals with disabilities can be shown to stem from specific social barriers and structures, rather than specific impairments. These barriers and structures encompass negative attitudes and perceptions but also more observable barriers such as policies and the organization of social spaces. This model of disability creates a distinction between *disability*—the loss of opportunities to engage in myriad aspects of society on equal footing—and *impairment*, one or more conditions that cause a long-term change in, or loss of, function. Rather than focusing on what is wrong with a person, the focus of the social model is on how strictures of information, access, and participation are embedded in everyday life and serve *to disable* those with impaired functioning. By the reckoning of this model, in order for full participation to be possible, social structures, relationships, and beliefs must be changed.

Individuals with disabilities in Senegal experience significant levels of exclusion in terms of health care, education, housing, employment, and other basic human services. La Loi d'orientation sociale, adopted by the Senegalese parliament in 2010, is the result of many years of advocacy to address the systemic discrimination experienced by individuals with disabilities in Senegal. Certain phrases (indicated in italics from highlighted excerpts of the law) illustrate dichotomy and evident tensions between the medical and social models of disability. I begin my analysis of key phrases and labels embedded within the text of the law, written in its entirety in French (and translated by me) with the title: *La Loi d'orientation sociale n° 2010–15 du 6 juillet 2010 relative à la promotion et à la protection des droits de personnes handicapées.*[12] Throughout the law, phrasings of this sort indicate a range of actions and measures intended to protect an especially defenseless population (*une politique publique en faveur de cette couche de la population particulièrement vulnerable* or "policies intended for a segment of the population that is particularly vulnerable"). These phrases include *la défense* (defense) and *la prise en charge* (support), and refer to a set of measures intended to improve access to better social and living conditions for people with disabilities.

The focus of the law is captured in this assertion: *Elle prend en compte les perspectives en matière de stratégies de réadaptation, de mobilisation des ressources et d'encadrement* ("It [the law] takes into account the perspectives related to rehabilitation strategies, mobilization of resources, and guidance"). The law has an undertone throughout that evokes the medical perspective on disability, which centers disability and/or difference in the individual rather than in inequitable structures in society. There is a clear emphasis on the provision of intervention services to address areas of impairment, an emphasis that tacitly implies a need for rehabilitation in order to meet societal standards of ableness. Special guarantees that favor people with disabilities, considered to be positive discrimination, are supported as well: *Ne sont pas considérées comme discriminatoires, les mesures incitatives spéciales en faveur des personnes handicapées qui visent à garantir l'égalité effective de chance et de traitment* ("Special incentives for people with disabilities which, guaranteeing equal opportunity and treatment, are not considered discriminatory"). This positive discrimination is formulated in the provision of access to medical services for free (for those with severe disabilities) or at a reduced price (for those with disabilities in general). A reduction in other fees includes reduced import taxes for materials, equipment, and vehicles intended for people with disabilities.

Despite the clearly medical-model undertone to the law, there are specific statements addressing rights that imply access to full citizenship for people with disabilities. For example, the law states, *L'Etat et les Collectivités locales, dans leur ressorts respectifs, assurent la pleine et entière participation des personnes handicapées à la vie sociale, économique et culturelle de la Nation* ("State and local governments in their respective jurisdictions, ensure the full participation of people with disabilities in the social, economic, and cultural life of the Nation"). The focus on full participation can be seen within specific domains. For example, in the domain of education, the law states, *L'Etat garantit le droit à l'éducation, l'enseignement, la formation et l'emploi pour les personnes handicapées* ("The State guarantees the right to education, training, and employment for people with disabilities").

The law also includes various labels to describe people with specific disabilities. There is a distinction made between those with milder versus more severe disabilities, and additional levels of supports are available for those with more significant disabilities. Ironically, the overall description of disability categories incorporates an acknowledgment of societal barriers, evident in the following excerpt: *Par personnes handicapées, on entend toutes les personnes qui présentent des incapacités physiques, mentales, intellectuelles ou sensorielles durables dont l'interaction avec diverses barrières peut porter atteinte à leur pleine et effective participation à la société sur la base de l'égalité* ("People with disabilities are defined as all individuals who have physical, mental, intellectual or sensory impairments, and who, when faced with various barriers, are prevented from achieving their full and effective participation in society on an equal basis"). This general description of categories of disability focuses on areas of impairment in the body and mind, without incorporating a value judgement on the person possessing the "incapacity." Other labels, particularly those referring to people with intellectual or more significant disabilities, serve to set apart those with significant disabilities as a distinct subgroup needing additional care (addressed in the next section). Examples of other labels used to describe people with disabilities in the law include *les malades* (patients or literally "the sick"), *une personne lourdement handicapée* (a severely disabled or handicapped person), *souffrent d'invalidité sévère* (they who suffer from a severe disability).

A novel component of the law includes the provision of a card identifying individuals with disabilities and assuring them access to key societal structures and rights. This seems to be an attempt to address, and directly acknowledge, some of the challenges faced by those with less visible, less understood, intellectual and social disabilities such as autism, traumatic brain injury, learning disabilities, and behavioral disabilities.

Specifically, the law states, *Toute personne handicapée reçoit une carte spécifique prouvant son handicap et appelée <une carte d'égalité des chances>* ("Every person with a disability will receive a specific card providing proof of his disability, called an 'equal opportunity card'"). The card assures the cardholder specific rights and access to *des droits et avantages en matière d'accès aux soins de santé, de réadaptation, d'aide technique, financière, d'éducation, de formation, d'emploi, de transport, ainsi qu'à tout autre avantage susceptible de contribuer à la promotion et à la protection des droits des personnes handicapées* (specifically, "rights and access to health care, rehabilitative intervention, technical and financial assistance, education, training, employment, transportation, and any other advantage which may contribute to the promotion and protection of the rights of people with disabilities").

This card does not require that services, spaces, and structures are modified to address the range of abilities of its users. Instead, it assures the cardholder the right to access the spaces and places that are available, access being a basic right. The provision of this card addresses the commonplace practice of exclusion experienced by people with disabilities; it does not, however, address the root causes or reasons for this exclusion. Opening the door does not ensure that the door will remain open, in other words, nor that the individual will not be escorted out of that same door when faced with inaccessible processes, procedures, attitudes, and values.

In addition to discussing examples of cultural conceptions of disability embedded in the recently adopted La Loi d'orientation sociale, I will next present and analyze labels representative of people with disabilities collected during interviews and observations throughout the participatory evaluation in the Wolof language. A bit of historical background: Prior to colonial influences, Wolof was spoken in the Senegambia area in the West Atlantic region of the African continent.[13] Movement due to migration and trade resulted in an increase in the number of individuals speaking the language, and it is now one of the dominant and primary national languages spoken by the majority of people in Senegal. The prominence of Wolof has been attributed to the interactions between colonial administrators who tended to be installed in large urban areas where there was a concentration of the population speaking Wolof. Because of its prominence, Wolof has become a necessity for communication for other ethnic groups migrating to Senegal to engage in commerce, work, and education, particularly in larger cities.

My data-gathering phase uncovered many phrases used to describe people with specific difficulties related to their senses. These phrases implied dysfunction, or simply lack of function, reflecting a more ableist orientation where a person "without" is implicitly compared to the normative standard "with." Examples include *dafa gumba* ("he is blind"), *dafa moumah* ("he is mute"), and *dafa tukh* ("he is deaf"). These labels were also used in French during observations and interviews. Examples include *personnes qui présentent des incapacités physiques, mentales, intellectuelles ou sensorielles durables* (people with physical, mental, intellectual or sensory impairments), *aux aveugles ou malvoyants* (blind or visually impaired), and *sourds* or *sourds muet* (deaf or deaf-mute). These labels reflect missing functions related to the senses and do not, on the surface, convey a value judgment based on perceived worth; hence, they are a problem both of translation and semantics.

An exhaustive examination of the uses and perceptions of these labels within specific cultural contexts is beyond the scope of this chapter; however, these contextual uses and their subtleties of meaning exist and are worth mention. For example, the statement *gumba du jitte yoon* ("a blind person should not lead the way") implies both literal and figurative connotations about the limitations of a person without sight, implicitly in comparison to those who have sight. Another contrast made in French between those with and without disabilities is the differential meaning inherent to phrases *les handicapées* and *les valides,* literally "the disabled" or "the able-bodied." Here, the concept of ableness is codified in the actual language used to refer to those without disabilities, who are viewed to be complete, fully able persons, as opposed to those who are missing some key function.

Differing notions of intelligence influenced by cultural values are embedded in language and beliefs about who is considered mentally whole, able, and worthy. What does it mean, for instance, to not "think well"? What are the implications for engagement in society? How people from different cultures are socialized to think about thinking differs and needs to be considered when people within specific cultures are deemed unable to think well according to that culture's norms and expectations.

Research has shown that ideas about intelligence and the culture of thinking vary by culture; basic cognitive processes may differ from one culture to the next.[14] When discussing cross-cultural distinctions, it is important to avoid simplistic comparisons. Being born to a particular cultural context does not limit a person from learning and assuming cognitive styles from other experiences and engagement with other cultural groups. However, it is important to acknowledge that cultural experiences do influence patterns of thought and ways of seeing the world that differ across groups, and that show up in what is valued in a person. While cautioning against overly simplistic notions that individuals from a particular cultural group share specific thought patterns, Etienne Benson cited research providing an example of potential culturally driven trends in cognition: "People in Western cultures . . . tend to view intelligence as a means for individuals to devise categories and to engage in rational debate, while people in Eastern cultures see it as a way for members of a community to recognize contradiction and complexity and to play their social roles successfully."[15]

Several phrases related to ideas about thought, reason, and intelligence demonstrate nuances in values-driven conceptions embedded in the actual Wolof language. Phrases related to thinking and cognition in Wolof, collected during discussions about the role and place of individuals with disabilities in Senegal, were varied and have differing connotations. For example, respondents used *amoul xam-xam* to refer to a lack of knowing or knowledge. In contrast, the phrase *xel bi nekhoul* is directly related to the quality of thinking an individual possesses. *Xel* refers to the mind, thinking, and thought. The phrase states that the mind or quality of thought is not good, implying deficient thinking. In the phrase *dafa doff* ("he is crazy"), a value judgment of a person's mental state is made. This person is not viewed to be in his or her right mind, and the implication is that the problem lies within the person. The individual's actions and behaviors do not align with societal norms, subtly hinting at a belief that a person who is acting crazy is doing so of his or her own volition. This person is not missing or lacking something concrete, such as knowledge or quality of thinking, as implied in *xel bi nekhoul*; rather he or she is lacking control and sense. He or she is viewed to have agency over his or her behavior and thus is making the deliberate choice to act outside of the societal norms.

Further examples of language embedded in policy include efforts to incorporate use of more "appropriate" terms and phrasing, evident in the increasing use of *les enfants à besoins éducatifs spéciaux* ("children with special education needs"). In the West, people-first social and political language constructions are intended to name a person separately from his or her disability, thereby deemphasizing his or her condition and attributing it to a variety of humanity encompassing more than a disability. The people-first language quoted above reflects what is considered more acceptable Western parlance (though its use is still inconsistent), and implies that a disability can be detached from the whole of a person. This language also negates the understanding that a person's essence of self is formed as a result of the totality of his or her life experiences, including experiences and interactions with a world built around able-bodied norms and the individuals or in-groups that embody them. The use of language in French acknowledging disability as part of selfhood is seen in terms such as *les handicapés* found in colloquial and policy language; however, when people with disabilities are instead totalized as "the disabled" (and the disability is framed as marginalization resulting from a world that is built only for those who fit norms), it is possible to read terms like *les handicapés* as a rejection or reframing of people-first language.

Despite the clearly medical emphasis and the focus on protection present throughout La Loi d'orientation sociale, I question whether it is automatically problematic that this law explicitly acknowledges the need for protection and care of an especially marginalized population. In the developing world, people significantly marginalized—because they are desperately poor—can constitute numerical majorities; which is to say, the majority of the population may not, or does not, have assurance of access to employment, health care, and so on. Yet people with disabilities, as a group, are still more deeply impacted. In Western contexts, where barriers to basic physical and legal structures are essentially disrupted, the focus tends toward (and has the luxury of attending to) deeper structures. Within a country like Senegal, the law (even with its location of disability within the individual) is nevertheless especially progressive because it assures, at least in principle, a significantly marginalized population services to which 90 percent of the larger population lacks access.

The medical model of disability remains strong and is evident in social institutions, such as schools. The need for care and protection embedded in the language of social and political discourse could also be a reflection of strong cultural values placed on family and personal health. This focus on family and understanding of behavior within the social context of the family directly contrast with many Western communities, where more individualistic and competitive relationships are often the norm. The emphasis of national legislation and local actions in support of individuals with disability should occur in tandem with efforts to reframe language and perceptions of disabilities, while also cultivating greater focus on creating systems of care and support that draw upon the cultural assets already present.

NOTES

1. Carleton Aslett-Rydbjerg, "Inclusive Education: Early Lessons Learned from Sengal: L'etude de faisabilite—Education speciale et integratrice" (paper, World Bank, NDF no. 306, November 13, 2003).

2. See Elizabeth R. Drame and Kaytie Kamphoff, "Perceptions of Disability and Access to Inclusive Education in West Africa: A Comparative Case Study in Dakar, Senegal," *International Journal of Special Education* 29, no. 3 (2014): 69–81.
3. Susan J. Peters, "A Historical Analysis of International Education Policy and Individuals with Disabilities," *Journal of Disability Policy Studies* 18, no. 2 (2007): 98–108.
4. Suzanne G. Lamorey, "The Effects of Culture on Special Education Services: Evil Eyes, Prayer Meetings, and IEPs," in *Inclusion for ALL: The UN Convention on the Rights of Persons with Disabilities*, trans. Deborah Zeigler (New York: IDebate Press, 2010).
5. Fiona Kumari Campbell, "Exploring Internalized Ableism Using Critical Race Theory," *Disability and Society* 23, no. 2 (2008): 151–162.
6. For more on critical disability theory, see Diane Pothier and Richard Devlin, eds., *Critical Disability Theory: Essays in Philosophy, Politics, Policy, and Law* (Vancouver: University of British Columbia Press, 2006).
7. Susan Bassnett, "Culture and Translation," in *A Companion to Translation Studies*, ed. Piotr Kuhiwczak and Karin Littau (Clevedon: Multilingual Matters, 2007), 20.
8. Margaret Wetherell, Stephanie Joyce Ann Taylor, and Simeon J. Yates, eds., *Discourse as Data: A Guide for Analysis* (London: Sage, 2001).
9. James Paul Gee, *An Introduction to Discourse Analysis: Theory and Method*, 2nd ed. (London: Routledge, 2014).
10. See Jennifer Fereday and Eimear Muir-Cochrane, "Demonstrating Rigor Using Thematic Analysis: A Hybrid Approach of Inductive and Deductive Coding and Theme Development," *International Journal of Qualitative Methods* 5, no. 1 (2006): 80–92; and Prachi Srivastava and Nick Hopwood, "A Practical Iterative Framework for Qualitative Data Analysis," *International Journal of Qualitative Methods* 8, no. 1 (2009): 76–84.
11. Pothier and Devlin, *Critical Disability Theory*.
12. For the full text of La Loi d'orientation sociale, see Secretariat General du Gouvernement, *Loi d'orientation sociale n° 2010–15* (July 6, 2010), www.jo.gouv.sn/spip.php?article8267.
13. See "Wolof," overview provided by the Penn Language Center at the University of Pennsylvania, https://plc.sas.upenn.edu/wolof.
14. Etienne Benson, "Intelligence across Cultures: Research in Africa, Asia, and Latin American Is Showing How Culture and Intelligence Interact," *Monitor* 34, no. 2 (2003), www.apa.org/monitor/feb03/intelligence.aspx.
15. Ibid.

11 • THE TRANSLATOR IN THE TEXT

SUZANNE JILL LEVINE

When we first learn to speak as children, we are learning to translate.
—Octavio Paz, "Translation: Literature and Letters"

Like many of my contemporaries, I discovered literature and admirable authors in my childhood, in those first tentative encounters with books like Lewis Carroll's *Alice in Wonderland*, discovering the magic of the written word. A little later on, there was the adventure of learning and reading in a foreign language—French—in junior high school (now called middle school), and in high school was where the idea of translation first came to mind. I grew up in a New York Jewish family with its share of jokesters and music lovers as well as a beautiful sister who in her youth was a successful actress. A form of humor we practiced at home around the kitchen table was the playful mimicry of speech styles and accents, living as we did, until I reached the age of sixteen, in a diverse immigrant neighborhood in Upper Manhattan. All this would come in handy (I now see) to the tinkering translator I would become.

To speak about the translator in the text, or how I became engaged with the translational nature of being a writer, I return to early adulthood and to one of the first writers I translated. In my book *The Subversive Scribe*, I wrote, "You often seek in the foreign what you are drawn to, perhaps unknowingly, in the familiar." Translation, as we know, is synonymous etymologically with metaphor and means movement from one place to another. I began to translate in my late teens, motivated by a love of literature but also a desire to discover other cultures, to be translated, to travel to foreign lands, which also meant an internal voyage, to begin to explore oneself through the words of others.

At age twenty-two, then in graduate school at Columbia University, I met the person who would be my first partner in life, with whom I would soon travel to England: Emir Rodriguez Monegal, a major scholar of Latin American literature and a prominent Uruguayan literary critic who in 1968 had been appointed chair of the Spanish department at Yale University. It was with Emir that I would get to know great writers from Latin America and become further immersed in Hispanic culture. I not only had lived in Madrid, Spain as a junior in college but had spent the summer of 1968 in Cali, Colombia—not too distant from the birthplace of Gabriel García Márquez where, through an exchange program, I had been an intern at a factory. That summer I made a literary discovery, almost as great for me as Hispaniola had been for Christopher Columbus: in Cali, among my new acquaintances, a young poet gave me a book I couldn't put down: it would become in English *One Hundred Years of Solitude*—soon to be translated by a professor at Columbia University, Gregory Rabassa. The eminent Gregory Rabassa was a significant force in bringing a number of great works to the attention of readers in the English-speaking world, and this extraordinary novel convinced me that Latin American literature was a rich path I wanted to follow. The hyperbolic language of Gabriel García Márquez coupled with Emir's critical enthusiasm led me to an even more significant writer, whom Mario Vargas Llosa has called "the father of the Latin American novel": Jorge Luis Borges. Here was an Argentine writer who, unlike most Argentine intellectuals who looked to France for as the fount of culture, was an Anglophile.

In swinging London, in 1969, I met the Borgesian, metafictional author of the first book I would translate. He was Guillermo Cabrera Infante, a recently exiled Cuban who, in 1965, had been fired from his post as director of the literary supplement of the official Revolution newspaper, *Granma*. Cabrera Infante had come to fiction writing, or fictional memoir writing, as a film critic in Havana before the revolution. He was also the son of the founders of Cuba's Communist Party. At first a collaborator in the revolution, he had been sent into exile in 1964, having participated in a protest against censorship and Stalinist cultural policy inside the island. He was now a *gusano,* as Fidelistas called the Cuban exiles. It was curious that Fidel used the same term that Hitler had used with racist venom and propagandistic zeal against the Jews of Europe—*gusano* meaning vermin or worm—for a man he deemed a traitor, a Trotsky to Fidel's Stalin.

Fidel banished Cabrera Infante—who came to identify with Trotsky and his fate—in a diplomatic way, literally, by appointing him to a minor diplomatic post in the Cuban embassy in Brussels. While in his office in the dreary basement of this building, the writer heard the sad news about the tragic death of one of Cuba's great musicians, a torch singer named Freddy Rodriguez, and this is where the real writing of *Tres tristes tigres* began. When explaining this carnivalesque novel, a very funny but also very sad book, about Havana as a city of the night, Cabrera Infante especially emphasized to critics that it was a "betrayal": *traduttore traditore.* He framed it as an original Roman comique that was really a failed translation of Petronius's *Satyricon,* translating the fauna of ancient Rome's nightlife into the night owls of Havana on the eve of Revolution. Cabrera Infante also refused to call it a novel, and always called it a book, in part because it departed from the traditional novel but also because for him it wasn't fiction, but closer to autobiography, though one could argue that most fiction is autobiographical.

Set adrift from the revolution, writing in exile as a cultural attaché in Brussels, he finished *Tres tristes tigres*, with its apparently nonreferential title from a limerick in Spanish; the book would catapult him into literary fame as a new member of the Latin American "Boom." *Three Trapped Tigers*, as we translated the title, was a true carnevale to the Havana Infante, a neo-baroque satire filled with literary and filmic allusions, a collage of voices and narratives and puns exploding with subversive intent. The Boom, which referred to newly discovered Latin American writers such as Carlos Fuentes and Julio Cortázar whose work was considered experimental, was a concept Emir and some of his contemporaries had coined during his tenure as editor of *Mundo Nuevo*, the first international Latin American literary journal in English. Although this term served to make readers aware of these emerging writers, Cabrera Infante was not a fan of terms like Boom and hated even more so the much-used literary-critical term "experimental," which he felt should be reserved for scientists in their laboratories. He also considered himself a Havanan or *habanero*, rather than Cuban, and cultivated a cosmopolitan approach to life, culture, and literature. When John Updike reviewed our translation in the *New Yorker*, he denigrated the author for attempting to be a Cuban Joyce.

Updike's condescending thesis seemed to question why writers from Cuba would produce avant-garde literature or poetic innovation when what readers needed was social realism, that is, to learn about everyday life in Cuba, which had importance now that Cuba had had its revolution. The irony is that *Three Trapped Tigers* is probably the most realistic novel about Havana ever written. In any case, Updike's review seemed symptomatic of a bias on the part of the Anglo-American literary establishment (nowadays, one could argue, supplanted by the "global" literary establishment) in its view of Hispanic culture, seeing its value as anthropological or political but not poetic or aesthetic, with certain exceptions. Now, curiously, Cuba has a "global" value in which a Cuban Joyce might be accepted; however, a buzzword such as Joycean, at this point, translates into a reductive sound bite. Ultimately the value of Cuba pertains to cultural tourism and the marketplace, fundamentally the same value it had during the Cold War, before the revolution.

On the eve of the revolution, Cuba was virtually a bilingual country. After the island was "discovered" by Spain in the fifteenth century, it was then colonized from the late nineteenth century until 1959 by its giant and very close neighbor, the United States. In the mid-1960s, what was not only innovative but in the deepest sense relevant to this political reality in Cabrera Infante's polyglot book was that it was written in a Spanish invaded by English. Wordplay and Cuban *choteo* (sexual double entendres) burst with Joycean extravagance from its pages in various languages, in which, even closer to the spirit of Lewis Carroll, nonsense made more sense than most anything else. Its epigraph, a quotation taken from our old friend Carroll himself, announces that the book's driving theme is translation and/or memory as a treasonous translator: "And she tried to fancy what the flame of a candle is like after the candle is blown out." Memory was Cabrera Infante's translator of Cuba's sound and living speech into writing, and writing was what remained of his country, for him, for the rest of his life, in exile.

In our first conversations, Guillermo and I learned that we were fellow fans not only of Lewis Carroll but, more importantly, of Groucho Marx. That is, we were devoted to puns and could chat for hours about Hollywood films, recalling dialogues and imitating actors. We met at the time he was co-translating *TTT* (as Cabrera Infante would nickname the book, stressing its "explosion" onto the literary scene) with an English poet whose Spanish was rudimentary and who wanted to convert Cuban slang into British cockney. Cabrera Infante, an Anglophile like Borges, loved London, but he didn't want his street savvy Cuban characters to speak cockney. As he was not happy with this situation, he asked me, his fellow Marxist, to take over from the poet and to help him translate the book. A detailed account of our collaboration can be found in *The Subversive Scribe: Translating Latin American Fiction*.

In *Three Trapped Tigers* the reader learns that words conceal as much as they reveal meaning; on almost every page one encounters how, in the realm of intimate life as well as in politics and history, lies can be accepted as truth, and truths as lies. As coauthor of the translation, I was co-creating a necessarily "treasonous" English version conscious of its counterfeit: of how a writer must explore what is not said, must become an interpreter, a translator, and must look through the surface to see the secret design. Some translators from the Spanish told me that they envied me *Three Trapped Tigers* as it was so playful and as I was free to invent; that is, they envied a position not usually open to translators, in which I was "authorized" by the author to be creative in ways that would be unconventional and not acceptable in a run-of-the-mill translation. What was lost in spoken Cuban was gained in literary and even sometimes a foreigner's English, in the Benjaminian spirit of translation as a creative mode. The English version was, indeed, thirty pages longer because of our, as he put it, closelaboration (a portmanteau)—words kept begetting other words with Babelic excess. Indeed we wanted the title page to read "closelaborated," instead of translated, but the publisher (Cass Canfield Jr., senior editor at Harper & Row, which today is HarperCollins) put his foot down: we, author and translator, were invading sacred—that is, editorial—territory by trying to change the title page. Publishers had the last word when it came to a book's cover.

I always return in such discussions to my early translation venture with Cabrera Infante because it clearly dramatizes the creative side of translation. Many poets have spoken this way about translation, but I think my book *The Subversive Scribe*—which originally came out in 1991—was one of the first in which the Poundian or transcreational approach was associated to a work of prose. Again, this all largely had to do with the fact that the era during which I began translating was not only during the Boom of the Latin American novel, but also the boom of deconstruction and poststructuralist theory. The writers I translated early on were not social realists but meta-fictionists; in addition to Cabrera Infante's *Three Trapped Tigers*, I also allude here to works like Severo Sarduy's *Cobra* and Manuel Puig's *Betrayed by Rita Hayworth*. For these writers, the subject of narrative was a fragmented subject, and the self was constituted by a free-floating discourse.

Literary translation, like the modernist novel, is by necessity a self-conscious act, a mirroring of a text already written, in which the translator must constantly make difficult decisions in an attempt to bring fragments together in a whole, knowing that it can never be completed. By strategically trying to take the author's place, the translator's very existence questions and pays homage to authorship, subverting the figure of the author whose creative "product" as a translation—now that it is discussed as such—has become explicitly what it always implicitly was: a dialogue of texts, a relationship between perceiver and perceived. Translating with Cabrera Infante confirmed for me early on that translation is an "act of writing," never finite without a reader, always an act of interpretation, and no different, philosophically, than the task of the original writer. When it comes to collaboration with an author, whether or not the author is physically present, you are always collaborating with an "other" to create yet another text.

My next translation, Manuel Puig's *Betrayed by Rita Hayworth*, had a front-page review in the Sunday *New York Times* Book Review, a miraculous event as it was a difficult book by an obscure author. Manuel wrote me a letter telling me that all his friends at a party in Buenos Aires were saying that they wanted "to be translated by Jill." In his campy, hyperbolic style, that same letter said, "Bioy Casares, Silvina Ocampo, and a bunch of other people are dreaming of being translated by you." With the exception of Bioy's famous friend Jorge Luis Borges, almost all the writers I translated were marginal in the sense of being on the periphery of the Latin American Boom; that is, they weren't magical realists. Both Infante and Puig were more like hyperrealists, exciting pioneers in their use of the spoken languages of their regions, and in the dynamic role of popular culture in their works. Because both were avid moviegoers and fans of American movies since childhood, both had a great command of vernacular English, even though they spoke it with an accent. Again, we must remember: historically, English was an important element in their national cultures for political, social, and economic reasons. Both Puig and Cabrera Infante wrote in English, but not at the level of their written Spanish, though Susan Sontag was a big fan of Cabrera Infante's "foreigner's English." Working with them was interesting from the perspective of their comfort with English and their freely creative attitude toward the translation of their texts.

I have been arguing here for the almost oneness of author and translator, but I am speaking of a special circumstance: my own as the author's collaborator in this case. There is of course a big difference normally between the authors of translations, that is, translators and The Author. When working together on a text, a translator may consult but the author will always be the consultant. Quoting French translator Albert Bensoussan, who writes with a flourish of puns inspired by Infante on the unequal roles of author and translator in shifting terms of gender and sex: "Femelle . . . le traducteur rend en son langage l'auteur publiable, mais il est oubliable. L'auteur s'ouvre, le traducteur se ferme. . . . L'auteur se crée, le traducteur secret. . . . Le traducteur n' est que voix de passage."[1] Here Bensoussan was reiterating the age-old handmaiden metaphor: the translator is female, even when he's a male.

In my own writing about translation but also in my translations I have tried to desex or at least to question this traditional assumption. Working from the borderlessness (or at least continuity) between translation and original, I wrote in *The Subversive Scribe*, "Then perhaps we can begin to see the translator in another light, no longer bearing the stigma of servant, of handmaiden. Translation, saddling the scholarly and the creative, can be a route through which a writer/translator may seek to reconcile fragments: fragments of texts, of language, of oneself."[2] Anne Malena, a Canadian translator, considered my book "A Translator's Apologia": "briefly pondering the feminized translator, traitor . . . as self-betrayer fallen under the spell of male discourse, translating books that speak of woman as the often treacherous or betrayed, Levine's apologia then is to 'take her own back,' so to speak, to subvert the notion of the translator and female betrayer, in fact to embrace betrayal and the pleasures of 'transcreating.'"[3]

Even when not translating in collaboration, as when I translated a novella by the polyglot and prolific Mexican Carlos Fuentes, translation can still be seen as creative collaboration, with the translator transforming the text in another literary context. I speak here specifically of his *Zona sagrada, Holy Place* (literally *Sacred Zone*), which came out in 1972 in a collection of three novellas, called, unfortunately, *Triple Cross*. Carlos had suggested a great title for the anthology of these three cross-dressing-themed novellas, *The Baudyville Trio*, which would have been more in the spirit of this eccentric group. *Triple Cross* made the book sound like a spy thriller, definitely the wrong signal to its possible readers. The most accessible of the three fictions was *El lugar sin limites* (*Hell Has No Limits*) by José Donoso, Carlos's childhood friend, and the third was a neo-baroque tour de farce, a kind of profane and petite *Divine Comedy* of Cuba, called *De dónde son los cantantes*, which became, in English, *From Cuba with a Song*. This was the work of a young gay Cuban writer in exile in Paris, Severo Sarduy, one of the most difficult writers I would translate.

This far-out project, very iffy for any publisher, was another example of Carlos's generosity with his fellow writers. While it was a way to get one of his own more obscure small works into translation, he was also helping the newly discovered Sarduy, as well as his dear friend Donoso, whose *Hell Has No Limits* was a brilliant novella and a courageous work at that time in the Latin American context, as its protagonist was an effeminate gay man and cross-dresser.

I worked on Carlos Fuentes's novel in the summer of 1971, and in a letter to me Carlos wrote that I made him "read like Henry James," both an ambiguous compliment and appropriate remark in that the style of *Zona sagrada* was self-consciously convoluted. We became friends as we collaborated on the translation, and our correspondence is a source of insights, certainly revealing Carlos's polyglot sophistication, as in this letter written to me from Mexico City, expressing his concern about the dialogues of Claudia, the character who was based directly on the famous Mexican actress Maria Felix:

> I have only one basic desire: that the Claudia-Mito dialogs should be a lot harder, rougher, biting, more vulgar. As long as he narrates in the 1st person, the Jamesian tone with baroque overtones is just perfect; when the mother and son engage in verbal battle, there should be (as in the Spanish original) a marked difference; Claudia, particularly, should be much more bitchy and almost gangster-like in her speech: like something out of Raymond Chandler or Ross MacDonald.[4]

Carlos's guidance was invaluable: by suggesting that I translate Claudia's snap-diva with a flair reminiscent of the sharp dialogues in Raymond Chandler, he was right on target. As the author, he had been influenced by the hard-boiled American detective genre or roman noir. Indeed, one of the books that most influenced him in its style and treatment of social and political corruption was Dashiell Hammett's *Red Harvest*. These writers' works were popular in the movies, and they often worked as screenwriters; as I've mentioned, Carlos was fascinated by Hollywood and the world of cinema. Like many writers he felt that the ultimate homage would be a film based on his work. Like Emir, Cabrera Infante, and Puig, he took a fond camp delight in not only film divas but especially the B movie actresses, in Mexico as well as Hollywood.

> You'll be amused to know that the shooting of ZONA SAGRADA starts on Aug. 23, with Maria Felix & Son. The goings on makes the novel pale; the Star, in real life, is almost murdering the kid with minor and major cruelties. He will arrive on the set pale, withered and choro: Let Emir in on a strictly private, Latin American joke: Ruth will be played by Gloria Marin, another ex-wife of Jorge Negrete El Charro Cantor. Nostalgia and camp. It's almost like having Greta Garbo and Virginia Bruce play opposite each other (Emir will say: Garbo played opposite Ina Claire, and that's really trivia!) Let me mull over the title problem . . . HOLY PLACES? TEMPLE?, SHRINE?, HOLY PLAY?, PICTURE AND SOUL?, oh damn.[5]

For Fuentes, *Zona sagrada* was, as he suggests above, a trip down memory lane via classic cinema, a cynical fictional portrait that traced nostalgically the image of his favorite Mexican diva to her mythic origins as a goddess, from ancient Greece as well as from pre-Columbian Mexico. One can also think of the translator as nostalgic: lost between past and present, recasting what cannot be totally recovered, between one culture and another. This analogy made sense to me after reading about the cineaste Henri Langlois, who founded the famous Cinémathèque Française. He spoke of the film buff—which I consider myself to be, and certainly what Cabrera Infante, Puig, and Carlos Fuentes were—as a nostalgic being, who lives with a sense of loss or exile, a sense of childhood's lost paradise and of the past as another country, because the images with which we become enamored are already in the past. Indeed, essentially, they are ghosts. With nostalgia I miss most of these writers I knew and translated, now gone to the other world. One of my more recent translation projects is a posthumous novel by the aforementioned José Donoso titled *Lagartija sin cola* (*The Lizard's Tale* or, literally, *Lizard without a Tail*). For me as translator, this project carried with it a measure of reincarnation, in part because, like most posthumous works, the original was unfinished.

Retracing the pilgrimage of editor and poet Julio Ortega, who had turned Donoso's dossier of found manuscripts into a publishable work, I visited the Firestone Library in Princeton, where many Latin American writers' papers are held. Among Donoso's papers I found some answers to the initial enigma of how to approach this incomplete work. One of the answers concerns the title. Among his original titles in the manuscript was *The Lizard's Tail* (*La cola de la lagartija*). Because another novel from Latin America (written by Argentine Luisa Valenzuela in the 1970s) bears this title, Julio Ortega made a slight variation, giving the title a more explicit image, which in turn is related to a significant image in the novel: the lizard's shedding of its tail as a mode of survival.

Donoso had started this project in 1973, and in his notebook tracking this work in progress I was able to discover that the original project consisted of sections of three related storylines (the titles of the other two were, respectively, "Pap Test" and "The Visa"). Here the Chilean author spoke of wanting to achieve stylistically a "classical effect," for the book to be written in a complex way but to flow for the reader. Donoso, who had learned English in a private school in Chile where he first met fellow classmate Carlos Fuentes, spoke English fluently with a slight British accent and, in this work as in other novels he wrote, he includes phrases or words in French, Italian, and especially English. In his notes, in the midst of complaining that Spanish wasn't easy to conquer, Donoso made the startling assertion: "I would give my life to write in English."

I tried very hard to follow his wish in giving his book a life in English he hopefully would have welcomed. In this spirit, I gave his title another turn of the screw—to allude to Henry James, the Anglo-American author both he and Fuentes greatly admired—by rendering it as "The Lizard's Tale." By doing this, I sought to call once more upon Fuentes's childhood friend as posthumous collaborator. I would like to end here by quoting Jorge Luis Borges's short meditation "The Enigma of Edward Fitzgerald," Fitzgerald having been the original English translator of Omar Khayyam and creator of the *Rubaiyat*: "All collaboration is mysterious. That of the Englishman and the Persian was even more so, for the two were quite different, and perhaps in life might not have been friends; death and vicissitudes and time led one to know the other and make them into a single poet."[6]

NOTES

Epigraph source: Octavio Paz, "Translation: Literature and Letters," in *Theories of Translation: An Anthology of Essays from Dryden to Derrida*, ed. Rainer Schulte and John Biguenet, trans. Irene del Corral (Chicago: University of Chicago Press, 1992).

1. See Albert Bensoussan, *Confessions d'un traître: Essai sur la traduction* (Rennes: Presses universitaires de Rennes, 1995), 71. "Le traducteur subit, soumis, subjugué. Femelle, même s'il est parfois amazone. Pris, prisonnier, enferré, enserré. Ne s'appartient plus. Aliéné, absorbé, ravi et dépossédé de sa propre parole. Parole de l'autre, l'auteur, la hauteur. Le traducteur est inférieur, postérieur, postsynchronisé. Le traducteur rend en son langage l'auteur publiable, mais il est oubliable. L'auteur s'ouvre, le traducteur se ferme, le premier s'éclot, le second se clot. L'auteur se crée, le traducteur secret. Le traducteur n'est que voix de passage" (The translator renders in his language the author publishable but he is forgettable. The author creates himself, the translator remains secret. . . . The translator is only a voice of passage). From Suzanne Jill Levine, "Epilogue: Traduttora, Traditora," in *The Subversive Scribe: Translating Latin American Fiction*, 2nd ed. (Champaign: Dalkey Archive Press, 2009), 183.
2. Levine, "Epilogue," 183.
3. Anne Malena, "A Translator's Apologia," *TranscUlturAl* 1, no. 2 (2009): 182.
4. Letter from Carlos Fuentes to Suzanne Jill Levine, November 1971.
5. Ibid.
6. Jorge Luis Borges, *The Selected Non-Fictions*, ed. Eliot. Weinberger, trans. Esther Allen, Suzanne Jill Levine, and Eliot Weinberger (New York: Penguin, 1999), 368.

ACKNOWLEDGMENTS

This volume grew out of a conference that took place at the Center for International Education at the University of Wisconsin–Milwaukee (UWM) in April 2015. Organized by Patrice Petro and Lorena Terando, this three-day event began with a lecture by Professor Lydia Liu, under the auspices of the UWM Institute for World Affairs. As is the case with many edited volumes, *At Translation's Edge* is a deeply collaborative effort, involving the talents of the editors and authors included here as well as those of many others who assisted with tasks both large and small. The editors wish to thank Professor A. Aneesh, Director of the Institute of World Affairs, who helped secure Lydia Liu's participation at the conference, and UWM Professors Lane Hall and Lisa Moline, who created distinctive artwork to represent and promote the event.

The conference itself was thoroughly interdisciplinary, with scholars in attendance from a range of disciplines, spanning comparative literature and translation studies to media studies and educational psychology. The impetus for the gathering was an effort to bring translation studies into dialogue with other disciplines and to provide space for an extended conversation with a shared vocabulary of key concepts, historical encounters, and disciplinary trajectories.

Following the conference, the organizers enlisted Nataša Ďurovičová, who was a participant in the conference, to join them in editing the volume itself. The three editors worked tirelessly on putting the collection together. This was no small feat, given institutional budget cuts at UWM, a major move of CIE's Vice Provost Petro to UC Santa Barbara, and many other unforeseen challenges that were managed by the editors across two academic centers and three academic institutions: the Center for International Education at UWM, the Carsey-Wolf Center at UC Santa Barbara, and the editors' home institutions of UWM, UCSB, and the University of Iowa. The editors are indebted to several individuals who made this volume possible. Graduate project assistant at UWM Mark Brand provided outstanding logistical support to the conference itself and assisted in copyediting at an early stage; at UCSB, Associate Director of the Carsey-Wolf Center Emily Zinn and UCSB graduate student researchers Alexander Champlin and Naomi DeCelles helped to prepare the final manuscript for publication, through careful review and expert copyediting.

Taken together, the essays assembled here take up questions of translation in its most expansive, interdisciplinary, and exploratory sense: translation as exchange, migration, and mobility, including cross-cultural communication and media circulation. While traditionally addressing the movement and history of ideas, languages, and cultures, translation for many of the authors in this collection is also a concept invoked not only to trouble and set on edge conventional approaches to the study of language and literature, but also to account for the forces, processes, and politics that precipitate the act of translation itself.

NOTES ON CONTRIBUTORS

OLGA BEHAR is a professor in the College of Communication and the Department of Humanities at the University of Santiago de Cali, Colombia. A journalist by training, she has held public office in Colombia and serves as editorial advisor to the Plataforma de Periodismo. Her books include *Las guerras de la paz* (1985) and *Noches de humo* (1987 and 2011), *El clan de los doce apóstoles* (2011), and *El caso Klein* (2012). She is a past recipient of the Premio Nacional de Periodismo Simón Bolívar in 1980 and the Primer Primio del Circulo de Periodistas de Bogotá for the best book written by a journalist in 2012.

JOHN CAYLEY is a professor of literary arts at Brown University. He is a pioneering practitioner and theorist of digital language arts. He is also a poet, translator, and small publisher with a BA in Chinese Language and Civilization. He won the inaugural Electronic Literature Organization's award for Poetry in 2001; translated the work of Gu Cheng, Yang Lian, Bing Xin, and others; and assembled a book-length study of the artist Xu Bing's *Tianshu* or *Book from the Sky*. His recent and ongoing projects include *How It Is in Common Tongues* (an outcome of *The Readers Project* with Daniel C. Howe—thereadersproject.org), *imposition* with Giles Perring, *riversland*, and *what we will*. He works with code, network services, big data, and writing for immersive virtual reality ("the Cave").

ELIZABETH R. DRAME is an associate professor and chair of the Department of Exceptional Education at the University of Wisconsin–Milwaukee. She coordinates the Autism Spectrum Disorders Certificate program, and her research interests include educational outcomes for students with disabilities in inclusive schools in the United States and abroad, social justice and equity issues in special education, and teacher quality. Her recent publications include "Perceptions of Disability and Access to Inclusive Education in West Africa: A Comparative Case Study in Dakar, Senegal" (2014), "Participatory Research in Support of Quality Public Education in New Orleans" (2014), and "We Make the Road by Walking: A Collaborative Inquiry into the Experiences of Women in Academia" (2012). She is coeditor of *Collaborative Practitioners, Collaborative Schools* (2012).

NATAŠA ĎUROVIČOVÁ is the house editor of the International Writing Program at the University of Iowa, where she publishes *91st Meridian*, the program's online journal and book series. Her research interests include early sound, voice in cinema, Central/East European cinemas, film historiography, theories of space, translation in hybrid media, and the politics of translation. As a film scholar, she works on language transfer in old and new media, as well as cinema in its national and post-national formations. Her publications include *World Cinemas, Transnational Perspectives,* coedited with Kathleen Newman (2009), "Los Toquis, or Urban Babel" (2003), and "Local Ghosts: The Human Body and Early Sound Cinema" (2003).

DEBORAH FOLARON is an associate professor in translation studies at Concordia University, Montreal, Canada. She is cofounder and coeditor of *Translation Spaces: A Multidisciplinary, Multimedia, and Multilingual Journal of Translation,* which seeks to explore the diverse spaces of encounter and translation that are emerging as a result of globalization and technologies. In 2011, she launched the multilingual website *Translation Romani.* Localized into ten languages (English, French, Portuguese, Spanish, Italian, German, Turkish, Hungarian, Czech, and Romani), the site presents two worlds of knowledge, Romani and translation, in relation to one another and to other languages and cultures of the world. Her current research focuses on translation theories and practices in the context of contemporary digital society, multilingualism, and less-translated minority languages, with a focus on Romani.

SUZANNE JILL LEVINE is a professor of Spanish and Portuguese as well as director of translation studies at the University of California, Santa Barbara. She has translated the work of Latin American writers such as Guillermo Cabrera Infante, Manuel Puig, Julio Cortázar, José Donoso, Silvina Ocampo, and Adolfo Bioy Casares. Her books include *The Subversive Scribe: Translating Latin American Fiction* (2009), *Manuel Puig and the Spider Woman: His Life and Fictions* (2000), and her five-volume edition of Jorge Luis Borges's poetry and essays (2010). Her most recent translations, *Mundo Cruel: Stories by Luis Negrón,* won the 2014 Lambda Prize for Fiction, and she is past recipient of multiple PEN awards, National Endowment for the Arts and Humanities grants, and a Guggenheim Foundation fellowship.

LYDIA H. LIU is a theorist of media and translation living in New York. She is Wun Tsun Tam Professor in the Humanities at Columbia University and the director of the Institute for Comparative Literature and Society. She has published extensively on literary theory, translation, digital media, Chinese feminism, and empire in English and Chinese. Her books include *The Freudian Robot: Digital Media and the Future of the Un-conscious* (2010), *The Clash of Empires: The Invention of China in Modern World Making* (2004), an edited volume titled *Tokens of Exchange: The Problem of Translation in Global Circulations* (1999), as well as a coedited translation with Rebecca Karl and Dorothy Ko titled *The Birth of Chinese Feminism: Essential Texts in Transnational Theory* (2013).

MARGARET A. NOODIN is an assistant professor of English and American Indian studies at the University of Wisconsin–Milwaukee, where she also serves as director of the Institute for American Indian Education. She is the author of

Weweni: Poems in Anishinaabemowin and English (2015), author of *Bawaajimo: A Dialect of Dreams in Anishinaabemowin* (2014), and editor of *Ogimaakwe Mitigawaki* (2011). Her poems and essays have been anthologized and published in *Sing: Poetry from the Indigenous Americas*, the *Michigan Quarterly Review*, *Water Stone Review*, and *Yellow Medicine Review*. She is past president of the Studies in American Indian Literatures Association, and current president of the MLA Division of Language Change and member of the MLA Delegate Organizing Committee.

PATRICE PETRO is a professor of film and media studies at the University of California, Santa Barbara, where she also serves as the Dick Wolf Director of the Carsey-Wolf Center and Presidential Chair in Media Studies. She is the author, editor, and coeditor of twelve books, most recently *The Routledge Companion to Cinema and Gender* (2017), *After Capitalism: Horizons of Finance, Culture, and Citizenship* (2016), *Teaching Film* (Modern Language Association of America, 2012), and *Idols of Modernity: Movie Stars of the 1920s* (2010). She is past president of the Society for Cinema and Media Studies, the United States' leading professional organization of college and university educators, filmmakers, critics, scholars, and others devoted to the study of the moving image.

MARTHA PULIDO is a professor of translation at the Universidad de Andioquia, Medellín, Colombia, and is currently a visiting professor in the postgraduate program on translation studies at Universidade Federal de Santa Catarina, in Florianópolis, Brazil. Her work includes *Filosofía e historia en la práctica de la traducción* (2003) and the translation into Spanish of *Los Traductores en la Historia* (2005) and *Filosofía de los acontecimientos* (2002). In 2011 the City of Medellín and Alliance Française-Medellín published her translation into Spanish of *Ágata de Medellín* by Jaques Jouet, and her most recent translation is *Orden y tiempo en la filosofía de Michel Foucault*, edited by Diogo Sardinha (2014). She is the founder of the journal *Mutatis Mutandis*, and her current research focuses on the history of translation.

NAOKI SAKAI is Goldwin Smith Professor of Asian Studies at Cornell University, where he teaches comparative literature, Asian studies, and history. He has published in the fields of comparative literature, intellectual history, translation studies, the studies of racism and nationalism, and the histories of textuality. His book-length publications include *Translation and Subjectivity* (1997), *Voices of the Past* (1991), and *The Stillbirth of the Japanese as a Language and as an Ethos* (1995). He serves on the editorial boards of numerous publications in the United States and abroad, and he is the founding editor of the project *TRACES*, a multilingual series in five languages: Korean, Chinese, English, Spanish, and Japanese.

LORENA TERANDO is an associate professor of translation and interpreting studies at the University of Wisconsin–Milwaukee. She has worked in various capacities in the translation industry, including as a member of staff at the English

Translation Service of the United Nations. The courses she teaches range from industry-specific or literary translation workshops in French and Spanish to English, to translation theory. Her research focuses on the voice of translator as witness in the testimonials written by women in situations of conflict, and explores trauma, loss, and memory. She translated María Eugenia Vásquez's *My Life as a Colombian Revolutionary: Reflections of a Former Guerilla* (2005), and her most recent translation of Elvira Sánchez Blake's *Espiral de Silencios* (2009) is under review.

RUSSELL SCOTT VALENTINO is a professor and chair of the Department of Slavic and East European Languages and Cultures at Indiana University Bloomington, and currently serves as president of the American Literary Translators Association. His recent books include *The Woman in the Window* (2014) and *The Man Between: Michael Henry Heim & a Life in Translation* (coedited with Esther Allen and Sean Cotter, 2014). From 2009 to 2013, he served as editor-in-chief at the *Iowa Review,* where he continues to serve as a contributing editor. He is the founder and senior editor of Autumn Hill Books, a contributing editor to the *Buenos Aires Review,* and recipient of NEA literature fellowships for translation in prose (2002) and poetry (2010).

YIMAN WANG is an associate professor of film and digital media at the University of California, Santa Cruz. She is the author of *Remaking Chinese Cinema: Through the Prism of Shanghai, Hong Kong and Hollywood* (2013). Her articles have appeared in *Quarterly Review of Film and Video, Film Quarterly, Camera Obscura, Journal of Film and Video, Literature/Film Quarterly, Positions: East Asia Cultures Critique,* and *Journal of Chinese Cinemas.* Her recent book contributions include chapters in *Silent Cinema and the Politics of Space* (2014), *Sinophone Cinemas* (2014), *China's iGeneration: Cinema and Moving Image Culture for the Twenty-First Century* (2014), and *American and Chinese-Language Cinemas: Examining Cultural Flows* (2014). She is currently working on two book projects: one on Anna May Wong, and the other on animality in cinema.

INDEX